Guidance in Spiritual Direction

Books by the same author:

CANA IS FOREVER

SINS OF PARENTS

IN PURSUIT OF PERFECTION

BLAME NO ONE BUT YOURSELF

WHAT TO SAY TO THE PENITENT

REFLECTIONS ON THE PASSION

LEAVEN OF HOLINESS

LITTLE STEPS TO GREAT HOLINESS

GUIDANCE IN SPIRITUAL DIRECTION

by Charles Hugo Doyle

THE NEWMAN PRESS
Westminster, Maryland
1959

Nihil Obstat: H. Griffin
Censor Librorum

Imprimatur: J. H. MacDonald
Archbishop of Edmonton
December 14, 1956

First published 1958
Second printing, January, 1959

Library of Congress Catalog Card Number: 57-11810
Printed in the United States of America

TO THE MEMORY OF THE LATE

Right Reverend Monsignor Edward R. Gaffney, P.A., V.G.

A ZEALOUS PRIEST AND A THOUGHTFUL FRIEND

I dedicate

THIS BOOK IN GRATEFUL REMEMBRANCE

Contents

Guidance in Spiritual Direction

1

Launch Out Into the Deep

IT IS strange how an isolated act, or a passing association with a person or an event can immortalize some men who might otherwise have been born, lived, and gone to their graves cloaked in anonymity. What reason, for instance, would the world have to know that Simon of Cyrene ever lived, save for the fact that he was seized by the Roman soldiers and made to help the Saviour of mankind carry His Cross to Calvary? Would we have ever heard of, or had cause to remember Major André, save that he was associated with Benedict Arnold? How wisely Lord Greville spoke, when he said: "Surely no man can reflect, without wonder, upon the vicissitudes of human life arising from causes in the highest degree accidental and trifling. If you trace the necessary concatenation of human events a very little way back, you may perhaps discover that a person's very going in or out of a door has been the means of coloring with misery or happiness the remaining current of life."

It is fairly certain that Ananias would never have been known to posterity except for the fact that he was the instrument chosen by God to counsel and direct the Apostle to the Gentiles—the great St. Paul. There is small doubt but that Ananias was probably a leading figure in the small Christian community at Damascus. He may even have gone to Damascus from Jerusalem as a part of the dispersion of Christians which came upon the heels of the persecution which followed the death of St. Stephen. If the flight to Damascus from Jerusalem was carried out with the idea that the

Christians would be relatively safe there, that hope was quickly to be destroyed, for word soon came that Saul, a most formidable foe of Christianity, was on his way with a band of soldiers to crush them. Apprised of this, Ananias was waiting for the persecutor. How or when Saul would strike he did not know. Little did he realize that Jesus Christ had confronted Saul on the road to Damascus and had set in motion the marvelous events that were to follow.

It was in a fearful mood of uncertainty that Ananias went to bed on the third night after the feared persecutor should have reached Damascus. On this night he saw a vision of the Lord, and He said unto him: "Arise and go into the street that is called Strait and seek in the house of Judas one named Saul of Tarsus. For behold he prayeth."[1] When we reflect that Ananias was expecting Saul of Tarsus as the persecutor coming to arrest him and take him with the other Christians bound to Jerusalem, we are not surprised that Ananias replied as follows: " 'Lord, I have heard by many of this man, how much evil he hath done to Thy saints in Jerusalem. And here he hath authority from the chief priests to bind all that invoke Thy name.' And the Lord said to him: 'Go thy way: for this man is to me a vessel of election, to carry my name before the Gentiles and kings and the children of Israel. For I will show him how great things he must suffer for my name's sake.' "[2]

The vision Ananias had seen moved him deeply and all the fear that the name Saul of Tarsus had once conjured up for him was dispelled. Hastening into the street, he found the house of Judas, and the sight that he beheld as he looked at Saul must have completely disarmed him—for he saw a blind man. And Saul in turn must have welcomed his visitor, for whilst he could not see him, he had been told by Christ when he was thrown from his horse, in answer to his question: "Lord, what wilt Thou have me do?" that he was to "Arise and go into the city: and there it shall be told thee what thou must do."[3]

How Saul's sight was restored and how he was baptized is too well known for me to comment upon here. The point I want to make, however, is that Christ did not reveal His plans for Saul at the moment of his wonderful conversion, but rather indicated that

[1] Acts 9:11.
[2] Acts 9:13–16. [3] Acts 9:6, 7.

he was to place himself under the direction of Ananias, who, in turn, would be guided by heavenly lights to complete the work of his conversion. More than a few great spiritual writers see in this strange procedure confirmation of the importance of spiritual directors for all those in pursuit of perfection. It was to Ananias that God had given the power to cure Saul's blindness, both physical and spiritual; and not a few other saints attribute their great spiritual progress to the wise direction given them by spiritual directors. So important is this matter that the great Pope Leo XIII wrote as follows: "God in His infinite Providence has decreed that men for the most part should be saved by men; hence He has appointed that those whom He calls to a loftier degree of holiness should be led thereto by men, in order that, as Chrysostom says, 'we should be taught by God through men.' We have an illustrious example of this put before us in the very beginning of the Church, for although Saul, who was breathing threatenings and slaughter, heard the voice of Christ Himself, and asked from Him, 'Lord what wilt Thou have me to do?' he was nevertheless sent to Ananias at Damascus: 'Arise and go into the city and there it shall be told thee what to do.' This manner of acting has invariably obtained in the Church. All without exception who in the course of ages have been remarkable for science and holiness have taught this doctrine. Those who reject it assuredly do so rashly and at their peril." [1]

The Abbot Cassian who spent years among the monks of the Holy Land and Egypt, has grouped their teachings along with his own on the matter of spiritual direction. For instance, in his work *Book of Institutions*, he exhorts the young cenobites to bare their hearts to the elder charged with the direction of their lives and to disclose to him without false shame their most secret thoughts, and submit themselves entirely to his decision as to what is good and what is evil.[2]

St. John Climacus, writing to the monks of the East in *Ladder of Paradise*, says to beginners: "that those who wish to leave the land of Egypt for the Promised Land and subdue their disorderly passions, stand in need of another Moses to serve them as a guide."

[1] Apostolic letter, *Testem benevolentiae*, January 22, 1899.
[2] Cassianus, *De coenobiorum institut.* iv. 9.

To those advanced on the road to perfection, the saint declares, "that in order to follow Christ and enjoy the holy liberty of the children of God, one must humbly deliver the care of one's soul to a man that is the representative of the Divine Master; and that such a one must be chosen with care, because he must be obeyed in all simplicity, in spite of the shortcomings that may be detected in him; for the sole danger lies in following one's own judgment." [1]

St. Bernard advises novices to have a guide "to enlighten them, direct them, console them and encourage them." Not alone to beginners but also to advanced souls the saint prescribes direction, saying: "I know not what others think about themselves on this matter; for myself, I speak from experience and I hesitate not to say that I find it easier and safer to direct many others than I do to guide myself." [2]

St. Vincent Ferrer, the great Dominican saint, says the following about spiritual direction:

> A person who has a director by whom he allows himself to be guided, whom he obeys in all his actions, great and small, will more easily and quickly arrive at perfection than he ever could by himself, even were he gifted with an extraordinary degree of intelligence and supplied with books explaining the nature of all the virtues and the means of acquiring them.
>
> I should go still further and say that our Lord, without whom we can do nothing, will never bestow His grace on one, who having at his disposal a man capable of instructing and directing him, neglects this powerful means of sanctification, believing himself to be self-sufficient and that, by his own powers, he is capable of seeking and discovering the things necessary for salvation.
>
> This way of obedience is the royal road leading men securely to the summit of that mysterious ladder over which the Lord seems to be leaning. It is the way trodden by all the holy Fathers of the desert. And, in general, all those who have tended toward perfection have followed this path.[3]

According to St. Gregory the Great, the fact that in some excep-

[1] *Scala paradisi,* I, 4. [2] *De diversis, sermo* VIII, 7.

[3] *A Treatise on the Spiritual Life* with a commentary by Ven. Mother Julienne Morrell, O.P., translated by the Dominican Nuns of Corpus Christi Monastery (Westminster, Md.: Newman Press, 1957), p. 92.

tional cases the Holy Ghost Himself teaches the soul without human help in no way abrogates the general law.

Julienne Morrell, a Dominican religious at the beginning of the seventeenth century, gives us an excellent commentary on the foregoing words of St. Vincent Ferrer. Writing on the necessity of a spiritual director, she says:

> Our Saviour Jesus Christ is, of course, our real and sovereign Master, infinitely wise and adequate to teach and instruct us in all that is necessary and useful to our salvation and perfection. For He is that divine Teacher sent by the eternal Father down to earth to set mortal man upon the road to salvation, He of whom Isaias speaks when he says: "Thy eyes shall see thy teacher. And thy ears shall hear the word of one admonishing thee behind thy back; this is the way, walk ye in it: and go not aside neither to the right hand, nor to the left." [1]

He fulfilled this literally, exercising with the greatest skill the office of heavenly Master and true Counsellor, when, as the Prophet says, he was seen upon earth and conversed with men. Moreover, He still performs the same office daily in the interior of our souls in an entirely spiritual, mystical manner.

Nevertheless, He who by His infinite wisdom disposes all things sweetly to the great profit of our souls, has very wisely ordained that men should govern and teach other men; both those who govern and teach and those who are taught and governed are meant to derive wonderful advantages and profit as well as signal merit therefrom: and those who govern or teach by practising charity, benignity, patience and many other virtues; those who are under their guidance by the exercise of humility, submission, obedience and mortification, acquiring thereby rich treasures of grace and glory. For the sovereign Lawgiver bestows upon them His entire blessing, remarking that they bind themselves to the law of another man's will in order to fulfill more perfectly the law of His charity and divine love.

Thus, according to the advice of our holy author [St. Vincent Ferrer], and the common consent of all the Doctors, he who would attain to perfection should not be governed by his own head nor

[1] Isai. 30:20–21.

trust his own judgment, however great capacity, experience or learning he might have; but should submit humbly (for it is a great act of humility) to the direction of a good spiritual father.[1]

After reading the foregoing, it might appear at first glance that spiritual direction is absolutely necessary for spiritual perfection. It must be stated here that, as Tanquerey remarks, "Direction, although not absolutely necessary for the sanctification of souls, is one of the *normal means* of spiritual progress." [2] This we have established by citing proofs from authorities, such as the saints, doctors of the Church, Pope Leo XIII, and other like sources. That such a contention is reasonable is based on the nature of spiritual progress. Progress in holiness is a long and painful journey over rough seas. To venture on any body of water without a pilot who knows the danger spots is sheer folly. St. Francis de Sales points out that a man who is his own physician has a fool for a patient: "Why should we wish to constitute ourselves directors of our own souls," says the saint, "when we do not undertake the management of our body? Have we not noticed that physicians, when ill, call other physicians to determine what remedies they require?" [3] In the realm of art, how many great artists can one find who have not had formal training in painting? And in like manner, how can one hope to master the difficult task of being perfect without a spiritual tutor? Beginners need guidance so that they may know what penances to perform and someone to keep them from going overboard in this matter, as well as an impartial judge of their progress. Those who are well on their way to perfection also need guidance in the inculcation of the virtues and the means of practicing these virtues. Even the person enjoying the delights of contemplation needs direction, as St. John of the Cross says: "God so desires that man place himself under the direction of another, that He absolutely does not want to see us give full assent to the supernatural truths He Himself imparts, before they have issued out of the mouth of man."

Now, thus far, we have noted only the moral necessity of spiritual direction, and with this firmly established, the next step

[1] *A Treatise on the Spiritual Life, op. cit.*, p. 93–94.
[2] *The Spiritual Life* (Westminster, Md.: Newman Press, 1945), p. 257.
[3] *Sermons recueillis,* IX, 95.

is to treat of the necessity of *many* priests taking up the important work of giving direction. Nearly every priest will agree wholeheartedly with the premise that spiritual direction is morally necessary if some souls are to be guided properly and quickly to perfection; but these same priests usually, politely but firmly, refuse to shoulder the task, giving as an excuse, either that they are not holy enough, or that they are not sufficiently schooled in the art of direction of souls, or both. When you point out the fact that there are, for instance, some 158,000 sisters, 8,000 brothers, 32,000 seminarians (religious and diocesan), and some 241,000 [1] college and university students in the United States alone, the problem takes on immense proportions. The direction of the 158,000 sisters alone is a staggering challenge, yet spiritual directors must be found for them if they are to be guided to perfection.

Hear Dom Chautard say:

> The proof of the fact that many subjects in religious communities, contemplative as well as active, merely *vegetate*, for lack of spiritual direction, is to be found in the radical change we have frequently observed in tepid souls who have returned to the fervor they had at profession as soon as they finally found a conscientious director. Some confessors seem to forget that the consecrated souls in their charge are obliged to tend to perfection and have a real need of help and encouragement to achieve the words of the psalm: "In his heart he hath disposed to ascend by steps . . . they shall go from virtue to virtue," [2] and to become, after that, true apostles of the interior life.[3]

Seminaries must soon come to grips with this problem and institute a realistic course in ascetical theology that will be adequate to the burning need for more and more specialists in the art of spiritual direction. The Junior Clergy Examinations might well include questions on ascetical theology along with moral and dogmatic theology. Seminars should be instituted in each diocese, led by experts in this essential branch of theology. I would not consider a person an expert simply because he could quote chapter and verse

[1] This number includes the non-Catholic students.

[2] Ps. 83.

[3] *The Soul of the Apostolate* (Trappist, Kentucky: Abbey of Gethsemani, 1946), p. 171.

of Tanquerey; but rather one who besides that, is so convinced of the importance of spiritual direction that he has submitted himself to the direction of another. St. Francis de Sales and St. Vincent de Paul were experts in the science of direction of souls, but that did not keep them from seeking spiritual direction for themselves.

Not a few young priests, I fear, emerge from our seminaries today imbued with the notion that to be a successful twentieth-century priest, one must be a combination saint and recreational director.

Is it not just possible that we have over-emphasized the importance of sports and amusements in our efforts to win young people away from improper places of entertainment and dangerous associations, and because they flock to our parochial socials in large numbers we are deluded into thinking that there is nothing more we need do? "Amusements to virtue," says David Thomas, "are like breezes of air to the flame—gentle ones will fan it, strong ones will put it out."

Today, when juvenile delinquency makes daily headlines it is possible that some of the junior clergy may be goaded into thinking that it is up to them to provide the youth of the parish with a full program of sports and all will be well. When St. Philip Neri set out to convert Rome, lukewarm and indifferent with the spirit of the Renaissance, we do not read that he opened any recreational youth centers, but rather, that he gathered a few young people around him and set about to so indoctrinate them, that they preached by good example, and made Jesus Christ live again on this earth by spreading about them the good odor of His virtues.

It is said that on one occasion Pope St. Pius X asked a group of cardinals: "What is the thing we most need, today, to save society?"

"Build Catholic schools," said one.

"No," said the pope.

"More churches," said another.

"Still no."

"Speed up the recruiting of priests," said still another.

"No, no," said the pope. "The *most* necessary thing of all at this time is for every parish to possess a group of laymen who will be at the same time virtuous, enlightened, resolute, and truly apostolic." [1]

Dom Chautard, in his wonderful book, *The Soul of the Apostolate*, a work so highly valued by St. Pius X that he often warmly recommended it and called it "his bedside book," tells of two great priests engaged in the French Catholic Action Movement—one, Father Jean-Joseph Allemand and the other, Father Timon-David, and lays the success of their work to the fact that they picked, out of countless thousands of youths, a small group capable of desiring and seriously practicing the interior life. They enkindled in the souls of these youths a white heat of love for our Lord, inspiring them with the ideal of the evangelical counsels, and then, finally, at the right time, gave these youths a zeal for souls, in order to use them to reach their comrades more effectively. But the whole secret of the success of these two priests' work really revolved around spiritual direction. Father Allemand undertook the *individual* direction of each youth, and excelled in arousing holy enthusiasm for perfection, and in convincing them that the best proof of devotion to the Sacred Heart is to imitate the virtues of our Divine Model.

As for Father Timon-David, he was also an excellent spiritual director, and he had a special knack of setting hearts on fire with love of virtue, and was not content in his guidance of souls with the principles of moral theology proper to the purgative life, but steered souls toward the illuminative life. Both these great priests considered that *personal direction, for each member, once a month, was indispensable.*

If priests who have charge of youth groups would stress more forcefully the importance of the apostolate of good example, and impress upon young people that they ought not only shun the acts forbidden by the Commandments but that they are called to taste of the splendors of the evangelical virtues, there is no limit to the possibilities for good in the individual, in his home, his parish, and his country. This was the very mode of procedure that proved so effective in the early Church. The apostles concentrated on individuals and small groups and the virtues they strengthened in their followers struck the pagans with astonishment, even then most

[1] *L'Ami du Clergé*, Jan. 20, 1921.

prejudiced against Christianity, so that they were forced to cry out: "What is this religion that can give such light and strength and fire to the hearts of men?" In any case, for God's sake let us not make spiritual development secondary to physical development or the winning of championships.

This apostolate should not be reserved only for youths but it must extend to other parish organizations made up of adults—the main theme being *the transformation of society by means of chosen souls.* Fathers and mothers would have a greater influence upon their families if they could but find proper spiritual direction. For lack of spiritual direction many children never know the joy of throwing themselves wholeheartedly into the practice of the interior life. And who can know how many priestly and religious vocations fail to blossom forth because of the lack of proper direction? In parishes where there are no vocations, you can look for priests who know only how to give absolution. Indeed, the Church would have many more saints if generous souls, especially priests and religious, received more serious direction.

Dom Chautard makes this pointed observation calculated to strike fear into the heart of any priest when he writes: "Would it be rash for us to fear that many priests will receive a frightful shock at the Last Judgment when they find out that they are, to a certain extent, responsible for the mediocrity and even the loss of souls, because they neglected to study the art of spiritual direction and would not take the trouble to practice it? They may have been good administrators, wonderful preachers, full of solicitude for the sick and the poor, but they have nonetheless neglected this outstanding feature of our Lord's own strategy: the transformation of society by means of chosen souls. The little flock of disciples chosen and formed by Christ Himself, and afterwards set on fire by the Holy Spirit, was enough to begin the regeneration of the world." [1]

Until seminaries and those in authority, then, meet the problem of adequate training in the art of spiritual direction, the priests already in the ranks must stir themselves to assume this great responsibility and prepare themselves for it by prayer and study. Who can shirk this duty who reads these words of Father Godinez:

[1] *The Soul of the Apostolate, op. cit.,* p. 172.

Hardly ten in a thousand called by God to perfection heed the call; of a hundred called to contemplation, ninety-nine fail to respond. *It must be acknowledged that one of the principal causes is the lack of spiritual directors.* Under God, they are the pilots who conduct souls through this unknown ocean of the spiritual life. If no science, no art, how simple soever, can be learned well without a master, much less can anyone learn this high wisdom of evangelical perfection, wherein such great mysteries are found. This is the reason why I hold it morally impossible that a soul could, without a miracle or without a master, go through what is the highest and most arduous in the spiritual life, without running the risk of perishing.[1]

I am afraid that spiritual writers who so earnestly speak of the need for directors, scare off potential directors by over-stressing the ancient quotation of St. Teresa, that "not one in a thousand is capable of so sublime a task," or St. Francis de Sales' remark that "not one of ten thousand" can measure up to the task. With all due respect to these two great spiritual lights, and to modern ascetical scholars as well, I feel that the extensive basic spiritual training of our ordained religious priests, as well as the advancement in all fields of study in our diocesan seminaries today would seem to fit our modern clergy to act as spiritual directors in far greater numbers than at present estimated. We are not to be surprised that certain saintly persons in ages past held the task of spiritual direction in such reverential awe. They had a similar attitude toward the priesthood itself. Indeed if the moral standards of the early Church were imposed as rigidly today as in ages past, the numbers in the ranks of the clergy would be somewhat decreased. Note these lines from St. Alphonsus: [2] "For eleven centuries, all who fell into mortal sin after baptism were excluded from the priesthood. This we learn from the Council of Nice,[3] from the Council of Toledo,[4] from the Council of Elvira,[5] and from the Fourth Council of Carthage.[6] And if a priest, after his ordination, had fallen into sin, he was deposed and shut up in a monastery, as may be observed from several canons." [7]

[1] *Praxis theologica mysticae* (Paris: Lethielleux, 1920).
[2] *Dignity and Duties of the Priest*, ed. by Rev. E. Grimm, C.SS.R. (Brooklyn: Redemptorist Fathers, 1927), pp. 52–53.
[3] Can. 9, 10. [4] Can. 2. [5] Can. 76. [6] IV Can. 68.
[7] *Corp. Jur. Can.*, dist. 81.

Perhaps if we look at this problem from the angle of qualities we may see that there is no real reason for the small number of spiritual directors. St. Francis de Sales says that a director must have three principal qualities. "He must be full of *charity, knowledge* and *prudence;* if he lacks any of these qualities there is danger." [1] Now, are these not qualities demanded in every priest and not reserved solely for spiritual directors? For instance, it is certain that when St. Francis mentioned charity he had in mind that such charity ought to be born of supernatural and paternal affection for those confided to any director, but is not every priest expected to have such charity even as an ordinary confessor? St. Alphonsus says that all confessors "require a great fund of charity in receiving all the poor, the ignorant and the vicious." [2] "You are not," says Hugh of St. Victor, "appointed judges of crimes, to chastise, but, as it were, judges of maladies, to heal."

Regarding knowledge, it is true that a spiritual director ought to have special training in ascetical theology, but Tanquerey says that "even in the case of *sinners,* the priest must know ascetical theology to teach them how to avoid the occasions of sin, how to struggle against their passions, resist temptations and practice the virtues opposed to the vices they must avoid. No doubt moral theology suggests these things, but ascetical theology coordinates and develops them." [3] But is there any reason why a priest ought to be ignorant of ascetical theology? Certainly not. The three things ascetical experts prescribe as essential for the direction of souls are not impossible, for they state one needs only a manual, the reading of the masters, and the practice of the Christian and priestly virtues. If I might add a fourth, it would be a longer and stronger course in ascetical theology in our seminaries, and post-graduate courses in it in our universities. The authorities whose duty it is to handle such matters might well make a move to emulate the great Pope Benedict XV who ordered established a chair of ascetical theology at two of the great theological schools of Rome. St. Pius X believed a course in ascetical theology to be more important than lectures on sociology.

[1] *Introduction to the Devout Life,* translated by Michael Day, Cong. Orat. (Westminster, Md.: Newman Press, 1956), p. 17.

[2] *Dignity and Duties of the Priest, op. cit.,* p. 274–275.

[3] *The Spiritual Life, op. cit.,* p. 36.

As to manuals, it is strongly suggested that the reader procure a copy of both *The Spiritual Life* by A. Tanquerey, and *Theology of the Spiritual Life* by Joseph de Guibert, S.J. Both of these works are excellent and either one or both will do much to open up new avenues of approach to this problem.

The study begun in the seminary must be continued and perfected in the ministry and such study must include not only dogmatic and moral theology but ascetical theology as well. This is essential if one is to be an effective confessor, to say nothing of a spiritual director. St. Lawrence Justinian addressed these words to *all* priests: "Many graces and not a little knowledge are needed by him who desires to raise souls to life." [1] The priest who feels he lacks the knowledge necessary to be a good spiritual director ought to set to work to correct this situation. He can study an authoritative manual and he can fortify himself with the words of the great spiritual giants such as St. Thomas, St. Teresa, St. John of the Cross, and St. Francis de Sales, to mention only a few. In this way his knowledge will be increased, his heart warmed, and his mind enlightened by faith. After years of consistent study the feeling of inadequacy may still endure but one may find consolation in the words of Thaulerus, who said that "a soul intending perfection ought to seek out an experienced servant of God, though it cost her a journey of many German miles. But if such a friend cannot be found, then will a simple *confessarius* serve, no matter how ignorant, for even by such men doth the Holy Ghost speak by reason of their office, so that they may securely be submitted to and obeyed, even in things which they do not well understand." [2]

There is little excuse, however, for ignorance of such an important work; and there is small chance of such a condition existing in a priest who is bent on the practice of the Christian and priestly virtues himself, under the care of a wise director. There is no better way to understand the different stages of perfection than to go through them yourself. Once a priest has grasped the fundamentals of ascetical theology and has himself been under direction, he ought not to dread the office of spiritual director. He will, how-

[1] *De compunct.*, p. 2.
[2] In F. Augustine Baker, O.S.B., *Holy Wisdom* (New York: Harper & Brothers, n.d.), p. 79.

ever, never be an effective director until and unless he undergoes the *experience of practicing the same prayer and other interior exercises that he prescribes and teaches.* No matter how well a priest practices discursive meditation, it will not help him very much when he is called upon to direct souls tending to contemplation. The experience gained by tending to contemplation himself will be invaluable in the direction of others. The study of contemplative books may earn one the title of being "learned," but the actual experience in *practicing* such prayer will make him a much more effective guide. It is the judgment of Gerson, St. Teresa, St. John of the Cross, and Seraphinus Firmanus that little trust is to be given to learning without personal experience, but much to personal experience though without learning. Dom Baker, writing on this consideration, says that "to this purpose it is observable that for the most part the instruments that God hath been pleased both in ancient and modern times to employ in the instructing and guiding souls to the perfection of contemplative prayer, have been persons of small learning but great personal experience in prayer, such as were St. Anthony, St. Benedict, St. Francis and St. Teresa." [1]

St. Teresa, speaking of fervent souls, puts it this way: "For this end it is very necessary that he should have a director, who ought to be a person of experience [practicing the same prayer and other exercises he prescribes and teaches] . . . My opinion has always been, and will be, that every Christian should continue to be guided by a learned director [learned in the mystic ways] if he can, and the more learned the better." [2]

St. John of the Cross says in like manner that some directors, unlearned in the mystic ways "disturb the peace of this quiet and hushed contemplation which God has been giving these souls by His own power, and they make their penitents meditate and reason and perform acts, not without causing them great displeasure, repugnance and distraction. . . . And thus one who rashly errs, being under an obligation to give reliable advice—as is every man,

[1] *Ibid.*, p. 76.

[2] *Autobiography*, translated by David Lewis (Westminster, Md.: Newman Press, 1951), p. 102–104.

whatever his office–shall not go unpunished by reason of the harm he has done." [1]

Now this is the very sort of quotation calculated to terrify the ordinary priest and cause him to fly from anyone suggesting his being a spiritual director. The very important point I want to make is that such ignorance *can* be dispelled by the study of ascetical theology, and this sort of a challenge can be and ought to be faced squarely by every priest. If one is fearful of great responsibility then he ought not assume the duty of a priest, for the very saints who speak so awesomely of spiritual direction speak in like manner of the very priesthood itself. Hear St. Isidore say, "Whoever leads people on the road of virtue must himself be holy and blameless." [2] And St. Gregory Nazianzen writes: "The priest must first be cleansed before he can cleanse others; he must first himself approach God before he can lead others to Him; he must first sanctify himself before he can sanctify others; he must first be himself a light before he can illumine others." [3] If a statement like the one made by St. John of the Cross cited above has the effect of scaring off some priests from the role of spiritual directors they ought not be too complacent in their role as simple confessors, for according to St. Gregory the Great, "a confessor has to render to God an account of as many souls as he has penitents." [4] So difficult and dangerous is the office of a confessor that the Council of Trent has called it "an office to be dreaded even by angels." [5]

The whole crux of this problem lies in the fact that spiritual direction is a science, as St. Gregory Nazianzen says: "To direct men seems to be the greatest of all sciences," [6] then as a science it *can* be learned. As to the method of acquiring this science, we have already mentioned the four things needed to accomplish this great goal, namely: adequate seminary training, a manual, reading and study of the masters, and the practice of the virtues. The sad part is not that all priests cannot become great spiritual directors, but rather that some *will not*, because of faulty reasoning, indifference, fear, or flight from moral responsibility.

[1] *The Living Flame of Love*, 1st red., III, 45–48; *Complete Works*, translated and edited by E. Allison Peers (Westminster, Md.: Newman Press, 1953), III, 78–79.

[2] *Offic. eccl.* I. 2, c. 5. [3] *Apol.* I. [4] *Moral.* I. 24, c. 30.

[5] Denzinger-Rahner, 899. [6] *Apol.* I. 18.

Presuming, then, that as St. Francis de Sales says, the charity necessary for a director is present, and that one has done his best to study a formal text on ascetical theology, then the third requisite laid down by the saint ought not to be too difficult to fulfill, namely, prudence. Prudence is a moral virtue and affects the understanding, whose action precedes the operation of the will, and then it presides over the duties of the other virtues so as to be their rule, according to which all are directed. Cicero defined it as "the knowledge of things to be sought and things to be shunned," while others briefly express it as the right manner of doing things. Father de Guibert, S.J., says, "To an extent this quality is inborn; it can be increased by curbing hastiness in judging, by reviewing the directions one gives, and by asking advice; also by being careful to allow for the differences between souls, by guarding against prejudice, and by avoiding *a priori* conclusions. However, if one's natural lack of good judgment is so great that it cannot be rectified, then one is wholly incapable of undertaking spiritual direction." [1]

Now how many priests do you know whose judgment is so poor as to bar them from the task of a spiritual director? And your own judgment—would you admit to unrectifiable imprudence? You wouldn't have gotten into the priesthood without normally good judgment. And when it is not as good as it might be, Father de Guibert has given aids for its improvement, such as curbing hastiness in judging, reviewing the directions one gives, and asking advice. Now that doesn't seem too impossible, does it? And let those who might seize upon the lack of such a quality as an excusing cause for not taking on the task of spiritual direction when the necessity arises, remember that St. Alphonsus writes: "that all priests must be persuaded that to hear *confessions,* great science and also *great prudence* are required; for without knowledge, without prudence, a confessor will do but little good and to some his ministry will be more injurious than beneficial." [2] In the light of the fact that prudence is a requisite for ordinary confessors, and they are legion, what happens to make so many priests excuse

[1] *The Theology of the Spiritual Life* (New York: Sheed and Ward, 1953), p. 167, n. 201.

[2] *Dignity and Duties of the Priest, op. cit.*, p. 274.

themselves on the score that they are not qualified to serve as spiritual directors?

The whole question boils down to the fact that the shortage of properly trained spiritual directors is an artificial shortage—one that could be remedied in one decade if seminaries would spread a good solid course in ascetical theology over the *whole four years* of the theologians' course, and if those who are now in the priesthood would today set about to make up what is lacking in their formal training in ascetics by study, and in their own spiritual life, by prayer, with the help of some other good director to guide them. Appearing to Mother Marie Ste Cécile de Rome, our Lord said, on April 22, 1927, "My priests should be other Christs . . . Many among them possess eloquence and human learning but they lack the fundamental science, holiness." [1]

I hope and pray that I have not over-simplified this matter, for that is the very last thing I would want to do. However, I do think it is time we rend the cloak of mystery surrounding spiritual direction and face up to the fact that a spiritual director is simply "the one to whom a person manifests his state of soul and to whom he offers himself to be habitually directed in the way of perfection." [2] We must see that many priests already possess the requisite supernatural charity and the prudence essential for such a task, and that everyone in the ministry could acquire by study and experience the necessary training to direct souls, with the pilotage of divine grace, over the unknown sea of the spiritual life. If such priests would only aspire to perfection themselves, the problem would be quickly solved; it should be noted that even if a priest is never called to be a spiritual director for a single soul, he is, nevertheless, according to the teaching of St. Thomas, not only obliged to strive after perfection, but he must possess perfection in a higher degree than the simplest religious.

Perhaps fewer priests would refuse to act as directors if they would but understand the work as Father Faber did. A director, according to Faber, is one who

[1] *Canticle of Love.* Autobiography of Marie Sainte-Cécile de Rome, R.J.M. (Dina Belanger) 1897–1929 (Quebec: Religious of Jesus and Mary, 1945), p. 222.
[2] La Reguera, *Praxis Theol. Myst.*, t. II, 8.

goes behind to watch God going before. He must keep his eye fixed on God, who is in the dimness ahead. He does not lead his charges. The Holy Ghost leads them. He holds out his hands from behind, as a mother does to her tottering child, to balance his uncertain steps as he sways overmuch, now on one side, now on another. He is not to have a way of his own, to be applied to everyone. This is what a novice-master does with his novices. He leads them by an acknowledged tradition, and animates them with the definite fixed spirit of the order, and models them, as a faithful copyist, on their sainted Founder. But this is not at all the function of a spiritual director. He only knows that we are in the way which is right for us when he sees God in front. He looks after our advance, and when he sees God increasing the distance between Himself and the soul, he spurs on the latter, discreetly, gently, yet firmly and uninterruptedly. He gains as much light from prayer as from his knowledge of character and his personal observation of ourselves. His office is very supernatural, but it is very natural also; and he will not direct well if he over-shadows the natural by the supernatural.

The great Faber has pointed words to say of those who make a big issue of this art of spiritual direction. He comments that it is a wonder their Guardian Angels do not impatiently break silence and say: "All things are God's gifts: go to, simpleton! and help your neighbor to the best of your abilities with a good-humored diligence, and neither make so much of it, nor throw a mystery around it." [1] Yes, above all, let us have no mysteries in direction.

The dual purpose of this book, then, is to interest more priests in becoming spiritual directors in the fullest sense of the word, and, at the same time, to provide, in as logical and simple a manner as possible, fundamental rules in spiritual guidance as found in the writings of the great masters of the spiritual life. If I might but succeed in the one or the other, I should feel richly rewarded for the work involved.

[1] *Growth in Holiness* (Westminster, Md.: Newman Press, 1950), p. 305–306.

2

Setting the Sights

IT IS related that God revealed to Macarius, the anchoret of Crete, famous for his austerities, devotions and sanctity, that there were two married women in a neighboring town of greater perfection than himself. He left the desert, staff in hand, in search of them. He found them, unknown to fame, unmarked by beauty or fortune, practicing the plain virtues of humility, patience, charity, self-denial and resignation, doing their domestic duties with cheerfulness, and maintaining a devotional spirit by ejaculatory prayer and frequent consecrations of soul and body to God.

It is consoling to realize that Christian perfection is possible to all Christians, nay more, it is required of all, as stated by Pope Pius XI in his Encyclical of January 26, 1923, on St. Francis de Sales.[1] Such teaching is borne out by the words of Christ Himself who proposes to all as the *ideal* of holiness the very perfection of our heavenly Father: "Be ye therefore perfect, as also your heavenly Father is perfect." [2] The Apostle John counsels: "He that is just, let him be justified still; and he that is holy, let him be sanctified still." [3] From all this we note the necessity of progress in perfection, and it was axiomatical with the saints that to act was characteristic of charity and that to halt was to recede. St. Bernard puts it this way: "Of necessity one must rise or else fall; if one tries to stop, one falls of a certainty." [4]

The great and saintly Father Lallemant, S.J., states that the

[1] *Acta Apost. Sedis*, XV, 50.
[2] Matt. 5: 48. [3] Apoc. 22: 11. [4] *Epist.*, XCL, n. 3.

motives which should excite one to perfection are: (1) The great advantages it brings with it: peace of soul, perfect liberty of mind, the delights of the love of God, the abundance of the riches of grace. (2) The assurance of our salvation, which is not to be had save in the way of perfection; whereas in the practice of it, salvation is morally certain.

As to the obligation incumbent upon *religious* of tending toward perfection, there can be no doubt. Such are bound to tend to perfection in virtue of their state, as is clearly stated by the Code: "Each and every religious superior as well as subject is bound to tend toward the perfection of his state." [1] St. Thomas teaches that it is not necessary to have attained perfection *before* entering the religious life, but one enters it precisely to acquire perfection.[2] And St. Alphonsus minces no words when he says: "If a religious takes the firm resolution of not tending toward perfection or of giving no thought whatever to it, he commits a mortal sin." [3]

As to the obligation incumbent on priests to tend to perfection there is no margin for doubt, either. The clergy, in virtue of their functions and of the charge which makes theirs the task of sanctifying souls, are bound to a higher interior holiness than that of the simple religious not raised to the priesthood. This is the teaching of St. Thomas. Hear him as he says: "By holy orders a man is deputed to the most dignified ministry, to serve Christ in the Sacrament of the Altar. For this a greater interior sanctity is required than even the religious state demands." [4]

The new Code of Canon Law is clear and explicit on this matter. It states: "Clerics must lead an interior and exterior life holier than that of the laity and give these the good example of virtue and good works." [5] Our Lord Himself exhorts His apostles and priests as follows: "So let your light shine before men that they may see your good works and glorify your Father who is in heaven." [6] St. Gregory comments that "the priest ought to be dead to the world and to all passions in order to lead a life altogether divine." [7] St. Isidore adds this consideration: "Whoever leads people on the road of virtue must himself be holy and blameless." [8] If further

[1] Can. 593. [2] *Sum. Theol.* IIa–IIae, q. 186, a. 1, ad 3.
[3] *Theol. moralis.* I. IV, n. 18. [4] IIa–IIae, q. 184, a. 6, ad 8.
[5] Can. 124. [6] Matt. 5: 16. [7] *Liber Regulae Pastoralis.*
[8] *De Offic. eccl.,* I. 2, c. 5.

proof be needed then these words of the *Imitation* should suffice: "Had you the purity of an Angel and the sanctity of St. John the Baptist, you would not either be worthy to receive or handle this Sacrament. . . . You have not lightened your burden; you are now bound by a stricter bond of discipline, and are *obliged to a greater perfection of sanctity*." [1]

Now, from all we have thus far noted, it must be more than evident that, as priests, we have little choice but to strive for perfection, and this obligation rests with each minister of God whether he be called to direct other souls or not. This being the case, let us set to this work with courage and unfeigned faith. As St. Paul counsels: "In all things let us exhibit ourselves as the ministers of God, in much patience, in tribulation, in necessities, in distresses . . . in labors, in watchings, in fastings, in chastity, in knowledge, in long-suffering, in sweetness, in the Holy Ghost, in charity unfeigned . . . as sorrowful, yet always rejoicing; as needy, yet enriching many; as having nothing and possessing all things." [2]

I cannot stress too emphatically the importance of the fact that the first step toward perfection is the ardent, sincere, and constant *desire* to attain it. This desire is simply an act of the will, which, aided by God's grace, constantly strives after spiritual progress. The importance of the supernatural, persevering, predominant, and practical *desire* for perfection is stressed by St. Teresa as follows: "Let us not stifle our desires. This is highly important. Let us firmly believe that with the divine help and our own efforts we, too, can in the course of time obtain what so many saints, aided by God, finally attained. Had they never conceived such desires, had they not little by little carried them into execution, they would never have risen so high. . . . Oh! how important it is in the spiritual life to rouse oneself to great things." Canon Arvisenet places these thoughts before his readers: "If thou ardently desirest perfection, this strong desire will be a spur to urge thee on from virtue to virtue, until at last thou arrivest at the summit of the Mount of Zion where thou wilt enjoy an intimate union with thy God. Desire therefore vehemently; purpose firmly, and renew this

[1] *Of the Imitation of Christ,* translated by Abbot Justin McCann (Westminster, Md.: Newman Press, 1955), p. 226–227.

[2] 2 Cor. 6:4–10.

desire and this purpose from day to day and from hour to hour. Thus, in a short time thou shalt be enkindled, in a short time thou shalt be on fire." [1]

That there should be no question as to just what is to be desired when one sets out to seek perfection, let us find a good solid definition of perfection. Whenever I think of definitions of perfection I think of the story David Hopkins tells about the woman who had never enjoyed many comforts or pleasures in her life. At long last, she took a long train trip and saw the ocean for the first time. As she stood with folded hands and stared, she observed: "That's the first thing I've ever seen enough of!" I feel the same way about definitions of perfection. They are about the only things ascetical writers have given us in abundance. We are short on methods but we have more than enough definitions of perfection.

Aristotle has given us a classical definition of perfection in general that can hardly be matched. To him, perfection in general is "that which cannot be surpassed in excellence and goodness in its own kind: just as a physician or a flute-player is perfect when he lacks nothing as regards the form of his proper excellence." [2]

To a Christian, perfection has a special religious or moral sense, and as such, St. Thomas says: "Essentially, the perfection of the Christian life consists in charity, first and foremost in the love of God, then in the love of neighbor." [3] Books have been written in explanation of the famous definition, but unfortunately, as often happens with those who write commentaries on St. Thomas, when one has finished reading the commentary, one has to look up St. Thomas to find out what the explanations mean. But taking St. Thomas' definition at first glance, it seems so simple and easy of attainment. In our circles, for instance, whom could you find who does not love God, or who (barring a few uncharitable words or acts) does not love his neighbor? It is not until one finds out, for instance, that the love of God of which St. Thomas speaks must be so strong that it is productive of an habitual renunciation of everything which impedes the heart from giving itself entirely to God, a love strong enough to break all purely natural attachments so that one habitually desires only that which God wills, and conse-

[1] *An Epitome of the Priestly Life* (New York: Benziger Bros., 1921), p. 26.
[2] Metaphysics IV. 16. 1021g. [3] *Sum. Theol.*, IIa–IIae, q. 184, a. 3.

quently, loves nothing except in God and for God–it is only, I say, when we contemplate what loving God really entails, that the whole scope of the matter of Christian perfection dawns upon us. It is so all-embracing that it implies a life of union with God by thought and love–a life completely filled with constant and affectionate remembrance of God. The perimeters are even stretched when we add St. Paul's inspired listing of the qualities of the love of which St. Thomas speaks: "Charity is patient, is kind; charity envieth not, dealeth not perversely, is not puffed up, is not ambitious, seeketh not her own, is not provoked to anger, thinketh no evil, rejoiceth not in iniquity, but rejoiceth with the truth: beareth all things, believeth all things, hopeth all things, endureth all things." [1]

Tremendous in scope as it is, it is God's command. Recall how, when on one occasion "a certain lawyer stood up, tempting Him and saying, 'Master, what must I do to possess eternal life?' But He said to him: What is written in the law? How readest thou? He answering, said: Thou shalt love the Lord thy God with thy whole heart and with thy whole soul and with all thy strength and with all thy mind: and thy neighbor as thyself. And He [Christ] said to him: Thou hast answered right. This do: and thou shalt live." [2]

St. Paul explains this doctrine of our Lord in his Epistle to the Colossians in these words: "Put ye on therefore, as the elect of God, holy and beloved, the bowels of mercy, benignity, humility, modesty, patience: bearing with one another, and forgiving one another, if any have a complaint against another: Even as the Lord hath forgiven you, so do you also. *But above all these things have charity, which is the bond of perfection.*" [3]

Little wonder then that the apostle should single out charity, since it is a love of friendship, which tends to union with God and its principal object is Infinite Perfection or Divine Goodness; thus considered in itself, charity is superior to faith and hope which do not unite us to God so perfectly as does charity. Again charity gives life and merit to the other virtues. It is, as the fathers say, the

[1] 1 Cor. 13:4–7.
[2] Luke 10:27; Deut. 6:5. [3] Col. 3:12–14.

form, the soul, the life of all the virtues. It is the root or the trunk of the tree of life.

It will be noted that here below our love of God cannot be absolutely perfect. In comparing Christian perfection here on earth to that which the elect in heaven enjoy, St. Thomas [1] says that God alone can love Himself infinitely, because He alone can have a comprehensive vision of His Essence; but the saints in heaven, without loving God as much as He is amiable, love Him with all their power, with a love that is always actual without any interruption. Such absolute continuity in love is not possible on this earth; sleep, in particular, does not so permit.

There is, however, a kind of Christian perfection which does not involve a continual actual yearning after God but only an exclusion of whatever is inconsistent with the motion of love toward Him, and such perfection can be attained in this life, and that in two ways. First, perfection may go to the extent of excluding from the heart all that is contrary to charity, as is mortal sin. Without this degree of perfection charity cannot exist, and consequently it is necessary for salvation. Second, perfection may go to the extent of excluding from the heart not only all that is contrary to charity, but all that hinders us from giving our undivided affections to God.

However, the mere exclusion of mortal sin, and even of deliberate venial sin, scarcely deserves the name of perfection. According to the principles formulated by St. Thomas, the perfection of charity excludes not only mortal sins and deliberate venial sins, but also voluntary imperfections, and the habit of acting in an imperfect fashion *(remisse)*, and of receiving the sacraments without fervor.

The saint notes too that among the perfect, charity toward their neighbor, which is the great sign of the sincerity of their love for God, extends not only to all mankind in general, but, when the occasion so presents itself, to all those with whom the perfect have contacts, not only to friends but to strangers and even to enemies. More than this, such fraternal charity in the perfect is found to be so intense that it can extend not only to the sacrifice of external goods but also to the sacrifice of life itself for the salvation of souls, and this based on the words of Christ Himself when He said:

[1] IIa–IIae, q. 184, a. 2.

"This is my commandment, that you love one another as I have loved you." [1] It is this very thing that we see in the apostles after Pentecost, when they were "rejoicing that they were accounted worthy to suffer reproach for the name of Jesus." [2] Likewise, this same idea inspired Paul to say: "I most gladly will spend and be spent myself for your souls." [3]

The definition of perfection as formulated by St. Thomas seems at first reading so easy of accomplishment, but, after a perusal of the foregoing, the work may seem to some too difficult or to others impossible of accomplishment. To all I hasten to say that the forming of the perfect likeness of God in our souls is not the work of an instant, a month, or a year. It is not produced like a statue of molten brass, which takes shape as soon as it is cast into a mould, but rather like a statue of marble, which needs many a blow of the hammer and many a stroke of the chisel, before it represents even the barest outlines of the model. But let us not be discouraged. If we but persevere unto the end, success will crown our efforts, and should death overtake us before the completion of our task, God Himself will give it the finishing touch of the Master's hand.

Unfortunately, the word "perfection" has a way of frightening some people and of leaving still others cold and unmoved. This fear may be the result of having read in the lives of the saints accounts of incredible trials, austere penances, cruel flagellations, and a near starvation diet. Thinking this to be the only way to perfection, some make such things an *end* rather than a *means*. "Fasts, vigils, meditation of Scriptures" writes St. Thomas, quoting a father of the Church, "detachment from and privation of every good, are not perfection but instruments of perfection, for the end of this schooling does not reside in these things, but through them the end is reached. . . . They are steps by means of which we endeavour to raise ourselves to the perfection of charity."

The coldness may be the result of some chance catch-phrase of an over-zealous novice-mistress who, for instance, says: "Perfection is doing all things well," the electrifying result of which will keep the dustless corridors shining, but what of the poor novice who does the dusting and polishing when she reads the life of St. Benedict Labré, and finds that this holy man couldn't (or

[1] John 15:12. [2] Acts 5:41. [3] 2 Cor. 12:15.

wouldn't) keep *himself* clean, and yet he is a canonized saint? Any perfection conceived outside of Christ Himself, and detached from Him, fits Tennyson's famous description:: "Faultily faultless, icily regular, splendidly null, dead perfection: no more."

Fear and coldness would be dispelled like mist in the face of the rising sun if directors, preachers and retreat-masters would stress the great short-cut to perfection, namely, the doctrine of sanctifying grace and of the abiding presence of God in our souls. How relatively easy it would be to raise souls above the petty trivialities of the present life, if the doctrine and the sublime truth of "O God as the Divine Guest of my soul, dwelling there night and day, desirous of receiving the unceasing homage of my intimate friendship and of my love" were explained and stressed in season and out of season! Oh, what good would flow from the deep conviction that while we cannot whenever we wish enjoy the company of the God-man on our altars, it is possible for all of us to withdraw like St. Catherine of Siena into ourselves to commune with the God of our hearts? What a pity that in our prayers we seek God very far from us in a distant heaven, instead of seeking and finding Him in our own heart!

By baptism, conferring sanctifying grace, we Christians were made participators in the divine life of God by being made children of God, for in baptism, we "have been clothed with Christ Jesus" [1] and "We have been grafted on Christ." [2] The doctrine of God's life within us and our incorporation with Christ is all too frequently forgotten by those whose duty it is to lead others to perfection and by those who are themselves called to perfection. Our incorporation into the Mystical Body is a wondrous thing, for you see, the thirty-three years of Christ's life on this earth could not satisfy His desire to glorify His Father, nor is He content to love His Father infinitely in heaven, and in our tabernacles. Hence, He deigned to make unto Himself a *Mystical Body* in which He continues to live, to love, and to glorify His Father. In a word, in order to love the more, Christ has united Himself to new individual natures, to millions of individual persons, so that the complete Christ is Christ united to the faithful who will love in Him and with Him to the end of time. From each

[1] Gal. 3:27. [2] 1 Cor. 12:27.

of us, Christ asks for another humanity, He asks for the entire possession of our being—our body and soul with all their powers to make them His own and live through them His life of devotion to His beloved Father. According to Sister Elizabeth of the Trinity, Christ says to each one of us: "My son, give me your heart that in you and through you, in a life of union, I may love, or, rather *we* may love the Father ardently: give me your mind, your eyes, your hands, your whole being. I wish, in you and by you, to live as it were a second life wholly of love, which will be the complement and continuation of My earthly life at Nazareth and in Palestine."

Dear reader, ponder well this thought. It can change your life and whenever and wherever it is preached and taught it will change other lives. It is atomic in its force! In every prayer we say, in every action we perform, in every suffering we endure, in our every act of love, we must come to realize that we are a member of Christ and that Christ wishes still to pray, act, love, and suffer in us. As a natural consequence, we shall instinctively try to rid ourselves of our vices and faults, in order to clothe ourselves with the mind and desires which animated Christ in His actions, sufferings and prayers during His life on this earth. This is what St. Paul had in mind when he told his followers to: "Put ye on Jesus Christ." [1] Paul had put on Christ, and did so so thoroughly that he could say: "For me to live is Christ, and to die is gain." [2]

When one has "put on Christ" to the extent that He fills the soul which has been emptied of self to make room for Him, when such a soul shows forth the virtues and the mind of Christ to all with whom she comes into contact, and when such a soul sees the same Christ in his neighbor: "For as many of you as have been baptized in Christ have put on Christ. There is neither Jew nor Greek: there is neither bond nor free: there is neither male nor female. For you are all one in Christ Jesus," [3] such a one could truly be said to be perfect.

Certainly, the striving after perfection would not be such an arduous and irksome task for some of us if, rather than imitating of Jesus, we strove to be transformed into Jesus, to become Jesus as it were, to be identified with Jesus not only present, but living and

[1] Gal. 3:27. [2] Phil. 1:21. [3] Gal. 3:27–28.

acting within us. Imbued with such an ideal, the soul would find joy in emptying herself so that Christ could live His own life in her, and for His sake and not for hers. When she would pray, she would know that she prayed in union with Christ and thus God would be wonderfully glorified, praised, thanked, and powerfully petitioned. When she suffered, she would delight in making up what St. Paul said was wanting to the Passion of Christ. The soul so consumed with such a doctrine would soon cry out with St. Paul, "I live, now, not I: but Christ liveth in me." [1]

The crux of this concept of *identification* with Christ rather than cold *imitation* of Him can be summed up in this formula: "To renounce ourselves in order to allow Christ to do all things in us." And was not this the very thing that St. Vincent de Paul practiced when he would say before each action: "How would Christ do this?"

Indeed, the imitation of Christ is somewhat cold and matter of fact, in comparison to identification with Christ. In the light of the Pauline teaching, to imitate Jesus is no longer to copy Jesus but to be transformed into Jesus, to become Jesus in a certain sense, to allow Christ to develop and reproduce Himself in the soul.

One could close this book here and have a formula for sanctity. If you never read another page beyond the foregoing and began the implementation of the great Pauline truth you would be well on your way to perfection. The works of the purgative way, namely, the uprooting of sins, vices, and defects, and the works of the illuminative way, to wit, the implanting of the virtues, are of no avail and have no real meaning when separated from Christ. "I am the way," He said, "and the truth and the life. No man cometh to the Father, but by Me." [2]

But the purgation of defects, and the acquiring and practice of the Christian virtues are not enough. The *unitive way* is the real crown of the spiritual life. The totality, the perfection, lies in the soul's readiness for the act of the love of God, for actual and intense union with Christ. It is here that the grand ideal of St. Paul—a life lived in Christ's Name, the spiritual way of identification with Christ—is so productive of the unitive form of spiritu-

[1] Gal. 3:20.
[2] John 14:6.

ality. It no longer is a question of merely giving ourselves to Christ but rather of a quasi-identification with Him so that we give Him our heart that He may look upon it as His own and cause His virtues to shine forth in it, and in this way continue His life on earth and satisfy His intense love for His heavenly Father. Hear St. John Eudes say: "As St. Paul assures us that he fills up the sufferings of Christ, so we may say in truth that a true Christian, who is a member of Jesus Christ, and united with Him by grace, continues and carries to completion, by every action performed in the spirit of Jesus Christ, the actions which Christ Himself performed during His life on earth, continuing His life and His actions, doing and suffering all in the spirit of Jesus, that is to say in holy and divine dispositions."

The idea of identification with Christ living in the soul of the Christian so seized the great Cardinal Newman that he composed the following prayer which admirably expresses his belief in this regard:

Dear Jesus, help me to spread Thy fragrance everywhere I go. Flood my soul with Thy Spirit and Life; penetrate and possess my whole being so utterly that all my life may only be a radiance of Thine.

Shine through me and be so in me that every soul I come in contact with may feel Thy presence in my soul. Let them look up, and see no longer me but only Jesus. Stay with me, and then I shall begin to shine as Thou shinest: so to shine as to be a light to others. The light, O Jesus, will be all from Thee. None of it will be mine. It will be Thou who shinest through me upon others. O let me thus praise Thee, in the way which Thou dost love best, by shining on all those around me. Give light to them as well as to me; light them with me, through me. Teach me to show forthThy praise and Thy truth. Amen.

If this sublime doctrine were only better known and practiced by the clergy themselves, if in sermons and conferences, and above all, in spiritual direction, it formed the topic of instruction, there is no doubt but that many souls would rise to great spiritual heights and would soon be admitted to one or other degree of mystical union, and they themselves would fulfill their vocation, which according to St. Pius X "is to form Christ in others."

Tempted as one might well be to stop here and to proceed no further, what follows will help you lay solid foundations and erect solid walls so essential to the completed edifice. If, however, you keep the Pauline ideal fixed in your mind and you read what follows in the light of it, your work as a spiritual director will be fruitful and rewarding.

3

The Purgative Way

THE highest summit of Christian perfection is *usually* reached only by degrees. So universal is this experience that ascetical theologians have followed the writer known as Areopagite,[1] who noted that the offices of the angels were to purify, illuminate and perfect, so he assigned a threefold state of spiritual life: that of beginners, that of proficients and that of the perfect, of whom the first class are purified, the second enlightened, and the last class made perfect. These three states have come to be known as the *purgative way*, the *illuminative way* and the *unitive way*.

You will note that I used the word *usually* when saying that Christian perfection is reached only by degrees. It is indeed possible by some miraculous intervention or extraordinary grace that a soul might be brought suddenly from the lowest depths of moral abjection to the sublime heights of charity, as may be seen in the case of St. Mary Magdalene and other penitent saints. On the other hand, we may find saints in whom the purgative state may predominate even to the end of their lives, and God sometimes withholds the favors of the unitive way from many faithful souls who have advanced generously in the degrees of the purgative and illuminative ways and who have all along preserved the fervor of holy charity, which is the essence and crown of perfection.

Notwithstanding the foregoing, most souls do follow the three different stages or ways to perfection, and so let us proceed as if it

[1] These writings were composed after the fifth century by some unknown author, not by the Areopagite of the first century.

were a rule to advance from the lowest to the highest, or, as St. Thomas puts it: that of beginners—the purgative way; that of souls already advanced—the illuminative way; and that of the perfect—the unitive way. And it is important to know the differences that exist between the three ways. This is particularly true for directors. It is obvious "that beginners and perfect souls are not to be guided by the same rules,"[1] for as Father Grou (1731–1803) says, "The grace given to beginners is not that bestowed on souls already advanced, nor is the one granted these the same as that received by those who have reached the heights of perfection."[2] Therefore let us apply ourselves to the study of the three ways or stages of perfection, beginning with the purgative way.

The purgative way is the way or state of those who are beginners, that is, those who have obtained justification, but have not their passions and evil inclinations in such a state of subjugation that they can easily overcome temptations, and who, in order to preserve and exercise charity and the other virtues, have to keep up a continual warfare within themselves. It is called *purgative* because the chief concern of the soul in this state is to resist and to overcome the unruly inclinations of the passions by nourishing, strengthening, and cherishing the virtue of charity. Tanquerey says these people must direct their efforts toward the *avoiding of sin*, above all *mortal sin*, and toward the conquest of evil inclinations, of the passions, and of all that could make them lose the love of God.[3]

Father Arthur Devine, C.P., suggests that the purgation can and ought to be done not only by the keeping of the Commandments, but by foreseeing the occasions in which the precepts oblige, so as to be ready by a prompt and well-disposed will to resist—and avoid any sins opposed to them. This state, although in one sense it is imperfect, in another sense may be called a state of perfection, because the soul remains free from the stain of mortal sin.

Purity of soul may be said to be the proper end of the purgative way. With this as a prime principle, the logical thing to do is to attempt to grasp the notion of (1) the gravity of sin, (2) the form

[1] *Articles d'Issy*, n. 34.

[2] *Manual for Interior Souls*, edited by Donal O'Sullivan, S.J. (Westminster, Md.: Newman Press, 1955).

[3] *The Spiritual Life, op. cit.*, p. 172.

of prayer best suited to this purpose, and (3) the acts which aid toward uprooting the remnants and habits of former sins, thus preventing one from ever returning to them, (4) abnegation of one's own will, and (5) conformity to the will of God.

It is not our intention to give here a lengthy treatise on the gravity of sin. It must suffice that we cite St. Thomas' definition of mortal sin as, "An act whereby we turn away from God, our last end, willingly attaching ourselves in an inordinate manner to some created good,"[1] and state that we know that mortal sin must offend God greatly since He condemns it so vigorously in Holy Scripture and punishes it so severely. Holy Scripture describes mortal sin as the most odious and the most criminal thing in existence since it is an act of *disobedience* to God, an act of *ingratitude* toward our greatest Benefactor, and an act of *injustice*, since by sin we openly violate the rights God has over us: "Whosoever committeth sin committeth also iniquity. And sin is iniquity."[2]

The fact that God punished mortal sin so severely gives us another idea of its gravity. All one has to do is to think of the punishment God inflicted on the rebel angels, on our First Parents, and to what an extent God's own Son had to suffer to atone for man's sins: "He was wounded for our iniquities: He was bruised for our sins."[3]

One has only to contemplate the sorry effects of mortal sin to sense its gravity. God is driven from the soul; sanctifying grace is lost and with it the galaxy of gifts and virtues (save faith and hope); the merits we have earned in the past are lost and may be regained only by perfect contrition or sacramental absolution. Moreover, while we remain in the state of mortal sin, we can acquire no merits for heaven. Should one die in the state of mortal sin, his portion is eternal suffering in hell with all its horrors.

The beginner in the purgative way will be benefited greatly by a serious reading of the Spiritual Exercises of St. Ignatius, First Week, First Exercise.

Sin, being a willful transgression of the law of God, may be mortal or venial. When the law we violate is not necessary to the attainment of our end, or when we violate such a law, but in a

[1] *Sum. Theol.*, Ia–IIae, qq. 71, 73, 85, 89. [2] John 3:4. [3] Isa. 53:5.

slight matter, or if the law is grave in itself, but we transgress it either without full advertence or without full consent, the sin is but venial and does not deprive us of sanctifying grace. Very Reverend F. J. Connell, C.SS.R., prefers to call venial sin "a more easily forgiven sin."

We ought to distinguish between venial faults of *surprise* and those committed with full deliberation and full consent. Even some of our great saints have fallen momentarily into faults such as carelessness in prayer, or uncharitable words or slight lies. When promptly deplored and repaired for by penance, the saints found them no obstacle to perfection. It is otherwise with deliberate venial sins, for such hinder spiritual progress and must be vigorously combatted.

The malice of deliberate venial sin is enormous, in fact it is, mortal sin excepted, the greatest evil. It is an act of disobedience to God; it diminishes the external glory of God; and it is an act of ingratitude to a loving Father. Its effects are most damaging since in this life it deprives the soul of many graces and gradually lessens its fervor and predisposes it to mortal sin. In the next life its effects are deplorable too, for in order to expiate for venial sin many souls have to spend a long time in purgatory and thus are deprived for that time of the vision of God.

The great Canon Saudreau says that as there are degrees in perfection there are also degrees in sin. It is not hard for us to see that some persons accidentally fall into grave faults, and perceiving their unfortunate state, rise immediately therefrom, while others again remain in the state of sin because they do not have the courage to extricate themselves. In one, the faith remains intact, due to such things as: a particular grace given by God; a natural attachment to religion; or the salutary influence of Christian companions. In the other, the remorse is strong, and, as we already noted, the sinner wishes to give up his sin but he has not the courage. He suffers the tyranny of his passions while he is the slave of sin; one moment he wants to rid himself of his plight, the next moment he relents and puts it off. So far he is not obdurate or obstinate in sin. But rarely will he remain so for long—the resistance to good, continual infidelity, finishes by rendering the graces less abundant and less efficacious, the voice of conscience is weakened, and the faith grows weaker, and finally, the passions so often given vent to become more and more demanding and tyrannical and then the sinner falls into a state of obduracy.

Such a state is deplorable since it is so offensive to God and dangerous for the soul. All arguments in favor of correction roll off such a person like water off a duck's back. The evil is not in the judgment but in the will. There are different degrees of obduracy. For instance, the first degree is that which results from ignorance, such as is found in a person of little or no religious training. The second degree is that which results from weakness and frequently such become discouraged over their constant falls. The third degree is that of indifference. These do not care whether what they do is permitted or forbidden. They just want a good time and seek it recklessly. Finally, there is the class of persons who delight in doing evil, and who are proud of their irreligion and evil acts.

The difficult task of the spiritual director is to inspire such persons as those just mentioned to better dispositions. There are two great means to be employed in the conversion of inveterate sinners, and they are *prayer* and *penance*. There is little use in trying on such persons means that would be effective with pious souls. One must try to get from the sinner an honest effort at regular and attentive prayers, pointing out that such prayers will touch the heart of God and obtain for the sinner light to see and strength to abhor this sinful condition. Every effort must be made to spur such a one on to a desire for perfection. Discussions on the eternal truths —heaven, hell, death and judgment are most effective. Warnings must be issued against the occasions of sin, whether places, persons or things. But remember, *the principal thing is to stress prayer.* "When a man begins to pray," says St. Augustine, "he ceases to sin; when he ceases to pray, he begins to sin." It must be always remembered, however, that the sanctification of a soul is above all else the work of God.

For true conversion three things are required: first, a knowledge of past guilt, so that the sinner is moved by God's grace and may realize the cruel tyranny of his sins. Next, a great fear should be conceived on account of the severity of the divine justice, and a great sorrow for having offended a generous and loving Father. Finally, comes an efficacious resolution of amendment, and sacramental confession, accompanied by satisfaction through acts and works of penance, to which also are added confidence in Christ and hope in His Blood, and love of so good a Redeemer and an ardent desire of obeying Him and following in His footsteps and embracing His Cross without counting the costs. Anyone attaining this stage of conversion may rightly feel himself dear and acceptable to God.

A sinner's conversion to God is the work of divine grace, which interiorly strikes and moves a man to enter into himself and be perfectly restored to his Creator. But such a convert ought to "Bring forth fruits worthy of penance." [1] Past faults demand that the sinner ought to maintain an habitual sorrow for his failures so that the mere perception of anything evil, whether in reading, conversing, or by any other means or ways, at once produces displeasure and sorrow. The second fruit of penance is the continual remembrance of sins, not as particular instances but in general: "My sin is always before me." [2] The third fruit is satisfaction and that is twofold: one, that some penalty unwelcome to the body may be undergone: "They that are Christ's," says St. Paul, "have crucified their flesh with the vices and concupiscences"; [3] the other and more excellent, that we may cultivate those virtues which we have heretofore violated. The fourth fruit is fear and circumspection lest we sin again. "Serve ye the Lord with fear, and rejoice unto Him with trembling." [4] The fifth fruit is solicitude and watchfulness in avoiding occasions of sin. "He that loveth danger shall perish in it." [5] The sixth is diligent care in plucking up the roots of sin. A good farmer is not content merely to cut down the weeds. He will not rest until he has destroyed their roots. We must do likewise, for after our sins are blotted out, their roots still remain in us. The seventh is to have a most lowly opinion and contempt of self. This should not be too difficult when we reflect how we, by our sins, have offended an Infinite God. The eighth is a firm resolution of amendment and an eagerness to improve. Only he is perfectly converted who, regretting his past sins, intends not to repeat what he may again regret. Finally, the last fruit is the love of God, that is, perfect conversion to God and aversion from all sins, and love of our neighbor.

[1] Luke 3:8. [2] Ps. 1:5. [3] Gal. 5:24. [4] Ps. 2:11. [5] Eccl. 3:27.

All we have said in this chapter to this point forms but a preparation for what the scholars and saints call the Purgative Way—the first of the three states of perfection. It must be carefully noted that the principal characteristic of the purgative way, or the state of beginners, is the purifying of the soul in view of attaining to intimate union with God.

The *Treatise on Heroic Virtue* contains this explanation: "The purgative way includes those who are in the state of beginners, who have obtained justification, but have not their passions in such a state of subjugation that they can easily overcome temptations, so that in order to preserve and exercise charity, and the other virtues which are essential to it, they have to keep up a continual warfare within themselves; and to this state belongs the purgative way, which of itself tends to dispose the soul for justification as regards past sins, to lead her to make satisfaction for them, and to preserve her from them for time to come."

Note well that in the spiritual life, *beginners* are those who habitually live in the state of grace, and who have a real desire for perfection, but who, nevertheless, have still certain attachments to deliberate venial sins, and, now and then, fall into them. Tanquerey lists beginners as: (a) innocent souls—children, young men and young women, who, not content with the mere avoidance of mortal sin, wish to do more for God and become perfect; (b) converts from sin, who after great sins, return to God and press forward in the ways of perfection; (c) the lukewarm who started out on the way to perfection but have fallen into a state of tepidity. Saudreau says that beginners include both children and converted sinners, but for all practical purposes we ought to include souls who have not made any progress because they are too indolent or because they think erroneously that perfection is not for them; souls who have a false concept of perfection and therefore entered on a false way of spiritual life, and finally, souls who were once fervent but have fallen into a state where they live habitually in fully deliberate venial sins.

No matter what the causes may be, three things must be effected in all beginners: (1) they should be led to desire, pray, and strive for higher perfection; (2) they should be taught to perform correctly the exercises of the interior life; and (3) they should be taught methods and encouraged to purge themselves of those things which impede the dominion of charity in them.[1]

1. How does one lead a beginner to desire perfection?

Such a desire may be implanted in various ways, for example, by exhortation; through spiritual reading, including especially the lives of the Saints; missions and week-end retreats; study clubs, etc. Prayer, unremitting prayer, must be urged. St. Ignatius urges upon beginners meditation on the four last things; and St. Alphonsus remarks that the saints owed their sanctity more to their prayers than to their works. Frequent confession and Communion must be encouraged.

2. What must be taught to inspire beginners to advance in perfection?

Beginners ought to be acquainted with the fact that in the spiritual life where there is no progress there is retrogression, or as St. Augustine puts it: "As soon as thou art content with thyself, and thinkest thou hast done enough, thou art lost." St. John's words are forceful too, for the saint was inspired to write: "He that is just let him be justified still, and he that is holy let him be sanctified still." [2] The director can and should endeavor to explain the fundamental principles of the spiritual life and to suggest certain readings and more especially to impart knowledge about meditation methods and to check progress in meditation at regular intervals. The predominant passion must be isolated and instructions given on how to subdue its force. The director ought to prescribe a daily examination of conscience, and over and over again, recall to the beginner's mind the real object of the spiritual life. To lose sight of the object is fatal.

3. How are beginners to purge themselves of whatever impedes their progress in the love of God?

Beginners must be taught that not only fully deliberate venial sins but even venial sins that are partially deliberate, render the soul less acceptable to God because they turn aside a part of human life from its one end, the service of God. The director may help the soul track down the more noticeable and external defects and

[1] *Theologia spiritualis ascetica et mystica* (Rome: Gregorian University Press, 1946), n. 330.

[2] Apoc. 22:11.

suggest means suited to the individual character and spiritual stature of the person involved.

Spiritual directors to novices must first ascertain what progress they have made in the interior life, and whether they have really begun to enter therein, or whether their advancement still consists only in avoiding the ordinary sins of young persons, together with a certain exactness in carefully performing their spiritual exercises of prayer, reading, and examination of conscience. Generally speaking, they have not made much progress in prayer. Further, the director must examine whether they be not ignorant of the ways of God, knowing no other perfection than that which they themselves practice, or whether they do not even perform those actions without any idea of perfection. In fine, he must learn, as far as possible, the disposition of their soul—all this information being necessary in order to judge in what way they must be directed, and to aid them in fulfilling the designs of God.

Here are some general principles on spiritual direction, the classification of different penitents and rules for initiating direction.

Generally speaking, direction (other than pulpit and catechetical direction) is inseparable from confession as long as the soul clinging to attachment to sin remains mostly in the purgative way. When the soul has begun to advance toward fervor, it becomes easier to give direction apart from confession. Some priests, in order not to confuse direction with confession, give it at the end of the confession.

The priest who is a director at heart will not only find out the inner causes of the faults a soul may have but also its various attractions. "He will analyze," says Dom Chautard, "the difficulties and repugnances it meets within the spiritual combat. He will show it the beauty of an ideal and will try it out, and select, and control ways of living that ideal; he will point out the pitfalls and illusions; he will give the torpid a good shaking, and will encourage and reprimand and console as required, but only to freshen up the will and steel it against discouragement and despair." [1]

The great author of *The Soul of the Apostolate* has drawn up a list of spiritual states that would be well for every spiritual director to study with painstaking care:

[1] Chautard, *op. cit.*, p. 168.

1. *Hardened in Sin.*

   Mortal Sin. Stubborn persistence in sin, either out of ignorance or because of a maliciously warped conscience.

   Prayer. Deliberate refusal to have any recourse to God.

2. *Surface Christianity.*

   Mortal Sin. Considered as a trifling evil, easily forgiven. The soul easily gives way and commits mortal sin at almost every possible occasion or temptation. Confession almost without contrition.

   Prayer. Mechanical; either inattention, or always dictated by temporal interest—such souls enter into themselves rarely and superficially.

3. *Mediocre Piety.*

   Mortal Sin. Weak resistance. Hardly ever avoids occasions but seriously regrets having sinned and makes good confessions.

   Venial Sin. Complete acceptance of this sin, which is considered as insignificant. Hence tepidity of the will. Does nothing whatever to prevent venial sin, or to extirpate it, or to find it out, when it is concealed.

   Prayer. From time to time, prays well.—Momentary fits of fervor.

4. *Intermittent Piety.*

   Mortal Sin. Loyal resistance. Habitually avoids occasions. Deep regrets if there is a fall into mortal sin. Does penance to make reparation.

   Venial Sin. Sometimes deliberate. Puts up weak fight. Sorrow only superficial. Makes particular examination of conscience, but without any method or coherence.

   Prayer. Not firmly resolved to remain faithful to meditation. Gives it up as soon as dryness is felt or as soon as there is business to attend to.

5. *Sustained Piety.*

   Mortal Sin. Never. At most, very rare, when taken suddenly and violently by surprise. And then, often it is to be doubted if the sin is mortal. It is followed by ardent compunction and penance.

Venial Sin. Vigilant in avoiding and fighting it. Rarely deliberate. Keen sorrow, but does little by way of reparation. Consistent particular examen, but aiming only at avoidance of deliberate venial sin.

Imperfections. The soul either avoids uncovering them so as not to have to fight them, or else easily excuses them. Approves the thought of renouncing them, and would like to do so, but makes little effort in that direction.

Prayer. Always faithful to prayer, no matter what happens. Often affective. Alternating consolations and dryness, the latter endured with considerable hardship.

6. *Fervor.*

Venial Sin. Never deliberate. By surprise, sometimes, or with imperfect advertence. Keenly regretted, and serious reparation made.

Imperfections. Wants nothing to do with them. Watches over them, fights them with courage, in order to be more pleasing to God. Sometimes accepted, however, but regretted at once. Frequent acts of renunciation. Particular examen aims at perfection in a given virtue.

Prayer. Mental prayer gladly prolonged. Prayer on the affective side, or even prayer of simplicity. Alternation between powerful consolations and fierce trials.

7. *Relative Perfection.*

Imperfections. Guards against them energetically and with much love of God. They only happen with half-advertence.

Prayer. Habitual life of prayer even when occupied in external works. Thirst for self-renunciation, annihilation, detachment, and divine love. Hunger for the Eucharist, and for heaven. Graces of infused prayer, of different degrees. Often, passive purification.

8. *Heroic Perfection.*

Imperfections. Nothing but the first impulse.

Prayer. Supernatural graces of contemplation, sometimes accompanied by extraordinary phenomena. Pronounced passive purifications. Contempt of self to the point of complete self-forgetfulness. Prefers suffering to joys.

9. *Complete Sanctity.*

Imperfections. Hardly apparent.

Prayer. Usually, transforming union. Spiritual marriage. Purifications by love. Ardent thirst for sufferings and humiliations. (Few and far between are the souls that belong to the last two, even to the last three categories.)

I have read at least eighty books on spiritual direction and related topics, and not one author has so concisely put down the points to be taken up in the direction of beginners in piety as has Dom Chautard in *The Soul of the Apostolate.* The book is a *must* for every priest and religious if it were for nothing else than its capacity to simplify the difficult. For instance, this great author reduces this problem of direction to four general rules as follows:

1. *Peace.* Find out if the soul has *genuine* peace, not simply the peace which the world gives, or the peace that results from absence of struggle. If it has none, try to give the soul a relative peace, in spite of all its difficulties. This is the foundation of all direction. Calmness, recollection, and confidence also come in here.

2. *A High Ideal.* As soon as you have collected enough material to *classify* the soul and to recognize its weak points as well as its strength of character and temperament and its degree of striving for perfection, find out the best means of reviving its desire to live more seriously for Jesus Christ and of breaking down the obstacles which hinder the development of grace in it. In a word, what we want here is to get the soul to aim higher and higher all the time: always *excelsior.*

3. *Prayer.* Find out how the soul prays and, in particular, analyze its degree of fidelity to mental prayer, its methods of mental prayer, the obstacles met with, and the profit drawn from

it. What value does it get out of the sacraments, the liturgical life, particular devotions, ejaculatory prayers, and the practice of the presence of God?

4. *Self-Denial.* Find out on what point, and especially how the particular examen is made, and in what manner self-denial is practiced, whether through hatred of sin or love of God. How well is the custody of the heart kept; in other words, what amount of vigilance is there in the spiritual combat, and in preserving the spirit of prayer throughout the day?

"All the essentials of direction," concludes Dom Chautard, "come down to these four points. Take all four, if you will, as the basis for a monthly examination, or confine yourself to one at a time if you do not wish to take too long." [1]

In résumé then, the characteristic of the state of beginners, or the purgative way, is the *purifying of the soul* so that it can *attain to intimate union with God.* With this clearly understood, it follows that we must determine the best means of accomplishing this great goal, and the learned ascetical theologians all agree that, fundamentally, they may be reduced to two: prayer and penance. Hence in the following chapters we shall treat of: (1) prayer for beginners; (2) penance to atone for past sins; (3) mortification to safeguard from future falls; (4) the destruction of the roots of capital sins in the soul; and (5) the struggle against temptation.

And now, let us turn our attention to *methods* in spiritual direction.

Spiritual direction in its broad and generic sense is nothing more than a moral influence exercised on some souls to lead them to God. In this general sense spiritual direction is practiced by the clergy in charge of souls in a parish, and by parents and teachers who are charged with the education of children.

In the strict sense of the word, we understand by spiritual direction that moral assistance given by a priest to a soul to help her avoid sin, to maintain her in doing good, and to make her achieve definite progress on the paths of virtue and perfection. Such moral assistance is exercised through elucidation, solution, advice, counsel, and exhortation—the action being on the heart, the spirit, and

[1] *Op. cit.*, p. 176–180.

the will—keeping in mind always dependence on and cooperation with the grace of God. Spiritual directors can say in all truth as St. Paul said: "We are God's coadjutors." [1]

Before going into details about the methods and means of giving spiritual direction it might be well to set down some counsels on how to interest people in seeking direction. Here are a few suggestions:

(1) Several times a year present to the people from the pulpit sound reasons for spiritual direction.

(2) Retreat-masters should stress the importance of spiritual direction in their conferences to religious, citing the teachings of the Church, the fathers and the saints in this regard.

(3) Preachers of closed or week-end retreats have a golden opportunity of presenting to their retreatants the importance, nature, and necessity of spiritual direction. Usually the people who have the sort of faith that moves them to make a retreat are easily disposed to convictions on the need for and advantages of direction.

(4) Directors and moderators of parish societies such as the Children of Mary, C. Y. O., Sacred Heart League, P. T. A. groups, altar societies, study clubs, confraternities, Third Orders, alumni and alumnae groups, will have wonderful opportunities to explain spiritual direction and to encourage individuals to seek it regularly.

(5) The preachers of parish missions could easily make spiritual direction the topic of at least one instruction.

(6) Catholic publications and diocesan newspapers could from time to time carry an article explaining the importance and advantages of spiritual direction.

To those who need source material for such sermons, conferences, and instructions, we would suggest a careful perusal of the opening chapters of *The Spiritual Life* by the Very Reverend A. Tanquerey, S.S., D.D., for here you will find enough matter for many such instructions.

Now, as to methods of giving spiritual direction we have to make several distinctions. Heretofore, you perhaps have thought

[1] 1 Cor. 3:2.

of spiritual direction only in terms of the confessional or parlor, and always in reference to individuals. It may surprise you to know that there are such things as pulpit direction, catechetical direction, and finally the familiar kind, namely individual direction in connection with confession or outside the confessional.

And what pray, you will ask, is pulpit direction? Well, without attempting to make the matter appear complicated, it means simply that you (1) explain the topic of the sermon as well as you can; that you suggest (2) a certain application to the personal needs of your listeners; (3) a recourse to prayer and the sacraments for aid to carry out the resolution taken as the result of the sermon; (4) discussion with confessor at one's next confession as to the resolution taken and how it was kept.

Let us take, for example, the story of the Good Samaritan. As the preacher, you no doubt would point out such facts as the following: The Good Samaritan saw a fellow-man in need; he did something promptly; he did something personally; he did it practically. And it *cost* him, too. It cost him time, trouble, and money.

The application might be something like this: "Did not our Lord say: 'Whatsoever you do to the least of My brethren you do to Me'?" [1] There is the difficulty: to recognize God behind the masks of men. Why, the most soiled and tattered wreck of humanity that shuffles along the street is more precious in the sight of God than all the material wealth in the whole world.

One Holy Thursday, Blessed Angela of Foligno, with her girl companion, went to the Cathedral. They heard Mass and received Holy Communion and made their thanksgiving. Then Blessed Angela nudged her companion and said: "Come on, it's all over here. Now let us go out and find Christ among the poor and the sick and the needy."

Our Lord is still out there among them. Will you pick one resolution from the following and make it your *point* for the week? May I suggest:

(1) You pick out one home where there is sickness and offer to drop around and straighten out the house or stir up a meal.

[1] Matt. 25:40.

(2) Greater patience and love toward an aged and infirm member of your own family and the performance of some act of charity toward him or her.

(3) A decade of the rosary for the sick, the poor, and those in prisons.

(4) A positive act of charity toward a poor family.

Make up your mind about your resolution and recall it to mind as I offer the Holy Sacrifice of the Mass. Offer your resolution when I offer the bread and the wine soon to become the Body and Blood of Christ. At Holy Communion when our Lord is in your heart, ask Him to bless your resolution and give you the grace to keep it.

At your next weekly confession tell the priest at the end of the confession just what resolution you took and how you kept it.

So there you have an example of pulpit direction. This method can be used in sermons on the Epistles, the Gospels, the Commandments, the sacraments, the virtues and the vices. For instance, after an instruction on charity toward our neighbors, the conclusion could run as follows: "Dearly beloved brethren, examine yourself and see wherein you fail in this virtue—especially (1) in your own particular judgments, your sentiments, your actions, (2) in the relations with the members of your family, your co-workers or your friends, (3) in your relations with your superiors.

"Make one concrete resolution on this matter before the Offertory of this Mass begins. Offer your resolution with the priest. Pray for grace and courage to keep your resolution. Renew it each morning this week. Examine yourself on it each night and confide to your confessor the next time you go to confession just what resolution you took and how you kept it."

The priest who would make use of pulpit direction should follow this formula:

(1) Explanation of the lesson.

(2) Application to the particular needs of the hearers.

(3) Requesting the listeners to pick their own point or resolution for the week from at least two or three stated resolves.

(4) Recourse to prayer and the sacraments for the grace to fulfill the resolution.

(5) Daily renewal of resolution or point chosen and daily examination as to execution.

(6) Mention of the point privately chosen to the confessor at end of weekly confession.

So much for pulpit direction. Let us turn our attention to another type of direction, namely *catechetical direction.* As you would suppose from its title, catechetical direction is designed to help children and youths spiritually, although it could be used in the instruction of converts with great effect.

Catechetical direction consists in:

(1) A general explanation of the lesson.

(2) Practical applications of the matter taught to the condition and age of the children.

(3) Emphasis upon practical applications and their adaptation to the conduct of each child in particular.

This is accomplished by—

(a) A review of the particular points already noted and written in a note-book.
(b) A secret choice made by each student of the one he feels particularly applicable to him.
(c) A determination on the part of the student to apply to himself the one point so chosen.

(4) An appeal to make use of prayer and the sacraments to assure the student he will have grace sufficient to keep the resolution so chosen.

(5) An individual private examination by the student on how the resolution was kept. This is done by—
(a) Recalling before the start of the next class the matter previously treated.
(b) Re-reading the points listed in the previous lesson.
(c) Leaving to the initiative of each pupil the control of his conduct in the particular point so chosen.

(6) Mention of the point privately and secretly chosen to the confessor at the weekly confession, stating how it was kept.

Let us work out together one example to show how catechetical direction works in practice. Let us say that the catechism lesson is on faith, and so the priest, the teacher, or the parents would naturally define faith, treat of its object, nature, necessity, and qualities. It is following these that the catechetical direction is initiated or in other words, there is a practical application of the lesson to the individuals in the class.

It could be initiated as follows: "When you pass the church the next time, what should your faith tell you?—My faith should tell me that our Lord is in the tabernacle. What should you do to conform to that faith?—I should tip my hat, if I am a boy, or bow my head if I am a girl, saying at the same time: 'Jesus in the Blessed Sacrament I believe You are really present in the Holy Eucharist because You have told me so and You can never deceive or be deceived.' "

Or again:—"At noon you are seated at the table ready to eat your lunch, what does your faith tell you?—My faith should tell me that all I find there and all that I have comes from God, so I ought to thank God by saying my grace before and after meals."

Or again:—"At night when you are all prepared for your rest, what should your faith tell you?—My faith should tell me that God has given me many, many graces during the day; He has protected me from evils and accidents; He has given me an Angel to watch over me—so I ought to thank Him by saying my night prayers with deep piety and reverence."

"So children, here are three points. Write them in your notebook:

(1) I shall always salute our Lord when I pass His house.

(2) I shall say my grace before and thanksgiving after meals.

(3) I shall say my morning and evening prayers with piety and reverence.

"Now you have three points. Take *one* point this week and

make a firm resolution to keep it. Do not tell your classmates which point you have chosen. That is your secret. But recall the point each morning, say a special prayer daily, or better still, go to Mass and Holy Communion, asking of God the special grace to keep your resolution. Examine yourself each night before you say your act of contrition on just how you kept your resolution.

"Next time you go to confession, if you care to, it might be well to mention that you took such-and-such a resolution at your catechism class and then proceed to tell your confessor how you succeeded and ask him if you should continue with the same point this week or pick a new one."

This, then, is an example of catechetical direction, and it remains for the clergy to be diligent in preparing at least *three* points that might serve as the students' practical resolutions, never neglecting, however, the appeal for prayer.

The third type of direction is by far and large the most effective —namely, the *personal direction* in conjunction with or outside confession.

Let us first treat of the direction of children and youths in the confessional. It should be stated at the outset that the direction of the young should revolve, principally, around:

(1) Prayer
(2) Mortification
(3) Duties of one's state in life

Here is an example of how prayer could be treated. The child having finished his or her confession, the priest could say:

"You have said, my child, that you have neglected to say your evening prayers?"

"Yes, Father."

"Have you forgotten them every night?"

"Yes, Father."

"Jesus is sad when a little boy or girl neglects to bid Him goodnight. Listen well now, for I will help you to say your evening prayers. Do you have a crucifix in your room?"

"Yes, Father." (If the answer is "No": "Ask your mother to put one there.")

"Who is nailed hand and foot to the cross?"

"Jesus!"

"Well now, this evening when you go to your room to get ready for bed, kneel down and look at the crucifix and say: 'My good Jesus, I love you.' Do you understand?"

"Yes, Father."

"You won't forget it?"

"No, Father."

"This, then, is your special little point to observe this week. Tell me, now, what are you going to do every night this week before you go to bed? Come next week and tell me how you made out."

"Yes, Father."

So much for the first direction.

The following week.

"Father, you told me to come back to confession and tell you how I said my night prayers."

"What special point did I give you?"

"To kneel beside my bed and face the crucifix and say, 'My good Jesus, I love You!' "

"Did you do that every night?"

"Yes."

"That is fine. Now, what are you going to do this week?"

"I don't know, Father."

"Well, this week you will kneel by your bed and look at the wounds in our Lord's hands, feet, and side and then say very slowly, word by word, the *act of contrition.* Do you know the act of contrition?" (If not, tell child to read it from his or her catechism.)

In subsequent weeks the spiritual director will direct his attention to the recitation of morning prayers, having added first the Lord's prayer, then the three Hail Marys. Later points to be assigned will be ejaculations, frequent daily remembrance of the presence of God, the nightly examination of conscience, more frequent Communion, prayers for sinners, prayers before and after meals.

Mortification:

As to mortification, the director will recall its utility and merit and so he will strive to strengthen the wills of those children under him by suggesting small acts.

"What was your particular point this week?"

"To do all and support all things for love of Jesus."

"Tell me something you do not like to do."

"I don't like to get up in the morning when it is cold outside."

"I understand, but the next time your mother calls you to get up and it's cold in your room, think for a moment how cold it was in the stable of Bethlehem and then hop out of bed and say: 'Dear Baby Jesus, I do this out of love for You.' "

Other suggestions: Taking the smaller cookie or piece of cake. Helping with the chores around the house, etc.

Duties of State:

Whole avenues are opened in this area: obedience, application to studies, respect for parents, love for brothers and sisters, going to bed on time, running errands when requested by parents, etc. It should be remembered that in giving direction to children and youths that *the point for the week* should be stressed and then followed up in the next session by questions on its observance.

In the case of adults, the priest must decide for himself whether or not to continue the common practice of the short instruction to the penitent at the end of his or her confession or do as a good many priests are doing today—introduce spiritual direction in its strict sense. For the penitent who approaches the sacrament of penance once, twice or five times a year, perhaps the instruction method will serve better, but for the person who confesses weekly or bi-monthly, spiritual direction seems indicated.

Here is a sample of spiritual direction prepared for the adult who is a weekly or bi-monthly penitent. (This is an initial instruction.)

"Father, it is a week (or fifteen days) since my last confession. Since then I have been negligent and distracted in my prayers. I have told some lies. I have often been angry and impatient with those with whom I work or live. For these and all the other sins of my life, etc."

"Do you go to Communion often?"

"Every day, Father."

"That is fine. Our Lord wishes you to be holy: are you prepared to cooperate in this work?"

"I would ask nothing more."

"Well, with God's help I can assist you in this work. Reflect a little now, and then tell me what is it in your spiritual life which causes you the greatest difficulty."

"As well as I can see now, it is my impatience and proneness to anger. I am very critical and cause others to lose their patience."

"I understand. Let us begin with the virtue of patience. From today until your next confession, you will do your best to combat this tendency to impatience and anger. Your special point this week will be to be kind and patient to all. When you awake in the morning say: 'My Jesus, I shall be kind and patient to all with whom I come in contact today for Your sake.' At each Mass and Communion you will ask for the grace to keep this resolve. Often during the day you will say: 'My Jesus, meek and humble of heart, make my heart like unto Thine.' When you kneel down to say your night prayers—place yourself in the presence of God and say: 'Lord, help me to examine my conscience on my special point taken at my last confession.' Saturday next, after your confession, you will tell me how you observed your given point."

In subsequent confessions the direction could continue with this virtue, or when the confessor sees fit, go on to the others, as treated in a later chapter.

Regarding religious and the clergy, the task should be easier, especially if retreat-masters would stress the importance and advantages of spiritual direction. For instance, when a religious complains, as religious frequently do, about a certain coldness toward the sacraments of penance and the Holy Eucharist, what a wonderful opportunity is presented the confessor to give spiritual direction. How consoling and instructive it would be if the director could cite the cause of such coldness as listed in the writings of St. Francis de Sales, namely, *want of due preparation!* The saint named three things as essential preparations for the reception of the sacraments of Penance and the Holy Eucharist:

(1) purity of intention
(2) attention
(3) humility.

Think of the points that such a trio would provide for weekly scrutiny, counsel and exhortation and guidance. The careful perusal of the rest of this volume will supply unlimited material for use in spiritual direction.

I would be naïve indeed, if I did not realize that long before this, some reader has come to the conclusion that the writer is the most impractical person imaginable, for how in these modern days can one find time to give individual spiritual direction? Let me say that at this writing I have been a priest for some twenty-eight years and I've been in small prairie parishes and in off-Broadway city churches and I know from experience that there were times when one could do little else but give a salutary penance, absolution, and open the slide on the opposite side of the box. In retrospect, I wonder if I would not have done more spiritual good if I had taken time to give my penitents more than a stereotyped instruction?

The longer I live, the more I see the need for spiritual direction on a large scale, and so I'm now convinced, that as priests, we must make ourselves more available to those desiring or needing spiritual guidance. For instance, could you imagine a doctor hoping to see, examine, and treat all his patients in only four and a half hours every Saturday of the year? Yet, this is what we do with our spiritual patients. They have to get to confession on Saturday from a four to six P.M. and seven-thirty to nine P.M. period. Now, could we not extend the opportunity for confession and direction by making ourselves available before and after morning Masses? Could we not set aside an hour after supper, two or three nights a week for those desiring spiritual direction? In certain instances could we not be available by appointment? A decision on this very vital matter is up to the individual confessor and his conscience.

The Curé of Ars raised to spiritual heights a small country parish which had fallen into a dangerous spiritual lethargy and he did it from his confessional. You and you alone must decide whether the spiritual life of your parish will be better served by the time spent in the confessional, or that expended on social affairs and sports programs. For God's sake and for the sake of souls, I trust it is the former.

4

The Purgative Way and the Prayer of Beginners

THE small child in school will tell you if asked: "What is prayer?" that it "is talking to God." The same question put to a St. John Damascene would elicit this answer: "Prayer is an elevation of the soul to God." [1] These are the two aspects of prayer, and by joining them you produce a clear-cut answer that prayer is *an elevation of the soul to God to offer Him our homage and to ask His favors, in order to grow in holiness for His glory.*

The great St. Paul, writing to Timothy, said: "I desire therefore, first of all, that supplications, prayers, intercessions, and thanksgivings be made for all men." [2] The Angelic Doctor, St. Thomas,[3] explaining this passage, says that prayer is the raising of the soul to God in order to obtain some grace. When the object of our prayer is some definite thing the prayer is rightly called *petition.* When the things are not definite, for instance when we say: "Help me, O God," then it is *supplication.* Entreaty is a holy insistence in order to obtain the desired grace, as when we say: "By Thy Cross and Passion deliver us, O Lord." Finally, *thanksgiving* is the thanks which we give for benefits received, and by which, says St. Thomas, we merit still greater graces.

There are four general classifications of prayer: vocal, mental, private, and public. Vocal prayer finds expression in word and act. Hear David say: "I have cried to the Lord with my voice . . .

[1] *De fide orthod.*, I. III, c. 24. [2] 1 Tim. 2:1. [3] IIa–IIae, q. 83, a. 17.

O Lord, thou wilt open my lips! and my mouth shall declare Thy praise." [1]

Prayer is private when uttered in the name of an *individual*, and it is public when offered in the name of *society*, such as that offered by priests in the daily recitation of the Divine Office. Our Lord Himself spoke of the efficacy of two or more gathering together in prayer and said, "There I am in the midst of them." [2] If this be true of a small group, then surely it is realized when a multitude come together to praise, thank, atone, and petition. St. Thomas says that the power of prayer is then irresistible: "The prayers of the many cannot go unheeded when they unite in one." [3]

Mental prayer must be treated at length here since most ascetical writers maintain that mental prayer is technically the prayer of beginners; in other words, the prayer of those in the purgative way, in which the soul is purified from its sins and corrects its faults. Rodriguez declares that it is the common teaching of the saints that each of the ways—purgative, illuminative and unitive—has a corresponding special mode of prayer. Suarez is of a like opinion, so we are on safe ground if we hold that *meditation* is the prayer of the purgative way; that *affective* prayer is the prayer of the illuminative way—a time when the soul is illumined by gaining an ever-increasing knowledge of the divine wisdom, and by the practice of virtue; and the *prayer of faith* (*contemplation*) is that of holy souls who live habitually in the presence of God and are united to Him by burning love.

Now it must be pointed out that, according to Father Joseph du Tremblay, there is no point of real separation between the purgative, illuminative and unitive ways, nor between the states of prayer corresponding to them. Often, he remarks, all three are practiced almost at the same time according to the influence of grace, but more time is devoted to one special form of prayer according to the soul's spiritual progress. Thus there is more meditation in the purgative way, and less in the unitive way.[4] The foregoing may serve only to confuse and in no way solve the problem, so for our purpose let us proceed as if the ways were passed through successively.

[1] Ps. 3:5. [2] Matt. 18:20. [3] *Com. in Matt.* c. 18.

[4] *Méthode d'oraison*, II, n. 13; quoted in Ludovic de Besse, O.S.F.S., *The Science of Prayer* (New York: Benziger Bros., 1925).

It would be a great blessing if we could resolve the mystery that surrounds mental prayer. It has, to some people, an awesome meaning, to others it is a spiritual favor accorded only to saints, while to others it is a practice only for intellectuals. Nothing could be more at variance with the truth; meditation is for all, the saints and the sinners, the intellectuals and the uneducated.

No doubt it is the words "meditate" or "meditation" that confuse most people. Meditation is only part of the entire procedure, and the misunderstanding is due to the fact that we call the whole exercise by one of its parts, and so the term *mental prayer* is a much more correct title. St. Teresa, in her inimitable way, defines mental prayer as "nothing else but being on terms of friendship with God, frequently conversing in secret with Him who, we know, loves us."[1] "Therefore," says Father Peter Thomas, O.C.D., "all that precedes meditation, all that accompanies it and all that follows it have for their primary end the stimulation of this conversation with Christ. Let us repeat it again–for it is of extreme importance–meditation, in its final analysis, should be basically a friendly conversation with Christ . . . Meditation, then, is interior prayer without aid of rosaries, prayer books or missals. It is the prayer in which we talk to God in our own words. It is distinguished from vocal prayer, which employs the words and sentiments of some saint, spiritual writer, or the liturgy itself."

Meditation or mental prayer may be defined as the *silent application and elevation of our heart and mind to God, to offer Him praise and homage, and to promote His glory by our advancement in virtue*. Sometimes the term *mental prayer* is applied to that form of prayer wherein pious affections and acts of the will are predominant, while the term *meditation* is applied wherein the reasonings and considerations predominate, and because of this, it is called *discursive meditation*. Spiritual writers suggest the latter for beginners, since, as a rule, they need it in order to acquire convictions or to strengthen them.

You will note that we define mental prayer as "a silent elevation of the heart and mind to God." "True prayer," says St. Gregory, "is not in the sound of the voice, but in the desire of the heart; not our words but our desires give power to our cries in God's hear-

[1] *Autobiography, op. cit.,* p. 60.

ing." In mental prayer, along with the elevation of the heart must go the elevation of the mind and these must produce acts of the will if mental prayer is to be fruitful.

The difficulties in initiating mental prayer will be dispelled if we keep before our minds the aim of this form of prayer as stated by St. Teresa: "To lead the soul to a friendly conversation with Christ."

The first Psalm makes man's happiness consist in meditation on the law of God: "On His law he shall meditate day and night . . . and shall bring forth fruit in due season." [1] "Meditation," says Dom Guéranger, has a twofold object: "To bring back to the mind truths well known but too much forgotten; to draw them out of the darkness and silence in which they are sleeping, and to give these truths a power of action which they can have only when recalled to mind and reflected upon. Meditation consists, therefore, in recollecting ourselves and considering attentively that supernatural truth, the impression of which has grown weak, and no longer sufficiently rules our lives to stamp them with its character and seal. As long as the soul has not become familiar with supernatural truths, or as often as she feels herself becoming less impressed by them and less powerfully spurred on, meditation, or a return to it, will be absolutely necessary. As we cannot see unless we look, so it is only by means of meditation that the soul either gains or regains the truth."

The advantages of mental prayer are multiple. St. Laurence Justinian, for instance, says that it "puts the tempter to flight, drives away sadness, restores lost virtue, enkindles devotion, and intensifies divine charity." Ascetical writers are unanimous in declaring that mental prayer enlightens one about the malice of sin and thus detaches a person from his sins and the causes thereof. St. Alphonsus teaches that a man may recite the Rosary or the Little Office of the Blessed Virgin, or perform other devotions and yet continue in the state of mortal sin. But for one who meditates, it is utterly impossible to persevere in sin, because he must of necessity give up mental prayer or sin. "Meditation and sin cannot exist together." [2]

[1] Ps. 1:2, 3.
[2] *Praxis confessarii,* n. 122.

As to the necessity for beginners to meditate, the proofs are multiple. In speaking of prayer in general the learned Lessius says it is an article of faith that for adults prayer is necessary for salvation.[1] Following St. Alphonsus Liguori, he is here speaking not of a "necessity of precept" which admits of exceptions in cases of ignorance, impossibility, etc., but of a "necessity of means." St. Alphonsus concludes thus: "All the blessed, except infants, have saved their souls by means of prayer. All the damned have lost their souls because they have not prayed. If they had prayed they would not be lost. In hell the source of their greatest despair is, and always will be, the fact that they could have saved their souls so easily by asking from God the graces which they needed, but now there is no longer 'time' in which to ask them."[2]

As to meditation, while it is a most effective means of sanctification, it is not necessary for the salvation of most Christians. For priests, meditation is morally necessary according to the teaching of Pope Saint Pius X who said: "It is of the first importance that a certain time should be allotted every day for meditation on the things of eternity. No priest can omit this without being guilty of serious negligence, to the detriment of his soul."[3] The great retreat-master Father Desurmont used to say in his conferences to the clergy, "that for priests in the world, it is either meditation or a very great risk of damnation." Therefore, while there is little doubt but Tanquerey is right in asserting that for diocesan priests who are absorbed in the activities of the ministry, the habitual exercise of mental prayer at an appointed time is morally necessary to their perseverance and to their sanctification,[4] we must take care not to fall into the error of the Quietists who taught that mental prayer was commanded by a divine precept. The question here is whether or not mental prayer is a *normal* means of sanctification, like spiritual direction. Guibert says mental prayer is a normal means of sanctification and that it cannot be neglected without grave harm being done to the soul's perfection.[5]

Such thinking seems to be in accordance with the teaching of the Church since she holds that mental prayer is the ordinary means

[1] *De just.*, 12, c. 37, d. 3. [2] *Chief Means of Prayer*, p. i., chap. 1.
[3] *Exhortation to the Clergy*, Aug. 4, 1908.
[4] *The Spiritual Life, op. cit.*, p. 324.
[5] *The Theology of the Spiritual Life, op. cit.*, p. 210.

by which she leads souls to the true interior life so necessary for them. St. Benedict's rule, for instance, mentions meditation many times. Before the sixteenth century, the General Chapter of the Dominicans legislated clearly on mental prayer and Louis of Granada asserted that anyone who does not engage in meditation at least once a day does not deserve to be called a spiritual person or a religious. The fact is that in his Bull confirming the spiritual exercises of St. Ignatius wherein mental prayer was an important exercise, Pope Paul III made special mention of it and not only did he approve and confirm the exercises but exhorted all the faithful to make use of them as very profitable.

And now hear the saints on meditation. "Mental prayer is a torch which on this earth of darkness shows us the road on which we should walk." [1] St. Thomas Aquinas confessed that all he knew he had learned in mental prayer. St. Teresa says that he that neglects mental prayer has no need of being taken to hell by demons: he will cast himself into it.[2] St. Augustine goes so far as to say that "meditation is the beginning and ground of all good." [3] And I know of no better quotation than that of St. Bernard with which to conclude this consideration. Speaking of the means of attaining perfection, the saint says:

> No one attains to perfection at a single bound. It is not by rapid flight but laborious climbing we must reach the topmost rung of the mystical ladder. Let us mount, therefore, with the two feet of meditation and prayer. For meditation will show what is wanting to us and prayer will obtain it. The former will point out the way, the latter will lead us along it. The fine, meditation will discover to our view the dangers which threaten us and prayer will enable us to avoid them.[4]

"I do not know any better means of saving ourselves than through mental prayer," said St. John Baptist de Rossi. "He who does not meditate will fall into temptation. The day wherein we have not meditated let us beware of sin." [5]

[1] Ps.-Bonaventure, *Diaet. sal.*, tit. 2, c. 5. [2] Cf. *Autobiography*, *op. cit.*, p. 151.
[3] *Sermo* 226.
[4] *First Sermon for the Feast of St. Andrew; Sermons for the Seasons and Principal Festivals of the Year*, translated by a priest of Mount Melleray (Westminster, Md.: Newman Press, 1950), III, 50.
[5] Quoted in Saudreau, *op. cit.*, I, 111.

The great St. Alphonsus admonishes as follows:

Take care to make a half hour's meditation as soon as possible in the day. For though meditation is not absolutely necessary, it is morally necessary, in order to obtain the grace of perseverance. Those who neglect it will find difficulty in persevering in the grace of God. The reasons for this are two-fold: the first is because the eternal truths cannot be seen by the eyes of the flesh, but only by the eye of understanding, which is reflection. Hence he does not perceive them who does not meditate; and for the want of perceiving them he will hardly arrive at a due appreciation of the importance of salvation, of the means which secure it, and of the obstacles which hinder it; so that his salvation will be placed in imminent risk. The second reason is because the soul that does not practice meditation will also be backward in practicing prayer. Now prayer is necessary not merely as a precept, but as a means to observe the commandments, since as a general rule, and speaking of adults, God gives His grace only to those who ask for it. But without meditation a person has a very faint notion of his own spiritual wants, and he is, moreover, but slightly impressed with the necessity of praying, in order to overcome temptations and to save his soul: thus he is led to pray little or not at all, and for want of prayer is eventually lost.[1]

Pope Pius XII, reflecting the traditional doctrine of the saints, wrote in his Apostolic exhortation *Menti Nostrae:* "It must be stated without reservation that no other means has the unique efficacy of meditation, and that, as a consequence, its daily practice can in no wise be substituted for."

What could be added to the foregoing that would more effectively prove the necessity of meditation for those who are pursuing perfection? Suarez was of the opinion that meditation should be practiced by all the faithful no matter what their state and that it ought to be proposed to all as a necessary means for perfection.[2] St. Vincent de Paul likewise believed and taught that persons of every condition ought to meditate.[3] Saudreau maintains that even youths of thirteen or fourteen are capable of meditation and ought to be given special training in methods and encouraged to use this

[1] *Thoughts on the Religious Life* (New York: Benziger Bros., 1907), pp. 338–339.

[2] *De devotione*, chap. IV, n. 9.

[3] *Life by Abelly*, I, III, chap. vii.

efficacious form of prayer.[1] When you think of it, isn't it strange that we priests do not teach our young people the science of mental prayer? We would be delighted to see the crude crayon doodles of a first grader and we would praise the child for his enterprise, but if a senior in high school handed in the same sort of work in art class we would be disturbed no end. Why, then, are we satisfied solely with vocal prayer in youths who could (and would) meditate if they only knew of its great value? A few mimeographed copies of methods and a careful explanation of them would be productive of serious and consoling results. With this in mind, let us turn our attention now to methods of meditating and mental prayer.

I heard recently of a young man who, with no experience in the field in which he sought employment, when the prospective employer said to him: "For a man who has had no experience you certainly ask a high wage," said in reply: "Well, the work is so much harder when you don't know anything about it." There is profound truth in that answer, and it is so true of meditation. If some of the mystery and false ideas of difficulties are swept away, it will be found, I am sure, that meditation is not so complicated as some are led to believe.

As to the best time for meditation, it must be stated that while it may be made at any time of the day or night, the scholars believe that the morning is most suitable since the body is rested, the distractions will be fewer, and the meditation can exercise a great influence on the whole day. As to *posture*, it is said that one's exterior attitude acts to influence the soul, and so the posture ought to be such that it is productive of humility and recollection. So one may kneel, sit or walk so long as one bears in mind the reverence due to God, especially when one speaks to Him directly.

As to the *place* where meditation is to be made, this depends on the individual for it may be made anywhere. If one searches a place where the least distractions are possible then that is a good place for mental prayer. For good reason, many of the saints chose the house of God as their favorite place for mental prayer since they felt drawn to the tabernacle where Jesus resides. For some good reason, many seminaries have morning meditation, not in the chapel

[1] *The Degrees of the Spiritual Life, op. cit.*, p. 126.

but in the study hall, to impress upon the students that one need not be in the presence of the Blessed Sacrament to meditate well. Some saints chose secret hide-aways for their mental prayer, and based the logic of their action upon these words of our Lord Himself: "But when thou shalt pray, enter into thy chamber, and, having shut the door, pray to the Father in secret: and thy Father who seeth in secret will repay thee."[1] But did not the same Jesus call the Temple "a house of prayer"?[2] Where convenient, I think most people who are able to do so might find the House of God a most apt place for mental prayer.

As to the duration or length of the meditation, opinions vary. We have already seen that St. Alphonsus advocated a half hour. St. Francis de Sales suggests beginning with a half hour and increasing it gradually to an hour.[3] Time, for some of the saints, was not a problem. For instance, St. Francis Borgia, who after spending eight hours a day in prayer, asked the favor of a quarter hour more. St. Rose of Lima spent twelve hours a day in prayer. Before giving direction as to the length of a meditation it would be well to take into consideration the vocation and state of life as well as the degree of habitual recollection and mortification of the passions. One fish at a time is good fishing, and anything from a half-hour to one hour is a happy medium for beginners. St. Benedict (God love him) insisted on frequent short, intense prayers rather than protracted and indifferent long sessions, but Guibert writes that a full hour of mental prayer will usually be necessary for those who wish to lead a true interior life but who are prevented from spending almost the whole day in prayer of one kind or another as do persons in contemplative orders.

As to the subjects used for mental prayer, Louis of Granada says: "There are no better or more efficacious subjects for meditation than those which treat of the notable articles and mysteries of our faith, such as the Passion and Death of our Saviour, judgment, heaven, hell, the divine gifts and the remembrance of our own sins, of our life and of our death. Each of these topics well pondered and considered has a great force to carry our heart to love and to fear God, to a hatred for sin and mistrust of the world."[4] The

[1] Matt. 6:6. [2] Luke 19:46. [3] *Introduction to the Devout Life, op. cit.*, p. 52.
[4] *Libro de la Oracion y Meditaciòn*, part. I, chap. I, n. 9.

other mysteries of the life of our Lord, the teachings of the gospel also furnish most ample material for mental prayer. The different virtues and the duties of one's state in life also provide a nearly inexhaustible source of meditation material. For beginners, it is suggested that they follow the Exercises of St. Ignatius.

For those who live in community life, it is not unusual to find that one meditation is read to the whole community and all are expected to use the material so dispensed. From experience, I have learned that, in not a few instances, the meditation takes on all the marks of spiritual reading, for pages and pages of some abstract or painfully dry tome are read to the religious. St. Teresa advises us that to meditate is to place ourselves in the company of Christ and reflect on Him in the state corresponding to our feelings at the time. When full of joy, meditate on His Resurrection, if sorrowful, join Him in Gethsemane, and so on. But when you think about it—who is full of joy at five-thirty in the morning?

If you are in a community where a set meditation is read to all, listen respectfully. If it touches your heart so much the better. If it fails to appeal to you, freely choose some different subject. "Let everyone choose the means which succeed best with him," says de Besse, "even though other people find these means unsuitable."

Those living in the world should use the greatest liberty in choosing a place or a time for mental prayer. Whether they pray in the morning, afternoon or evening; whether in their homes, on the train, or in a church; whether they use books, images or a crucifix, it matters little so long as they do it faithfully and fervently. The main thing is that they have a real appreciation of the advantages and need for mental prayer if they would make spiritual progress. Mark well the words of St. Bonaventure:

> If you would suffer with patience the adversities and the miseries of this life, meditate. If you wish to obtain the courage and the strength to vanquish the temptations of the enemy, meditate. If you wish to mortify your will with all its inclinations, meditate. If you wish to know the deceits of Satan and uncover his cruel plans, meditate. If you wish to live in joy and walk sweetly in the ways of patience, meditate. If you wish to rid your mind of vain thoughts, meditate. If you wish to nourish your soul with honey of devotion and have it constantly filled with good thoughts and good desires, meditate. If you wish to

strengthen your courage to pursue the ways of God, meditate. It is in mental prayer that we receive the union and the grace of the Holy Ghost who teaches all things. I will go further: if you wish to rise to the height of contemplation and enjoy the sweet embraces of your Spouse, meditate. We have heard of and seen and still see every day a great number of simple people who have received all the good things we have enumerated.

Thus speaks a great saint, so it behooves us all to set about learning to meditate and meditate well.

Blessed Eymard suggests that the meditation be made to suit the end desired, since,

Mental prayer is God's way of sanctifying us, therefore it must also bring about a reform in our ways. If the passion to be subdued is sensual, [he continues], we must in mental prayer see, first of all, the fatal consequences of our state in regard to eternal salvation; we must consider the supernatural punishments, the last ends, death, judgment, hell which we deserve, heaven which we close, the wrath of God. We shall thus be induced to be severe in our moral behavior and, as it were, a declared enemy of our passions.

If it is a matter of rooting up a sin from the heart, our tactics must be different. The heart is as refined and sensitive as the body is blind and brutal. The heart is all affection; it gives itself; it masters through love and is mastered by it. It acts only out of sympathy. We must take away its idol, change its affection, turn it away from the object of its sympathy. We must in mental prayer consider the nothingness of what the heart adores, the vanity of what it loves. Against the idols of clay, set the beauty of the Eternal God. But be very careful never to take away from what it has seen, without at the same time giving its love another object more beautiful, worthier, and sweeter than the first. It cannot remain empty. Take the world away from it only to give it God instead. Give it God, the Love of Loves, Jesus Christ, its Savior, infinitely good and infinitely loving.

If the sin to be rooted up is one of the mind, the way to go about it will again be different. Whereas the heart yields to sentiment, the mind wants to be convinced by reason and yields to evidence only. Reason with it. It takes a long time to convert it. Rarely and with difficulty may we score a complete victory over it. That is particularly true of pride. Let your meditation, then, be one of reason and light. Convince it that it is in the wrong. Point out to it the injustice of the end which sin does to God, its ugliness. Let it be convinced of its faults, and it will be forced to submit.[1]

There are numerous methods of making mental prayer, chief among them the Ignatian and the Sulpician methods. However, before examining meditation mechanics, it must be stated that certain points are common to all of them. There is always a remote, a proximate, and an immediate preparation.

Remote preparation lies in making our daily life harmonize with prayer. This is done in three ways: (1) mortification of the senses and of the passions. St. Francis Borgia used to say that prayer introduces divine love into the heart; but it is mortification that prepares a place for charity, by removing from the soul the world, which would otherwise prevent the entrance of love. Having once heard a person praised for his great spirit of prayer, St. Ignatius of Loyola said: "It is a sign that he practices great mortification." (2) habitual recollection; (3) humility.

Proximate preparation consists in three acts: (1) selection of a topic for meditation on the preceding evening; (2) recalling the general topic to mind upon awakening the morning of the day on which it is to be made; (3) approaching the time for the exercise with a strong desire to glorify God and further our own spiritual advancement.

Immediate preparation, which is actually the beginning of the meditation itself, consists in placing ourselves in the presence of God by recalling to mind the fact that God is everywhere and that He dwells within us and by acknowledging this Presence and imploring the aid of the Holy Ghost to help our feeble efforts to accomplish our august task. St. Teresa's immediate preparation for meditation consisted in an examination of conscience, then the recitation of the Confiteor, and ending with the Sign of the Cross.

As to the *body of the meditation* itself, methods may differ, but in general contain the following acts: (1) acts of worship, thus giving to God the religious homage due Him; (2) considerations of some mystery of our faith or some virtue, pondering them so as to stir up our will to regulate our conduct in consequence thereof;

[1] *In the Light of the Monstrance* (New York: The Sentinel Press, 1947), pp. 173–174.

(3) self-examination to see our failings in regard to the belief or practice of the mystery or virtue and to survey the progress yet to be accomplished; (4) prayers or petitions begging the grace to use the means conducive to uprooting of a vice or the implanting of a virtue; (5) resolutions whereby we determine from then on to do better.

Every meditation must have a *conclusion*, and this is very important. Every proper conclusion to meditation ought to include: (1) an act of thanksgiving for the favors received; (2) a review of the manner in which we have made our mental prayer; (3) the selection of some impressive thought or some strong text or maxim which will recall to us during the whole day the ruling idea of the meditation.

Ludovicus Blosius compiled this group of aspirations for use by those in the purgative way: "O Lord God, I, a most vile sinner, am not worthy to live on earth. Alas, I have wandered far removed from Thee, and I dwell in a region far removed from Thee and unlike Thee. Wretched and blind am I! I am nothing, I can do nothing without Thee. Ah, kind and sweet Jesus, have mercy on me. Wash me with Thy Precious Blood; cleanse me from all sin; heal me perfectly, that I may please Thee."

I cannot impress too deeply upon the reader that to meditate means, in general, nothing more than to reflect seriously upon some subject. Meditation as mental prayer is a serious reflection on some religious truth or event, united with reference and application to ourselves, in order thereby to excite in us certain pious sentiments —such as contrition, humility, faith, hope, charity, etc.—and to move our will to form good resolutions conformable to these pious sentiments.

In the actual exercise of prayer we meditate on the subject we have chosen; we draw conclusions from it; we make reflections on the past; we examine our present dispositions and form resolutions for the future. We stir up the affections, encourage ourselves to persevere and ask the assistance of God to this great end.

Discursive meditation is that mode of reasoning from the more to the less or from the less to the more. For instance: If the highest angel fell, if a creature so perfect, free from concupiscence and the corruption of original sin, possessed of more grace than I shall ever have, nevertheless, perished miserably, how fearful ought I to be of falling whatever the degree of perfection I may have attained?

Madame Cecilia, in her great work, *At the Feet of Jesus,* says that

meditation is an exercise of the faculties of our soul—memory, understanding and will. Do you complain you cannot meditate? Well, let me ask you: Have you ever received an affront that cut you to the quick? Then, perhaps, you did meditate; you thought over it for an hour or more. *Memory* recalled the facts, *imagination* supplied extra details and coloring, the *intelligence* discerned the motives, such as ingratitude, jealousy, pride; it considered the baseness and the unexpectedness of the insult; finally, the *will* took a firm resolution to avoid that person. Now what was all this but a meditation in which you employed all the powers of your soul? Moreover, it was probably made without a single distraction, which is a very rare occurrence when we meditate on a mystery of our holy faith.

Unfortunately the subject was not well chosen, but at least it may help you to understand that you are capable of making a meditation. Suppose that, instead of reflecting on a personal affront, you had chosen for a subject the insults received by our Lord at the court of Herod. You pictured the scene, recalled the facts, pondered them, weighed the motives, and then, stirred yourself up to imitate your Divine Model and prayed in a spirit of worship, petitioned for grace to act as our Lord did under similar circumstances—then you would have made an excellent meditation.

There is no great difficulty in making mental prayer but it is wise to follow some of the plans traced out for us by the masters of the spiritual life. The two best known plans are the Ignatian Method and the Sulpician Method. Let us begin by examining the one formulated by St. Ignatius and set forth in his Spiritual Exercises.

1. *Preparation:* Points determined. Question of memory. Fruit chosen.

   Recollection: suitable thought over-night and in the morning upon awakening.

   Preparatory prayer to the Holy Ghost.

2. *Preludes:* Recall of the truth to be considered. Composition of place (a fancied picture to help the imagination). Petition for the fruit of the meditation.

3. *Body of the Meditation:* Exercise of—

    Memory: Who? What? Where? Why? How? When? For whom? With what fruit? With what love?

    Understanding: What is the practical conclusion? Its motives? Becoming? Useful? Delightful? Easy? Necessary? What have I done hitherto? What shall I do henceforth? What obstacles are there? What means am I to take?

    Will: Affections throughout. Faith, sorrow, humility, confidence, hope, love, praise, thanksgiving. Resolutions taken at the end of each point: practical, sound and personal.

4. *Conclusion:*

    a. Colloquies: a special little conversation with God, Christ, our Blessed Mother, my patron saint or some other saint about the matter of the meditation, and a petition for the fruit which I expect from the mental prayer.

    b. Review: How have I made the meditation? Wherein and why have I failed or succeeded? What resolutions have I formed? Choice of a thought as a reminder of the meditation for the day.

Let us now examine the famous Sulpician method of meditation.

Preparation:

Evening. Choose the *subject* of meditation and the virtue to be considered in God, in Christ, or in one of the saints.
Determine the fruit to be derived from it. Try to keep it in mind before going to sleep; recall it when rising in the morning.

Morning. When you begin your meditation *realize* that you are in the presence of God and make intimate acts of contrition, humility, adoration and love.
Beg the Holy Spirit to bless this conversation with Christ and ask the Blessed Mother to obtain the grace for you to speak with her Son as she would, and to grow in the special virtue under consideration.

The Meditation Proper

ADORATION*

Christ before My Eyes
(Video)

CHRIST

Represent to yourself Christ (or one of the Saints) as a living, loving COMPANION. Consider His sentiments, words, and actions that reveal the virtue under consideration. Charmed by its beauty in your Divine Model, converse easily and familiarly with Him about it, expressing sentiments of faith, adoration, admiration, praise, thanksgiving, love, joy. Keep repeating these sentiments MANY TIMES.

COMMUNION*

Christ in My Heart
(Sitio)

SELF

Contrast yourself with Christ regarding this virtue, noting its relative importance in your own life, your personal conduct toward it in the past and for the future. This will be done in familiar converse, using such affections as humility, contrition, desire, confidence, love. Repeat these affections to Him MANY TIMES lovingly, tenderly, loyally, but simply. Listen, also, to what He has to say to you.

* The adoration and the communion should not be considered as two separate parts and follow each other, but should be interwoven throughout the entire meditation.

CO-OPERATION

Christ in My Hand
(Volo)

Look forward to the duties of the day and resolve with great earnestness to be faithful in meeting the opportunities that God will permit to prove the sincerity of your love for Him. If this resolution is related to the *particular examen*, it will have additional vigor. Submit it to Jesus and Mary for approval, and ask their help in carrying it out so that you may become more thoroughly one with them.

CONCLUSION

Select a striking thought to carry through the day for loving prayer. If possible, unite this with a thought from the Mass.

Thank God for the graces He has given you during this meditation, and ask His pardon for any faults or negligences committed.

Entrust yourself and your resolution to the care of our Lady.

There are other methods of meditation, for instance Bishop Bellord's Method, to name but one. However, to give more here would serve no good purpose and might only tend to confuse the issue. Those who do not find the Ignatian Method suitable could try the Sulpician Method and if both of these are found unsuitable, the director might search out other methods and suggest them to those under his care. Beginners should be carefully instructed in the form of mental prayer, and mimeographed or printed sheets showing a scheme or outline such as we have given above might be handed to the individual or used as a basis for a study-club.

Let it be clearly understood that just thinking of one of the eternal truths or the virtues is not mental prayer. Meditation in the mind, to bear fruit, must be accompanied by acts of the will. In meditation we exercise the understanding; in prayer, the will. One may meditate as long as one pleases and upon the most sublime subjects, but such meditation will be of small profit if one does not proceed to affections suitable to the thoughts entertained. "What then is the proper definition of prayer?" asks Gaetano da Bergamo,

> Simply this: As meditation is to think seriously on the things of God, so prayer is the devout turning of one's self to God by pious and humble affections. Praising, admiring, adoring God; fearing and loving God; trusting and hoping in God; humbling and resigning one's self to God; endeavoring to imitate Him. And as meditation no less than prayer should be directed to the well-ordering of our life, which consists in shunning evil and adhering to good, so in a general way, we may say of affections that they are various movements of the will—loving, desiring, seeking and resolving either to acquire some virtue or to correct or avoid some vice.

It is foolish to attempt to acquire the spirit of devotion and mental prayer until and unless we have blotted out the ideas of our past life, the images and the memory of innumerable things which foster our self-love and vanity. It is only our sins and our evil habits that prevent the will, in prayer, from flying instantly to the

Sovereign Good and being enkindled with love. This obstacle removed, the will would soon be all on fire without any long exercise of the understanding.

St. Teresa warns that perfection does not consist in thinking much but in loving much; and St. Vincent de Paul says:

> When we want a light we take a tinder box, strike it, and as soon as it flames up, we light the candle. Anyone who continued to strike the tinder after the candle is lit would act in a most ridiculous manner. Similarly, when the soul has been enlightened, what is the use of hammering the intellect over and over again in order to increase the number of arguments and holy thoughts? Surely it is a waste of time to do this when all our attention should be devoted to inflaming the will.[1]

Those who find it difficult to begin or are tempted to abandon this powerful means of salvation must have the courage to act against themselves and proceed to begin, and continue in it after the novelty has worn away and the yoke of perseverance begins to gall. Blessed are they who courageously persevere, for their salvation is secure.

[1] *The Degrees of the Spiritual Life, op. cit.*, I, 3, 2.

5

Penance and Mortification in the Purgative Way

IF SOMEONE, endowed with the gift of prophecy, had sought out St. Mary of Egypt at the time that she, beautiful, vain, and lustful, was the idol of all Alexandria, and had said to her: "Woman, listen to me; the time will come when you will not only reject your life of ease and sinful pleasure, but also, in the midst of a horrible wilderness, will lead the life which I will set before you. For forty-seven years you will not see a single human face; but surrounded by wild beasts, you will prefer their society to that of your present companions. You will take only three loaves of bread with you to the desert; and these, hard and stale, will serve for your food for sixteen years. When these are gone you will live like an animal on the wild herbs in the field and the water of the marshes, until you learn to live without any sustenance whatever. Besides, having no roof to shelter you, or warm garments to clothe you, you will shiver in the piercing cold of the winter nights, and be scorched in summer by the burning rays of the noonday sun. This I predict for you; and believe me, you will do it all."

Tell me, dear reader, if you had gone and told this to Mary of Egypt at the height of her sinful career, would she not have laughed you to scorn? Yet, it is an historical fact that she did choose it, and we have it on the word of the Abbot Zosimus, who was directed by God to bring her the last sacraments. And thanks to the grace of God, not only did it not appear to her on her deathbed a wearisome life, but easy, and full of joy.

Beginners in the purgative way are often frightened when they read in the lives of the saints of their austere penances, and they say to themselves, "I could never do anything so difficult." At the outset of the struggle, the task of doing penance and performing mortifications may rightly seem difficult, but we discount the grace of God. With His grace we can do all things He asks us to do, so do not let the thought of penance and mortification frighten you away from making spiritual progress. The chief penance and mortification God asks from most of us is a complete fulfillment of the duties of our state in life.

Penance, after prayer, is the most effective means for cleansing the soul of past faults and even for guarding it against future falls. Our Blessed Lord Himself declared He had come to call sinners to repentance: "I come not to call the just, but sinners to penance." [1] And He said that unless we do penance we shall perish: "But except you do penance, you shall all likewise perish." [2] So, on the word of the Son of God, penance is obligatory since by our sins God is offended and His rights are violated, and thus we are bound to make reparation for the outrage.

Penance may be defined as a supernatural virtue, allied to justice, which inclines the sinner to abandon and hate his sins because they offend God, while inclining him at the same time to form the firm resolve of avoiding sins in future and of atoning for those of the past. It is obviously, as one can see, a duty of justice toward God and a duty of charity to ourselves and to our neighbor. That it is a duty to God is self-evident since every sin robs God of some glory which is His due. But how is penance a duty of charity to ourselves and to our neighbor? It is a duty to ourselves, because sin leaves in the soul pernicious consequences against which it is necessary to react. Sin intensifies in us a disordered love for pleasure and weakens our will and thus makes future sins easier to commit. Nothing works as effectively against such disorders as the virtue of penance. For each sin we commit that has been remitted, there remains a temporal punishment and this punishment must be atoned

[1] Luke 5:32.
[2] Luke 13:5.

for in this life or in the next. It is to our advantage to make satisfaction in this life and penance is a very important way by which to accomplish this. That penance is important as an act of charity toward our neighbor is equally evident from the teaching of Christ Himself, of the Church, and the practices of the saints. When the apostles failed in their attempts to deliver the young man of the unclean spirit that had so frightfully tortured him, they posed this question to our Lord: "Why could not we cast him out?" Christ said to them: "This kind can go out by nothing but prayer and fasting." [1] Since this is positive proof that our works of satisfaction can contribute to the welfare of other souls, our charity ought to prompt us to do penance in behalf of others. "Prayer and mortification," says Saudreau, "are, in effect, the means often indispensable and alone capable of procuring the conversion of inveterate sinners." We know what the Curé of Ars said to the priest who said he could not convert his parishioners: "Have you fasted? Have you prayed? Have you taken the discipline? Until you have used all these means, do not think you have done your utmost." [2] Directors of souls might learn this lesson well and they ought to say this prayer daily: "My God, give me the courage to make many sacrifices for the salvation of many souls."

The Church gives evidence of her accord with the belief that our works of satisfaction can contribute to the spiritual welfare of others by sanctioning such pious confraternities and religious groups as those whose aim is the offering of prayers and works of penance for the conversion of sinners.

Some specially favored souls both in religious life and outside it are drawn to offer themselves as expiatory victims for the sins of others. Some are directly called to such service by God Himself, as was Sister Josefa Menendez. Father H. M. Vinard, S.J., in his introduction to her writings, says:

> To be a victim necessarily implies immolation, and as a rule atonement for another. Although strictly speaking one can offer oneself as a victim to give God joy and glory by voluntary sacrifice, yet for the most part God leads souls by that path only when He intends them to

[1] Mark 9:27–28. [2] *The Degrees of the Spiritual Life, op. cit.,* I, 19.

act as mediators: they have to suffer and expiate for those for whom their immolation will be profitable, either by drawing down graces of forgiveness on them, or by acting as a cloak to cover their sins in the face of divine justice. It stands to reason that no one will on his own initiative take such a role on himself.

To Sister Josefa our Lord said on one occasion: "Yes, pray for souls, for the seven of which I have given you charge. A few more sacrifices and they will return to Me." [1] To practice penance more perfectly, it is important that we unite ourselves to the atoning Christ, and we must join in His acts of satisfaction. "All penances," says Father Faber, "come to naught which do not rest on Christ."

Among the works of penance, fasting and almsgiving are highly ranked. The Church has established the Lenten fast, that of the Ember days, and certain vigils to afford all an opportunity of making expiation for their faults. With the advice of a director such periods of fasting could be extended so that besides the days of fast inspired by the law of the Church, those wishing to do penance may forego some food at each meal to this same end.

Almsgiving is both a work of penance and mercy and because of this double role is a powerful means of atoning for our sins. "Redeem thou thy sins with alms," [2] says Holy Scripture. There is little need to expand on this here.

Other works of penance include the willing and joyful submission to all the trials and crosses Providence permits to befall us. Along with this is another laudable way of doing penance and that is a careful and faithful discharge of the duties of our state in life. St. John Berchmans said: "My greatest penance is community life," to which thousands of religious will say "Amen." But no matter what the state, if the duties are done in a spirit of expiation and penance they will work unto the purification of the soul. Directors might impress that on their charges who are looking for penances to perform.

So far we have discussed penance, but what about mortification, and wherein does it differ from penance? Mortification, like penance, is a useful means of cleansing the soul from past faults;

[1] *The Way of Divine Love* (Westminster, Md.: Newman Press, 1949), p. 58.
[2] Dan. 4:24.

but its main purpose is to safeguard us from sin in the present and in the future, by lessening in us the love of pleasure. You will remember that we defined penance as a supernatural virtue, allied to justice, which inclines the sinner to abandon and hate his sins because they offend God, while inclining him at the same time to form the firm resolve of avoiding sins in future and of atoning for those of the past. Mortification, as the word implies, is a certain kind of death, a separation of the soul from carnal pleasures and may be formally defined as "a combat against our evil propensities in order to keep them subject to our higher nature and subject too, to the Will of God."

Mortification is not a negative thing. It is getting rid of self in order to allow Jesus to live His life in us, and to enable us to share His life fully. There is no chance of living such a life without that degree of mortification which is sufficient to prevent our lower appetites from leading us into sin. It is a certain fact that the threefold concupiscence (the inclination to avarice, impurity and pride) that remains with us, spurred on by the world and the devil, often inclines us to evil and endangers our eternal salvation unless we take steps to mortify it. Since we are obliged, as far as we can, to flee from proximate occasions of sin—persons, places and things, if from past experience such things are to us serious and probable danger of sin, then in most cases mortification is required, and mortification that is mandatory. Besides the practices of mortification imposed by divine law and the practices of mortification imposed by ecclesiastical law such as the fast of Lent, Ember days and vigils which bind those subject to them under pain of grievous sin (unless one has been excused or dispensed), there are others which, when temptations grow violent, certain individuals must undertake upon the advice of their director. These we shall see a little later on.

Of the necessity of mortification for perfection, proof abounds in the Holy Scriptures and in the writings of the saints. Since mortification consists in regulating and ruling our passions, our evil inclinations and our disorderly self-love, and perfection consists in the love of God unto sacrifice and the immolation of self, then we can see the full meaning of Christ's words: "If any man will come after Me, let him deny himself and take up his cross daily and follow Me." [1] Commenting on these words of our Lord, St. Basil calls attention to the fact that our Saviour begins His counsel with the words: "Deny thyself, and [then only], follow Me."

St. Paul tells his followers that "they who are Christ's have crucified their flesh with the vices and concupiscences." [2] Elsewhere he speaks of "Always bearing about in our body the mortification of Jesus." [3]

Many volumes could be used merely to cite the testimony of the saints. For instance, St. Jerome says: "In just the measure that you overcome self, will you advance in perfection." St. Francis de Sales says that "as salt preserves flesh from corruption, so mortification preserves the soul from sin."

But let us not labor a point that is so obvious; rather, let us make a cursory study of the practices of mortification. Before beginning such a study, it is important to lay down a few principles. (1) Mortification is a means and not an end, for perfection does not consist in self-denial but in charity, and so, mortification ought to be adapted to the end that it develops charity; (2) mortification must include the whole man, body and soul; (3) mortification must be practiced with discretion and prudence. St. Francis de Sales comments that "To weaken our body exposes us to temptation as much as to pamper it"; [4] (4) mortification of the interior faculties is of greater worth than the mortification of our exterior senses, although for practical purposes it is well to begin with those of an exterior nature.

In mortifying the body and its exterior senses the motive that is uppermost is that our Lord Himself recommended the moderate practice of fasting and of abstinence and the mortification of sight and touch. St. Paul was so convinced of the necessity of mortifying the flesh that he exclaimed: "But I chastise my body and bring it into subjection: lest perhaps, when I have preached to others, I myself should become a castaway." [5] And in the same vein the Church prescribes fasting and abstinence for her children on certain days. The saints never doubted the need for mortifying their bodies. For instance, St. John of the Cross strikes out at those

[1] Luke 9:23.
[2] Gal. 5:24. [3] 2 Cor. 4:10. [4] *Introduction to the Devout Life*, *op. cit.*, p. 150.
[5] 1 Cor. 9:27.

who are enemies of penitential works and even those that assume the guidance of souls, though despising mortification of the body and advising their penitents against it: "Believe not those teachers that cry out against mortification of the flesh. Believe them not, even if they should corroborate those teachings by miracles." St. Bernard had this answer for those who in his day thought lightly of bodily mortification: "We are cruel only to our body when we torment it with works of penance: but you are far more cruel to yourselves when you satisfy the concupiscence of the body, in that you doom it, with the soul, to everlasting pains in eternity."

Now, since there are books in abundance treating of the necessity of mortification in order to restrain the *flesh* and bring it into subjection, let us proceed rather to consider the means of mortifying the *senses*, all five of them, namely, sight, hearing, taste, smell and touch—along with regulation of the whole body, and, finally, the regulation of our exterior actions. Where a scriptural text applies, we shall cite it, and then state how each of the senses may be suitably mortified.

Since the eyes are said to be the windows of the soul, let us begin with them. "My eye hath wasted my soul," [1] says the prophet in Holy Scripture. So difficult is it to guard the eyes from causing us to sin, that it is advised that we pray for special grace as David did in these words: "Turn away my eyes that they may not behold vanity." [2] "Through the eyes," says St. Bernard, "the dart of impure love enters the heart." [3] There are looks that are mortally sinful and these must be abstained from under pain of grave sin. There are sights that are dangerous in that they of themselves would be apt to bring on temptation, such as indecently dressed so-called "entertainers" on television, in stage shows, books, newspapers, and in moving pictures. When we see such things, we must not gaze upon them. The earnest person in pursuit of perfection should repress idle, curious glances and mortify himself in even those things where no sin or danger of sin is involved. "What is not seen," says St. Francis de Sales, "is not desired." The eyes may be mortified in many ways. For instance, you are walking down the street and you would like to gaze at a pleasing window display. You could practice mortification by *not* glancing in at the windows on

[1] Lam. 3:51. [2] Ps. 118:37. [3] *De modo bene viv.*, s. 23.

the way downtown, delaying the act of looking until you are on the way home. In like manner, a letter from home, or from a friend, can also provide you with an opportunity to practice mortification of the sense of sight, if you deliberately delay opening same for an hour or two. Just try it. It is harder than you think!

A certain degree of success in mortifying the eyes in matters of indifferent things ought not embolden us so that we think we can take chances where these serious sins are vaguely possible. Learn from the example told by St. Augustine of Alypius. He went to a theatre, resolved not to look at any dangerous object, saying, "I will be absent though present," but being tempted to look, he, says the saint, not only prevaricated, but also made others prevaricate: "He opened his eyes, applauded, became excited, and left the theatre carrying sin with him."[1]

Philosophers call the sense of hearing, the sense of discipline, because through it, as through a door, the idea of truth and all wisdom enter into the mind. This door ought to be strictly guarded by the sentinel of self-denial, lest falsehood instead of truth, and folly instead of wisdom, force their way into the heart. God has granted us the sense of hearing so that we may acquire the mysteries of faith, lessons of salvation, and the doctrine of the gospel. This being so, we ought to keep out all things that are at variance with its purpose, nor may we open our ears to the truth of vanities.

The sense of hearing may be mortified by restraining our ears from light and frivolous songs; from jokes and idle words; from murmurings and detractions; from gossip; from all species of flattery. Well did St. Paul speak when he said: "Evil communications corrupt good manners."[2] It is a good practice to mortify one's curiosity by refraining from asking questions that would satisfy it and by repressing a desire for frequent conversations: "In the multitude of words there shall not want sin."[3]

A little twist of the dial to "off" on the television or radio set every now and again will provide a means of mortifying the sense of hearing.

Concerning mortification of the sense of taste or appetite, Father Rogacci, in his treatise entitled *The One Thing Necessary*,

[1] *Conf.* VI, 8. [2] 1 Cor. 15:33. [3] Prov. 10:19.

says that the principal part of external mortification consists in the mortification of the appetite. Hence, St. Andrew of Avellino used to say that he who wishes to walk in the way of perfection must begin to mortify the taste. St. Paul puts it bluntly in these words: "They are enemies of the Cross of Christ; whose end is destruction, whose God is their belly." [1] According to St. Thomas, the devil, when vanquished in his temptations to the indulgence of the appetite, ceases to tempt to impurity.

The sense of taste or appetite may be mortified in many ways: by taking smaller portions of some delectable food, or taking a little more of what one dislikes in the line of food; taking the smallest and least attractive portion; the strict observance of the fasts of the Church (if one's health permits); abstaining from alcoholic beverages and exotic foods and delicacies. To practice temperance, St. Bonaventure says that "we must avoid four things: first, eating out of the time of meals, as animals do; secondly, eating with too much avidity, like famished dogs; thirdly, eating too large a quantity of food; and fourthly, we must avoid too much delicacy." [2] It is important that one should consult his director before undertaking more in this regard.

As to the sense of smell, sin is not so frequently committed in this regard. However, this sense, too, is to be restricted. Immoderate use of perfumed soaps or perfume itself is often but a pretext for satisfying sensuality and such things can incite lust. Mortification of the sense of smell can be exercised in the patient endurance of disagreeable odors and smells when the occasion shall occur in the course of one's duties.

Finally, the fifth sense is that of touch. This is the most dangerous of all, since, diffused throughout the members, it assails the mind from every possible side. St. Alphonsus says regarding this sense that we must abstain from familiarity with persons of the opposite sex and use all possible caution and modesty with ourselves. This subject will be treated later under the capital sins, but it suffices here to say that the saints found it necessary to chastise their bodies to overcome temptations in this regard. "Mortify your body and you will conquer the devil," says St. Augustine.

[1] Phil. 3:18. [2] *De prof. rel.*, I, i, c. 36.

Not only the senses but the entire body must be regulated and mortified. This mortification embraces such things as puerile levity, frivolities, vanities, uncontrolled laughter, rapid motions and hasty gait; soiled garments or an unclean person lest they excite disgust in our neighbor; every indication of an unfriendly feeling; all boldness, petulance and hastiness in action and any affected or aspiring mannerisms. All exterior discipline consists in this, that we be *mature*, *humble*, and *kind*.

St. Alphonsus says to those who have not the courage to mortify their flesh by works of penance that they ought at least endeavor to accept with patience the mortifications arising from infirmities, the heat and cold, that God sends them; but even these ought to be reminded of the words of St. Anselm: "God will cease to chastise the sinner who voluntarily punishes himself for his sins." And these words of St. Francis de Sales are worthy of a respectful hearing: "The mortifications which come to us from God, or from man by His permission, are more precious than those which are the offspring of our own will. Hold it as a rule, that the less we do from choice or our own taste, the more shall we find in our actions of goodness, of solidity, of devotion and of profit."

Directors, the words of St. Francis de Sales notwithstanding, ought to suggest at least one single mortification of each of the five senses daily. A periodical check on this practice will help you know the depth of purpose of the person under your spiritual care, for every act of mortification done with the proper dispositions is a work for heaven.

And now to a study of interior mortification. We have a soul and a body. Exterior mortification is necessary in order to mortify the disorderly appetites and senses of the body, and interior mortification is necessary in order to mortify the irregular affections of the soul. Interior mortification is more excellent than exterior, both because it has a nobler object, the soul and its powers, and because the exterior ought to proceed from the interior. Mere external mortification can by no means beget true virtues in the soul; this is patent from not a few of those who, though devoted to an austere life, are stubborn, proud, unruly, and despisers of others. The exterior mortification, therefore, is joined to the interior, so that both may be the way to solid virtue. "What profit," says St.

Jerome, "to castigate the body by severe fasts, if one is puffed up with pride—unable to brook an insult or a refusal?"

It is necessary, first, to mortify the interior sensitive faculty, which is called phantasy or imagination. Since memory and imagination generally act in accord, memory-activities being accompanied by sense-images, it is necessary that these two interior senses be mortified. To check the wanderings of the memory and the imagination we must strive first to expel all *dangerous* fancies and recollections. Next, we ought to mortify *idle thoughts* so that we may have better control over evil ones. This can be accomplished by whole-hearted concentration on the work at hand. Day-dreaming and fanciful thoughts ought to be nipped in the bud. As Blount says: "As dreams are the fancies of those that sleep, so fancies are but dreams of those awake."

There are three kinds of thoughts which ought to be repudiated. The first is that of impure thoughts and thoughts that are likely to lead to gluttony, lust, envy, and other vices; unless such thoughts are promptly rejected, they may incite to mortal sin. The second kind is that of idle and unprofitable thoughts, such as curious inquiries into hidden things, whether of God or man. The third kind is that of such things as belong to nature, that is to say, constant thoughts of food, drink, clothing, habitation and other such things. Evil thoughts usually spring from one or more of the following: (1) our concupiscences; (2) the instability of the human heart; (3) from Satan, who is ever on the alert to suggest either vain and idle thoughts or evil and immodest thoughts.

The remedies against such thoughts are:

(a) Prompt recourse to prayer.

(b) Calling to mind the eternal presence of God.

(c) Manful opposition to their beginnings.

(d) By turning the mind to other things such as work, hobbies, good reading or recreation.

(e) Prompt revelation of such thoughts to one's confessor.

(f) Avoidance of idleness.

In man's nature and constitution we have seen that God designed the five *senses* to be avenues between the soul and the external world, and as such, they must be controlled in order that they may not lead us into sin.

The same all-wise God who gave man his five senses, likewise gave him what we term *appetites* which we define as restless, urgent cravings after certain objects, without which the bodily emotions cannot be satisfied. Certain appetites appertain to man's body for his preservation as an individual, such as hunger and thirst, and others for the preservation of man viewed as a social being, such as the sexual instinct.

In man's soul there is a twofold appetite: one is *intellective*, that is to say, it follows the perception of the understanding, and is called the will; the other is sensitive, which the knowledge of the interior sense precedes. Let us examine the differences between them.

The Intellective Appetite	*The Sensitive Appetite*
The will follows the guidance of reason.	The sensitive appetite follows the imagination or phantasy.
The action of the will is simply free.	The sensitive appetite enjoys only a certain obscure and imperfect freedom.
The will is an immaterial power residing in the essence of the soul.	The sensitive appetite is a corporeal faculty inherent in matter.
The will is directed to individual and general things, as well as to those that are free from matter or that are material.	The sensitive appetite is directed only to individual and material things.

In the sensitive appetite there is a twofold appetitive power: one for attaining what is suitable and avoiding what is hurtful, which is called *concupiscible;* the other for repelling what is hard to obtain or reject, and this is called *irascible*. With concupiscible power we pursue or avoid good or evil, as far as they are strictly good or evil; by the irascible power we treat good or evil, as they are respectively hard to obtain or reject.

According to the scholars, nearly all the evils, nearly all the damages to the soul, and nearly all crimes and imperfections spring from this twofold appetite. This being true, our chief work ought to be to wage war upon the inordinate affections of this appetite, to govern and restrain them so that they be made subject to the lawful command of reason as far as is possible in this life.

When the movements of the sensitive appetite toward some sensible good are vehement, and as a result the reaction on the bodily organism is more or less strong,[1] such movements are termed *passions*. In general then, passions are movements or acts of the lower sensitive appetite. The word *passion* itself comes from *pati*—"to be passive," indicating a receptive mood.

Scholars list eleven passions; namely, love, hatred, desire, aversion, joy, sadness, hope, despair, fear, courage, and anger. The first six passions take their rise in the concupiscible appetite, while the remaining five proceed from the irascible. Moral and ascetical writers are unanimous in declaring that all eleven passions must be bridled by the spirit of prayer and mortification, if one is to make progress in virtue.

The Stoics taught that the passions were thoroughly evil and that they must be annihilated. But the accepted doctrine of Catholic scholars teaches that bad passions cannot be entirely subdued while we live here on this earth; but they must be mortified and so recalled to duties of virtue, so that they may not only not hurt, but even be of service in our spiritual combat. This can be effected if we are careful by every means possible to check them when they first rise up against virtue, for it is easier to restrain the beginnings of affections than to govern their assault. The first rule is to cut them off by closing the exterior senses whereby they are inflamed; and the second is by beginning with the regulation of that affection by which we are more frequently assailed and this is accomplished by particular examen and/or consultation with our director.

Because of various groupings by different scholars the number of passions may seem to vary, but the majority hold them to be eleven in number, and Bossuet says that they all proceed from love: "Our other passions refer but to love, love which embodies or stimulates them."[2] Let us examine each of them in turn:

[1] Ia–IIae, q. 22, a. 3.

[2] *De la Connaissance de Dieu et de soi-même* (Paris: Téqui, 1908), c. 1, n. 6.

(1) *Love* is a strong desire for union with some thing or person that pleases us and so we are urged to possess it.

(2) *Hatred* is born of a desire to rid ourselves of some thing or person that displeases us.

(3) *Desire* is a yearning for an absent and not yet attained good.

(4) *Aversion* is a desire to flee some evil not yet present lest it become present.

(5) *Joy* is satisfaction arising from some present good.

(6) *Sadness* makes us execrate evil always present, either in reality or according to the conception of it.

(7) *Courage* makes us strive to repel an evil that is hard to repel.

(8) *Fear* is a trepidation of the soul regarding future evil difficult to be resisted.

(9) *Hope* is a passion of the soul concerning future good, arduous or difficult, but still possible to obtain.

(10) *Despair* is opposed to hope and arises in the soul when the acquisition of some good seems impossible.

(11) *Anger* is a passion which repels what hurts us and incites the desire for revenge.

When we glance over such a formidable array of passions we can see what appears as a potent force in disturbing and upsetting our spiritual equilibrium and forming roadblocks to perfection. Now, while some passions appear as evils, we must beware of thinking that God would bestow anything evil on our nature. *De facto*, passions are helpful to us when they are well-ordered, that is, when they are directed to good and when they are controlled and made subservient to God's will. They are really strong forces capable of stirring our mind and will to action, and are thus beneficial. It is only when our passions are ill-ordered that they are spiritually hurtful. You see, an ill-ordered passion is one which is directed toward some sensible good that is forbidden, or even directed toward some good which is lawful, but which is pursued with unreasonable eagerness or without reference to God.

Ill-ordered passions may weary and torture the soul, weaken

the will, and blemish the soul, and so they must be mortified. Hear St. John of the Cross say:

> I do not hesitate to affirm that one single disordered passion, even if it lead not to mortal sin, is enough to cause the soul such a state of darkness, ugliness and uncleanness, that it is incapable of intimate union with God so long as it remains a slave of this passion. What shall we say of the soul that is marred by the ugliness of all its passions, that is prey to all its appetites? Neither words nor arguments can make us understand the divers stains which all these appetites create in the soul. Each one of them in its own way places its share of filth and ugliness in the soul.

It is important, therefore, as you can see from the words of St. John of the Cross, that we do our utmost to curb our ill-ordered passions. This is done by means of prayer; by avoiding external acts that would stimulate or excite the passions; by diverting our minds to other things; by performing positive acts directly opposed to the disturbing passion, and finally by directing the passions toward God.

Let us examine a few ways of ordering disordered passions. Remedies for the passion of *love* [1] are the most difficult, since love checked presses the more. However, one's best defense is (1) the avoidance of beginnings; (2) all thoughts of the loved object not properly directed ought to be avoided; (3) the loved object should be shunned; (4) the mind is to be kept occupied with other thoughts; (5) one ought to guard the external senses from seeing and hearing anything that would excite the passion; and finally, (6) it is necessary to divert the love to God, to virtue, and to everlasting rewards.

This passion may be mortified by deliberately avoiding the company of someone to whom we are ardently attached, or whose company pleases us. Choosing a less agreeable person as a companion from time to time will help weaken this passion.

The remedies for the ill-ordered passion of *hatred* are: (1) to excite the mind to love through the consideration of some good in

[1] We are not treating here of lawful marital love or pure family affection, but rather of improperly directed love. Even when the passions are directed toward good, they must be made to obey the dictates of reason and the control of the will.

that which is hated; (2) by remembering that it is evil to exclude anyone from our love who is destined to eternal glory and whom God loves; (3) by forcing ourselves to think well of such a person and to speak well of him also; (4) to pray for such a person. "Love your enemies, do good to them that hate you," [1] said our Lord, and if we are commanded to love our enemies, whom ought we to hate?

This passion may be mortified by positive acts directly opposed to it. Acts to gain the good graces of someone we dislike and prayers for such a one are indicated.

The remedies for ill-ordered *desire* are: (1) to reflect that created things cannot satisfy us; (2) we ought to turn our desires for some unlawful good into a lawful ambition such as doing good for our fellowman or to becoming a saint or an apostle.

The remedies for the ill-ordered passion of *aversion* are the same as we have sketched above against hatred and are to be applied also to this. It may be stated here that it is praiseworthy to turn our aversion toward sin and vice and whatever leads to them so that we may loathe them. This passion may be mortified by using the same means used to mortify the passion of hatred.

The remedies against the ill-ordered passion of *joy* are: (1) to consider the brevity of this life and that earthly pleasures pass away quickly from us; (2) to avoid careless, talkative, and vain persons, and those with little or no relish for the divine. Even in lawful joys at recreations, etc., care must be taken neither to waste too much time nor must the mood be allowed to become so dissipated with immoderate joy that it is difficult to resume one's labors or that recollection is found troublesome. The time of recreation ought not permit us to forget respect for person, age, and rank. It must never be forgotten that true joy springs only from a consciousness of virtues.

The passion of joy may be mortified by denying oneself from time to time such things as music, delaying the reading of a delightful historical novel, or abstaining for a time from a pleasant hobby.

The remedy against the ill-ordered passion of *sadness* is in seeing in trials, losses, and difficulties splendid occasions for practicing

[1] Matt. 5:44.

patience, magnanimity, and other virtues, and as a means of winning divine favor. If our sadness is the result of envy, or jealousy, then these two enemies ought to be attacked at their source. If it is the result of repentance of past evil, then it is good insofar as it does not slip into useless and destructive melancholy. It would be well to apply the words of the Holy Ghost: "Drive away sadness far from thee. For sadness hath killed many, and there is no profit in it." [1]

Since the cause of much of our sadness is frequently not so much the evil itself that presses down upon us as our opinion and estimation of it, it follows that it is within our power to overcome this by self-discipline and by refusing to dwell upon what disturbs us. A deep realization that by yielding to sadness the evil is neither removed nor diminished, should convince us of its uselessness. The only sadness that is according to God and that has a salutary effect is that begotten on account of sins or the small progress in the pursuit of virtues.

This passion may be mortified by curbing the play of the imagination, by avoiding being hurt by another's slights, and by practices of humility.

The remedies for the disordered passion of *courage* are (1) humility, and (2) a discretion that would keep one from attempting what is above one's strength. Those who rely too much on themselves find, at last, how slender are human powers without God's assistance, from Whom all our sufficiency, all our strength proceed.

"True courage," says Shaftesbury, "is cool and calm. The bravest of men have the least of the brutal bullying insolence, and in the very time of danger are found the most serene and free," and Chapin asserts that "Courage is always greatest when blended with meekness; intellectual ability is most admirable when it sparkles in the setting of a modest self-distrust." [2]

This passion may be mortified by an abiding humble opinion of one's self and by recalling from time to time that true courage is the result of reasoning. Persons conscious of a disordered passion of courage in themselves ought to humble themselves and seek the

[1] Ecclus. 30:24–25.
[2] Edwin H. Chapin, *Duties of Young Men.*

advice of a director or confessor before assuming a too difficult or extraordinary mortification or penance.

The remedies for the disordered passion of *fear* are the same as for love, desire, and sadness. One who does not love or desire a certain good, does not fear its loss or desire its gain, and so, he who feels not an evil present, dreads not its happening.

It is profitable to read the lives of the saints, for therein we find many examples of persons like ourselves, who remained fearless in many of the circumstances that confront us and who swerved not from virtue on account of impending evil. Sometimes it may help to think that the evil we dread is not an evil, or not a great evil, or that it may not occur at all. One of the most effectual remedies of fear is true charity, by which one may love God and feel beloved by Him; for "if God be for us, who is against us?" [1]

The passion of fear may be mortified by positive acts against seclusiveness, timidity and other various kinds of retreat. Special emphasis must be laid on the importance of facing up to responsibilities and of resisting such dodges as inefficiency, "passing the buck," and above all, flights into unreality, as modes of escape in place of intelligent solutions to difficult problems.

The remedies for the disordered passion of *hope* are: (1) taking into account the vanity of things which we often hope for: "The hopes of a man that is void of understanding are vain and deceitful"; [2] (2) pondering of the lives of those who, deceived by vain hope, have miserably failed, such as Hitler, Napoleon; (3) contempt of the world and the despising of earthly things will be profitable, for no sane person hopes for what he despises.

The remedies for the ill-ordered passion of *despair* are (1) arousing the mind by reflecting on the example of those who even in the severest straits have courageously surmounted every difficulty; (2) urging ourselves to do what seems difficult, for, as Burke says, "a speculative despair is unpardonable where it is our duty to act"; (3) calling to mind frequently that God assists those who make an effort, and therefore confidence is to be stimulated by consideration of the divine power and goodness.

The passion of despair may be mortified by (1) stoutly withstanding any and all temptations to depression; (2) facing up to

[1] Rom. 8:31. [2] Ecclus. 34:1.

one's responsibilities, especially those relative to the duties of one's state in life; (3) resisting procrastinatory tendencies.

The remedies for the ill-ordered passion of *anger* are (1) attempting nothing in word or deed when we are roused to anger, but remaining quiet until the heat subsides of itself; (2) putting aside or lessening our opinion of the real or supposed injury; (3) reflecting calmly that a little later on we are likely to think otherwise of the injury; (4) reckoning the inconveniences which will follow in a much higher degree if we wish to avenge the injury; (5) frequent meditation on the patience of Christ.

This passion may be mortified by practices of self-control, silence, humility, toleration of injury and avoidance of occasions wherein contentions may arise.

In this whole matter of passions we must never lose sight of the fact that strong as our passions are, they may be starved into submission and conquered without being killed. The passions are like fire, useful in a thousand ways but dangerous only in two ways, through their excess or ill-ordering. St. John of the Cross says the passions

> are like restless and discontented children, who are ever demanding this or that from their mother, and are never contented. And even as one that digs because he covets a treasure is wearied and fatigued, even so is the soul wearied and fatigued in order to attain that which its desires demand of it; and although in the end it may attain it, it is still weary, because it is never satisfied . . . The soul is wearied and fatigued by its desires, because it is wounded and moved and disturbed by them as is water by the winds.[1]

The moment we allow any of our passions to lead us astray, our perfect union with God is impeded. This is certainly true of habitual attachments. They assault the will even if they be in themselves trivial. St. John of the Cross adds this comment, that "it makes little difference whether a bird be tied by a thin thread or a heavy cord; it cannot fly until either is broken."

Father Augustine Baker, O.S.B., reminds us that

> the only proper remedies against unquiet passions are, first, mortifica-

[1] *Ascent of Mount Carmel,* I, 6; *Complete Works, op. cit.,* I, 35.

tion of all inordinate affection to creatures, of all vain encumbering friendships, all factious partialities, all thoughtful provision for contenting of our sensual desires; but especially of that most dangerous, because most intimate, a thirst for unnecessary knowledge, and of all ambition to get victory or glory by disputing, writing, etc., as likewise of all anger, impatience, melancholy, fear, and scrupulosity; and, secondly, a studious care to preserve our souls in all peace, tranquility, and cheerfulness possible, not suffering any passions to be raised in our minds during our imperfect state, no, not although they should be directed upon good and holy objects, because they will obscure and disorder our spirits. And, therefore, we must avoid all violence and impetuous hastiness in performing our best and most necessary duties, which are discharged most efficaciously and purely when they are done with the greatest stillness, calmness, clearness of mind and resignation.[1]

There is little doubt but that nearly everyone has a decidedly ruling passion, or, as the scholars like to call it, a "predominant passion." The discovery and identification of our predominant passion is a most important work and an artful one, too, since secrecy usually covers it with camouflaged wrappings. The principal means to be used in ferreting out our predominant passion are (1) daily practice of self-examination; (2) fixing our attention upon symptoms and from these attempting to discover their principal cause; (3) carefully scrutinizing particular faults that continuously recur; (4) consultation with a confessor or director —a good spiritual guide can often discover a penitent's ruling passion before the penitent has discovered it himself. Father Faber says of the director, "He must help us in the search for the ruling passion. He must approve the discovery. He must guide us in the warfare which we must forthwith wage against our domestic enemy." [2]

Let us now turn our attention to the matter of disciplining and mortifying the higher faculties of our soul, namely, understanding, memory, and will. Understanding is given in order to know God; memory, to recall His goodness; will, to love Him. Because of the sin of our first parent, Adam, the understanding has become dim,

[1] *Growth in Holiness, op. cit.*, p. 81.
[2] *Holy Wisdom, op. cit.*, p. 99.

the memory fickle, and the will weak and corrupt. All too often the reason accepts the false for the true, the memory occupies itself with things by which it is ever made restless, and the will chooses evil for good. Interior denial, then, must be attended to, in order that the inner man may be renewed, who has been created to God's image and likeness.

It was Glanvill who remarked that "the understanding also hath its idiosyncrasies as well as other faculties," and because the understanding is the eye of the blind faculty of the will, it follows that it too must be mortified and disciplined. In ascertaining truth, the understanding should (1) avoid vain, subtle, and lofty speculations; (2) be withheld from delving into those things which contribute nothing to the glory of God, our own salvation or the salvation of our neighbor. On the positive side, we ought to (1) study with care and diligence all the things relative to our profession, duty, and state in life, and in particular, the things necessary for advancement in perfection and those necessary for salvation; (2) establish regular hours of study daily and never omit them except for serious reason.

Exactness of memory naturally follows discipline of the understanding, and in turn, memory itself must be mortified and disciplined, for as Basil notes: "Memory is the cabinet of imagination, the treasury of reason, the registry of conscience and the council-chamber of thought."

Since the sensitive memory does not differ from phantasy, so the intellective memory does not differ from understanding, it follows, therefore, that if the understanding is engaged in considering useful and holy things, the memory will preserve representations of these same things and will reproduce them when the need arises. Memory ought to suffer some discipline since Fuller compares it to a purse which he says, "if it be so over-full that it cannot be shut, all will drop out of it; take heed of a gluttonous curiosity to feed on many things, lest the greediness of the appetite of the memory spoil the digestion thereof."

The acts of the understanding, by which we advance to the exercise of actions, are (1) counsel and (2) supremacy. *Counsel* has two acts: inquiry and judgment. Inquiry is an act by which we reason about the means to an end by seeking them and examining how they will avail us in achieving that end. Judgment is an act by which, supposing inquiry by reason, it is decided what is to be done. After this follows *supremacy*, intimating and commanding the thing's execution.

The act called judgment needs discipline and control and these are best accomplished by:

(1) A firm and unalterable adherence to the teachings of the Church.

(2) Frequent solicitation of advice and counsel from elders, confessors, and spiritual director.

(3) Taking time before rendering decisions. "He that is hasty to give credit," says Holy Scripture, "is light of heart."[1]

(4) Deferring decisions when we are emotionally upset.

(5) Avoiding rash judgments.

(6) Praying for the help of God's grace in rendering just decisions.

(7) Making all decisions in the light of eternity.

The will is the faculty of the soul which exercises authority over all others and therefore, by its power, the goodness or malice of human actions exist. Its actions are volition, intention, fruition, choice, consent and use. The first three regard the end, the last three regard the means.

(1) *Volition* is that act by which we desire some good absolutely as an end.

(2) *Intention* is an act of the will concerning an end, proposed by the understanding, to be attained by suitable means.

(3) *Fruition* is pleasure from a good that is possessed.

(4) *Choice* is the selection of that means which the understanding has decided to be preferable to the rest.

(5) *Consent* is an act of the will by which it applies itself to whatever is proposed to it by the understanding as desirable.

(6) *Use* is the act by which the will determines the other faculties to action.

[1] Ecclus. 19:4.

And because this faculty, on account of its innate freedom, is everlastingly being carried after its own inclination and after whatever may appear pleasing to the individual, it must be checked and mortified. Mortification of the will consists in willing nothing but that which God wills, subjecting itself in all things and through all to the divine will, and by staunchly withstanding inordinate self-will.

St. Philip Neri used to say that sanctity consists in the mortification of self-will, while Blosius has asserted that he who mortifies self-will does an act more pleasing to God than if he gave life to the dead.[1] "Hence," says St. Alphonsus, "many priests and pastors, and even bishops, who led exemplary lives, and devoted their time and labor to the salvation of souls, not content with all this, have entered religion in order to live under obedience to others; believing—what is really the truth—that they could not offer to God a sacrifice more acceptable than the renunciation of their own will." The saint then adds these strong words concerning priests:

> All are not called to the religious state; but he who wishes to walk in the way of perfection (besides the obedience due to his prelate) must submit his will to the direction of at least a spiritual Father, who will guide him in all his spiritual exercises, and also in temporal affairs of importance which are connected with the sanctification of his soul. What is done through self-will is of little or no advantage to the soul.

Directors of religious might strive to make them see in their holy rule ample opportunities for the mortification of self-will. One practice of obedience is more meritorious than many penitential works and pious exercises prompted by self-will. Everyone striving for perfection could stand frequent reminders from the counsels of the saints, such as these words of St. John Climacus: "Let no day go by without trampling underfoot your own will"; or the words of St. Mary Magdalene dei Pazzi who said she "looked upon that day as lost in which she had not conquered in some way her own will." The great St. Catherine of Siena heard these words from our Lord: "Think of Me, and I will think of

[1] *Sac. an.*, p. I, n. 5.

thee; think of doing My will, and I will think of what is for thy good."

Here are St. Alphonsus' suggestions for conquering self-will:

(1) Prayer: he who prays, obtains all graces.

(2) Do violence to self with a determined will. A resolute will surmounts all difficulties.

(3) Make our examen on the passion that molests us, and impose a penance on ourselves as often as we yield to it.

(4) Practice mortification in small things, and even in things that are not sinful; for thus we shall acquire a facility of overcoming great difficulties.

The great Cardinal Bona has drawn up a list of what he calls "mortifications by which the soul is perfectly purified and is prepared for a happy union with God." Here is that list in outline:

(1) Mortification of all affections toward temporal things.

(2) Mortification of self-love.

(3) Renunciation of one's sensuality in food, drink, raiment, in mutual discourses and sensual conversations, in curiosity and equipment of cell, house, and all utensils.

(4) Perfect mortification of all affections of mundane, natural, and acquired love.

(5) The casting aside of all thoughts and images of created things, and a certain application to complete solitude.

(6) Rejection of any care and management whatever of temporal affairs, unless just necessity force us thereto, or on account of spiritual utility or obedience.

(7) Removing all bitterness of heart by the sweetness of divine love so that we may embrace all our opponents and persecutors with the same feeling of mind.

(8) Complete renunciation of pride and vain glory, in contempt of praise, honor, favor, and human recognition.

(9) Mortification of all affections toward spiritual, interior and sensible delights, such as grace, sensible devotion, interior

sweetness, visions, apparitions, and supernatural communications.

(10) Removing all scruples from the heart with entire confidence in God.

(11) Total eradication of all disquiet and impatience of heart in every outward adversity, whether it be disgrace, ridicule, calumny, or loss of temporal goods, friends, or relatives.

(12) Mortification of all self-will in complete resignation to all interior abandonment to be endured for love of God, even though it may be necessary to continue during one's whole lifetime without any interior consolation.[1]

Because we have considered mortification in the purgative way let us not think that it is to be confined solely to beginners in the spiritual ascent. Mortification is the work of a lifetime and must be as actively practiced in the contemplative as in the unitive and purgative ways. I wish I could tell you that once you have mortified a passion it would die and bother you no more, but sad to relate such is not the case. A monk once complained to the Abbot Theodore that, although he had combatted his evil inclinations nearly eight years, he had not succeeded in entirely destroying them. The Abbot answered: "O my son, you are lamenting over a war of eight years! I have spent sixty years in solitude, and in all that time no day has passed in which I have not felt resistance of my passions."

There is a great challenge here for everyone. "Conquer self!" This was what St. Ignatius Loyola constantly repeated to his spiritual children. We must say it over and over to ourselves and to those confided to our spiritual care. If you notice little progress in prayer, either in yourself or others, examine the matter of self-will and self-love, for as St. Ignatius says: "The principal reason that so few who practice mental prayer arrive at Christian perfection is because they take no care to conquer self."

Let us keep ever before our minds the words of St. Paul that "they who are Christ's have crucified their flesh with the vices and concupiscences."[2]

[1] *Cursus vitae spiritualis*, chap. XVII.
[2] Gal. 5:24.

6

The Purgative Way and the Struggle Against the Capital Sins, Temptations and Scruples

IN AN old book entitled *Histoires et Paraboles,* I came upon this story. A certain young man, in crossing a forest, was attacked by a frightful monster which in shape resembled a lion, but had seven heads like those of a serpent. Rushing at him from behind a bush where it had been lurking, it raised aloft its seven heads, from each of which darted forth a venomous tongue, which filled the air with horrible hisses. The youth, who was both strong and brave, was not disconcerted. Having no other weapon than a hatchet, which he carried at his side, he drew it forth and rushed at the savage monster.

At the first blow he cut off four of its heads, at the second he struck off another two and at the third he would certainly have completed his victory by cutting off the remaining head, had not the hatchet unfortunately slipped from his hand and fallen to the ground. At that very moment the beast, enraged by the wounds, rushed furiously upon him, bit him, stung him and seized him in its claws. In vain did the unhappy man struggle to free himself and call for help but his cries were unheard and the monster carried him to its den and devoured him.

There is no need of my reminding you that the foregoing story is pure fable, but, as Franklin once remarked, "Fiction or fable allures to instruction," so if the foregoing leads us into the important study of the seven deadly sins or capital sins as they are frequently called, it will have served its purpose.

The first care of anyone commencing to serve God, when he has taken measures to conquer mortal sins, must be devoted to the uprooting of evil habits, which he may have acquired by repeated evil acts. For after sins have been pardoned there remain as their offspring in the soul an evil habit and propensity to the same sins, resulting from the custom of sinning and against which a continual struggle must be maintained. One of the principal tasks, therefore, of beginners must be the entire destruction of vices, if virtues are to be planted in the soul and nature restored to its original state of freedom as far as the condition of mortality will allow.

It must be understood that vice differs from sin; for vice, taken strictly, is a habit, but sin is an act. Just as virtue is a habit effective of good action, so vice is a habit effective of evil action. Vice, therefore, is a quality, according to which a person can be called wicked, even when he is inactive. But there are seven capital sins, in which as in so many sources or roots, the other vices are virtually contained, and against which our first attack ought to be directed. Keep in mind that vices are habits of sin, while capital sins are inclinations to sin.

Just as a general would not dare rush into battle without suitable planning well developed far in advance of the attack, so in like manner, before engaging in the extirpation of vices, a certain adequate preparation is required. Adequate preparation must, of necessity, include:

(1) Fervent and frequent reception of the sacraments.

(2) Determination to uproot vice completely from the soul.

(3) Distrust of one's own strength and childlike dependence on God's grace.

(4) Self-scrutiny to know oneself and one's vices. This may be done by the practice of particular examination.

(5) A deep conviction that vices are cast out by the practice of the contrary virtues.

(6) The determination of one's predominant passion or vice.

(7) Counsel from and consultation with one's confessor or director.

With such a preparation initiated, the next steps involve: (1) the avoidance of the occasions of sin; (2) resistance to the beginnings of the vice being extirpated; (3) concentration of the attack upon one vice at a time, commencing with the most grievous; (4) when a vice appears to have been overcome, thanksgiving must be tendered God for His grace.

A word of warning must be interjected here. Be not deceived into thinking that a dormant vice is a dead one. Not infrequently, the will is prompt to combat vices, but the other faculties obey slowly and almost reluctantly. Cardinal Bona notes, "It also not infrequently occurs, God so willing it, that when most we seem to ourselves well disposed for combat, the matter succeeds least according to expectation: and when we quit the struggle, it often happens that we are suddenly filled with divine fervor. These are, no doubt, vicissitudes of things, acts of divine Providence, that we may learn not to be high-minded, but to fear." [1]

Spiritual directors would do well to warn beginners against two dangers: (1) the development of over-dependence on the grace of God, so that the work of extirpating vice is left entirely to it, a condition one might look for in the tepid and slothful, in the despisers of rules and precepts, and in those who make a great display of uprooting minor vices while ignoring the more serious ones; (2) the other danger is to those who develop unfounded anxieties and even scruples lest in the up-rooting of their vices they fail to fully correspond to or co-operate with God's grace. These latter individuals must be carefully instructed concerning the dangers of scruples and warned against discouragements.

With these things well understood, let us now turn to a study of the seven deadly or capital sins; but at the outset, let me say that it is not my intention to write a treatise on these sins, for there is an abundance of such works in print. I shall simply define the various sins, cite remedies, and indicate certain signs of their conquest.

[1] *Cursus vitae spiritualis,* part I, chap. 2.

The seven capital sins are: pride, covetousness, lust, anger, gluttony, envy, and sloth.

Pride is an inordinate love of self which causes us to consider ourselves, explicitly or implicitly, as our own first beginning and last end. It is said to be interior when confined to thoughts alone, and exterior when performed by word or deed.

Remedies for pride are: (1) humble prayer; (2) a deep conviction of our own nothingness—that we are nothing, can do nothing of ourselves, and that we are sinners; (3) frequent meditation on the words of Holy Scripture, "God resisteth the proud." [1]

Signs of eradicated pride are: (1) if a holy fear of God stirs us, and if we strive constantly to acquire humility; (2) if we firmly believe that only sins and evil proceed from us, and that all good things come from God; (3) if we subject ourselves to God, and for His love, submit likewise to superiors, equals, and inferiors; (4) if we covet in no way at all high station, office, and deem honors as worthless, that we may gain Christ; (5) if we suffer abandonment, neglect, and false accusation; (6) if we bear with delight and patient spirit every adversity and humiliation; (7) if we desire to be unknown, to be accounted as nothing, and in the innermost recesses of the heart be really convinced that we are unworthy of any honor, or any good, even life itself.

Covetousness is an inordinate love of riches and temporal goods. This vice is so evil that God says of it: "There is not a more wicked thing than to love money: for such a one setteth his own soul to sale." [2] Acts of covetousness must be examined from two view-points—the acts of those persons in the world and those proper to persons who by solemn vows have professed evangelical poverty.

Those in the world are covetous when they violate the tenth commandment; make bad use of this world's goods and do not share them with the poor and needy when the law of charity or justice so directs; when they seek temporal goods with such eagerness that they trample on the laws of God, of the Church, and of the state, for the sake of gain; and when they give their whole

[1] Jas. 4:6.
[2] Ecclus. 10:10.

hearts to the heaping up of wealth and are not prepared to relinquish it in any way and at any time that may please God.

Religious are covetous who cling with too much affection to necessary things, the use of which is allowed, and hold them as their own with obstinate tenacity; who receive and retain anything without permission; who have property or money without permission; who desire what is rare and superfluous in dress, in books and furniture in cells, thus shunning the inconvenience of poverty; who turn in spirit and thought to goods left in the world, and wish for them again; or who have many unnecessary things and then, when deprived of any article, feel annoyed and complain.

Remedies against covetousness are: (1) to be satisfied with a few things; (2) to seek to possess only the barest essentials; (3) to be faithful in turning in gifts and money to superiors if one is bound by the vow of poverty; (4) to meditate frequently on the worthlessness of earthly goods; (5) to be liberal in the sharing of what we do possess.

The signs of defeated covetousness are: (1) joy rather than depression whenever we suffer a material loss; (2) constant and abiding realization that whatever we do possess comes to us from God, and that we are only stewards bound to render a strict account for the use of material goods; (3) careful avoidance of all acts of injustice; (4) a willingness to share our goods with the poor and needy.

The signs that a religious has conquered covetousness are as follows: (1) rejection of unnecessary and superfluous comforts, and still better, even things deemed by others as necessities; (2) bearing with joy the inconveniences of the common life; (3) a heart rid of material attachments; (4) promptness in turning in to superiors all money and material gifts; (5) scrupulous observance of the rules regarding poverty; (6) keeping ever in mind the words of Julianus Pomerius: "Those riches we ought to seek which arm us against the attacks of the enemy, separate us from the world, commend us to God, enrich and ennoble our souls. . . . These are to be considered our wealth: modesty . . . justice . . . piety . . . humility . . . gentleness . . . innocence . . . purity . . . prudence . . . temperance and love."[1]

[1] *The Contemplative Life* ii. 13. 2; translated by Mary Josephine Suelzer, "Ancient Christian Writers," 4 (Westminster, Md.: Newman Press, 1947), p. 78.

Lust is a desire for impure and libidinous pleasure. Its kinds are too familiar to need enumeration here. What must be stressed, however, is that some embers of this vice remain after conversion even in spiritual persons and in those consecrated to God in religion; it is because of this that we must always be on our guard.

The relics of the vice of impurity which beset the beginner as well as the person well advanced on the road to perfection are:

(1) Impure thoughts not promptly expelled from the mind.

(2) Insufficient regard for personal modesty.

(3) Lack of proper control over the senses of sight and touch.

(4) Too much delicacy in denying our bodies ease, exotic foods, perfumes, clothing, etc.

(5) Dangerous reading material such as romantic books and amatory poetry.

(6) Over-familiarity with persons of the opposite sex. Now, while some of the foregoing are not mortally sinful, they most certainly prepare the way for sin and are basically akin to lust.

The remedies for the six vestiges of lust are naturally the practice of acts contrary to them. The first on the list is remedied by prompt action in the rejection of impure thoughts or desires. This can be quickly effected by ejaculatory prayer, the Sign of the Cross, use of Holy Water, etc. Constant thought of the presence of God is most effective in matters concerning personal modesty. The third is remedied by ridding the mind of all inordinate affection for persons or things so that one's thoughts are never excited by affection nor one's senses by thoughts or desires. The fourth is remedied by daily acts of mortification. The fifth is remedied by mortification of the imagination and the prompt rejection of material disposed to produce immodest ideas. The last is remedied by carefully avoiding the occasions of sin, coupled with prayer for strength to co-operate with God's grace in this regard.

The over-all remedies for lust are the sacraments, prayer, meditation and mortification, spiritual reading, frequent aspirations, lively realization of the presence of God, control over our five senses, and a clear and open manifestation to our spiritual father of all affections and besetting temptations.

The signs of extinguished lust are:

(1) A burning love of and desire for chastity.

(2) Only rare and sinless commotions of the flesh.

(3) Prompt and easy rejection of impure thoughts and desires.

(4) Ease in guarding the senses, especially sight and touch.

(5) If stings of the flesh subside from lack of attention and without any sense of pleasure.

(6) If those of the opposite sex in no way stir concupiscence in us.

In this matter, devotion to our Blessed Lady ought to be recommended and stressed. A practical devotion such as the rosary, or the practice of the Three Hail Mary's night and morning with the additional ejaculation, "O Mary, my Mother, preserve me from mortal sin this day (or this night)" (300 days Indulgence) is most assuredly indicated. One should be warned that such prayers must be continued even when there is every indication that lust has been fairly well extinguished, for there is no time in our life when one can be certain that our weak nature or the devil himself may not move to destroy the soul. "Blessed is the man who is always fearful." [1]

Anger is both a capital sin and a passion of the sensitive appetite respecting present evil. We will treat of it here as a vice in which sense it is defined as an inordinate desire for revenge. Its acts are mainly those of the will and thought and those of exterior deportment by words and deeds.

Anger is a brief madness, and a sort of insanity disturbing reason, and, to some extent, destroying human nature itself: "Anger resteth in the bosom of a fool," [2] and "The anger of man worketh not the justice of God," [3] are words of the Holy Ghost worthy of study and consideration.

The remedies for anger are remote and proximate. Remote remedies are (1) careful self-scrutiny to discover its presence or likelihood; (2) the arousing of an abiding hatred for it; (3) daily prayers petitioning resistance to it; (4) frequentation of the sacra-

[1] Prov. 28:14. [2] Eccles. 7:10. [3] Jas. 1:20.

ments; (5) spiritual reading, especially the lives of the saints; (6) counsel from superiors and spiritual directors.

The proximate remedies for anger are: (1) faithful practice of the virtue of humility, especially when subject to abuse, contempt or aggravations; (2) avoiding the company of tale-bearers; (3) uprooting suspicions from the heart, because they excite anger; (4) recourse to ejaculatory prayer when excitement to anger is felt; (5) use of soothing words when one is the subject of wrathful words or actions, recalling the words of Holy Scripture: "A mild answer breaketh wrath." [1]

If some word or action on our part offends another by accident rather than by design, a speedy reconciliation ought to be sought by explaining with all sincerity possible that no offense was meant, or if the situation demands it, by a sincere and humble apology.

The signs that anger is subdued are:

(1) Prompt restraint of the external manifestations of anger.

(2) Control of internal motions of anger, deeming them as contrary to the virtue of humility and unbecoming a child of God.

(3) Prayer for those who have offended us.

(4) Kind words and good deeds to those who have injured us.

(5) Control of ourselves, even when violently moved by the force of the action against us, being mindful of the words of Holy Scripture: "Be angry, and sin not." [2]

Gluttony is an inordinate indulgence in food and drink. This, according to the theologians, may be done in four different ways:

(1) Eating when there is no need, eating between meals, and for no other reason than that of indulging our greed.

(2) Seeking delicacies or daintily prepared meals, the more to enjoy their relish.

(3) Eating and drinking so much that the health is imperiled, or the exercise of judgment disturbed.

[1] Prov. 15:1.
[2] Ps. 4:5.

(4) Eating with too much avidity and in an indecent manner of the things set before us, and being entirely absorbed in food.

The remedies against gluttony are: (1) the practice of some mortification at each meal; (2) being satisfied with what is set before one at the table; (3) care taken not to cultivate a taste for rare and expensive foods; (4) purity of intention in eating and drinking or, as St. Paul says: "Whether you eat or drink . . . do all to the glory of God"; [1] (5) total abstinence or great restriction in the matter of intoxicating beverage; (6) moderation in the quantity of food or drink consumed.

The signs of conquered gluttony are: (1) pleasure over being served the smallest and least attractive portions of any food at the table; (2) no difficulty experienced in not eating between meals; (3) food taken without avidity; (4) the mind is easily turned to spiritual things proposed by the reading during meals, as in the case of religious houses; (5) when we are moved, at each meal, to take a little more of what we dislike and a little less of what we like, thus practicing the virtue of mortification. Some of the saints were wont to add an aspiration against gluttony to their prayers before meals, and an act of thanksgiving to their prayers after meals whenever they had been served anything they particularly disliked.

Envy is a tendency to be saddened by another's good as if that good constituted an affront to our own superiority. There are said to be four kinds of good that are productive of envy:

(1) Honors and riches.

(2) Qualities of the mind–science, learning.

(3) Qualities of soul–holiness and virtue.

(4) Grace and Gifts of the Holy Ghost in others.

The remedies against envy are: (1) control and repression of the first moments of envy in our soul; (2) seeing in another's preferment to an honor or office we ourselves coveted, the Will of God; (3) frequent meditation on the humility of our Saviour; (4) remembrance of the doctrine of the Mystical Body and awareness that the person we envy is incorporated with us therein; (5) seeing

[1] 1 Cor. 10:31.

in the deprivation of worldly goods or honors, a hidden blessing and something permitted by God for our spiritual good.

The signs of vanquished envy are:

(1) When we are happy when others have some special honors conferred upon them.

(2) When we suffer with others over their material losses.

(3) When we come quickly to the defense of someone whose office or good fortune we are tempted to envy.

(4) When we are the first to congratulate those who have surpassed us in honors or learning.

(5) When we hasten to help and console those who have suffered spiritual or temporal reverses.

Sloth is an excessive love of ease, comfort and idleness, whether of body or soul. It means a laziness or lethargy which leads to neglecting our spiritual or temporal duties.

The remedies for sloth of body consist in: (1) stirring up in ourselves the realization that work is necessary and imposed upon man by God Himself; (2) a careful discharge of all the duties of our state in life; (3) avoiding procrastination; (4) the setting up for ourselves, with the aid of our spiritual director, a rule of life; (5) frequent prayer for strength of will to do promptly and well what is prescribed by rule or commanded by those over us.

Sloth, when it is laziness of the soul, makes one lukewarm and negligent in the service of God. It is worthy of note that the word "sloth" comes from the Greek, meaning "sadness," so that it is easy to infer that sloth may depress a person so that he takes no pleasure in doing anything. Sloth is indeed a mortal sin when it leads to a loathing of all spiritual exercises since in the wake of such a condition there arise contempt of laws, rejection of discipline, scandals, apostasy and despair. Sloth may, on the other hand, exist without grievous sin, such as results from a spirit that is wearied, a spirit that is overburdened by cares, or one despondent over the vastness of the work of striving for perfection and so a weariness and disgust for spiritual things develops.

Remedies against the second kind of sloth are as follows: (1) the undertaking with a certain joy all the works of religion and charity; (2) meditations frequently made on the end of our life here on earth, which is to know, love and serve God and that it is through love, practice of virtue, and work that we shall reach heaven; (3) to have special intentions each day for which to offer our work and prayers; (4) daily reading of the lives of the saints.

The signs of vanquished sloth are:

(1) Prompt performance of the duties of one's state in life.
(2) When such duties are never omitted or curtailed except for grave reasons.
(3) When even spare time and periods of recreation are used profitably.
(4) When one never feels complaisant with his spiritual progress but rather daily proposes to himself new goals and prays for grace to meet the challenge.

For fear that some persons may confuse sloth with lukewarmness or tepidity, we had better note the difference here and now. Sloth is a disgust for spiritual practices to the extent that it disregards and even despises God's friendship. Lukewarmness, or tepidity as it is sometimes called, is distaste for piety and spiritual things in general, which causes a person to perform his religious duties in a careless, lazy manner. And note well too that *spiritual dryness* is different from both sloth and lukewarmness. Spiritual dryness is a certain difficulty or drag in performing our spiritual duties and is usually involuntary. Sloth and lukewarmness, on the other hand, are voluntary.

Lukewarmness or tepidity is called by Tanquerey, "a sort of spiritual languor which saps the energies of the will, inspires one with a horror for effort and this leads to the decline of the Christian life." [1]

This great author notes that lukewarmness may attack those in the purgative way or even perfect souls, but it frequently manifests itself in those found in the illuminative way. It presupposes, in fact, that a soul has already reached a certain degree of fervor, and that it gradually allows itself to become lax. Its chief causes are said to be defective spiritual nourishment, and/or the entry

[1] *The Spiritual Life, op. cit.*, p. 592.

into the soul of some noxious germ such as pride, avarice, worldliness, etc. Its degrees are numerous but in the main, it is called *incipient* if we preserve a horror for mortal sin while committing imprudences that may lead thereto. Deliberate venial sins corresponding to our predominant passion are frequently committed. *Extreme* lukewarmness is the lot of those who allow themselves to drift into a state of indifference about whether or not they are in the state of grace, and return to their former love of pleasures, and this to such a degree that at times they regret that such pleasures are forbidden under pain of grave sin.

Father Faber lists seven signs pointing to the presence of this dread spiritual disease:

(1) Great facility in omitting our exercises of piety.

(2) Negligent performance of our exercises of piety.

(3) The soul feels not altogether right with God.

(4) Habitual acting without any intention at all, good, bad or indifferent.

(5) Carelessness about forming habits of virtue.

(6) Contempt of little things and of daily opportunities.

(7) Thinking rather of the good we have done than striving for the future.

Father Faber gives one added sign of lukewarmness in religious and that is when they measure their spiritual stature by persons in the world, rather than with the great saints. He concludes with this frightening observation:

> I fear that this evil of lukewarmness is very common, and that, at this moment, it is gnawing the life out of many souls who suspect not its presence there. It is a great grace, a prophecy of a miraculous cure, to find out that we are lukewarm; but we are lost if we do not act with vigor the moment we make this frightening discovery. It is like going to sleep in the snow, almost a pleasant, tingling feeling at the first, and then, lost forever.[1]

The remedies for lukewarmness or tepidity are (1) careful and

[1] *Growth in Holiness, op. cit.*, pp. 434–437.

diligent daily examination of conscience; (2) recourse to our confessor or director and the opening of our heart to him; (3) fervent practice of the exercises of piety; (4) prayer for the strength of will that strives to refuse God nothing.

Spiritual dryness is defined as a privation of those sensible and spiritual consolations that make the practice of virtue and prayer pleasant and easy. This is indeed a most distressing cross but one not devoid of advantages. By such aridity we are humbled, and purified, and the acts of piety and the virtues practiced under such a handicap are most meritorious.

Remedies are not within our capacity if aridity is visited upon us by God Himself, and in such a case we ought humbly to accept God's will, and even thank Him for His interest in our spiritual struggles. God would not send us such a trial if it were not for our good.

Where spiritual dryness is the result of our own faults, we ought to search them out in particular examen and move to correct them. They can, you know, result from sloth, worldliness, lack of frankness with our director, "for if you lie to the Holy Spirit," says St. Francis de Sales, "it is not surprising if he refuses you his consolation." [1]

It is important for the director to point out to the soul so afflicted that spiritual dryness may be a great means of amassing merit, for it is more meritorious to pray without consolation than when it is present. He can point out to such sufferers that they ought to imitate our Lord, Who, being in agony in the Garden of Gethsemane, "prayed the longer." [2] It would be well for the director to interest himself in the result of his counsels in this matter. Simply because a penitent does not mention his consolations or his dryness, it is no indication that all is well. It is indicated that from time to time the director should ascertain whether or not the penitent understands this whole matter of consolations and aridity and his attitude toward each of them. It is to be noted that in time of aridity, persons often turn to vocal prayer exclusively, while others find that the aridity bothers them only toward the end of their mental prayer just when they should be endeavoring

[1] *Introduction to the Devout Life, op. cit.*, p. 230.
[2] Luke 22:43.

to draw good affections from a precedent motive considered by the understanding. Regarding the first of these two difficulties, it should be recommended that mental prayer would be more affective in time of aridity, and certainly it would be more meritorious because of the added difficulty involved. As to the second difficulty, it is suggested that if the heart is barren of affections during the meditation, some remedy could be found in by-passing the production of affections, and instead, exercise mere acts of the will, which are not so affective, or retire themselves to their internal discourse.

No sooner do we set out to eradicate vice from our soul than we invariably find ourselves beleaguered by temptations and these come from the foes of spirituality, namely, the world, the flesh and the devil. Now temptation is defined simply as a solicitation to evil, and according to St. Augustine, temptation has three phases: suggestion, pleasure, and consent. The suggestion consists in an evil proposal to the mind or the imagination. The pleasure follows as a natural consequence from the suggestion. Our lower nature naturally gravitates to such things and pleasure is experienced in them. If the pleasure has not been deliberately provoked, and the will rejects it as soon as its evil presence is detected, there is no sin. If the will withholds acquiescence in the pleasure and repels it, not only is there no spiritual damage done, but merit has been gained. If, on the other hand, the will delights in the evil pleasure, willingly retains it and enjoys it and consents to it, the sin is committed. But make no mistake, temptations *per se* are not sins, in fact, they are the raw material of glory, and the acceptance of them and their management is a great work.

It must be clearly understood that God never tempts us directly, but in His all-wise Providence He permits our spiritual enemies to tempt us while giving us the graces essential to resistance. By doing this, God wills to make us merit heaven; to humble us; to make us always watchful; to purify us and to test the strength of our love. Does not Holy Scripture prove this by recording these words to Tobias: "Because thou wast acceptable to God, it was necessary that temptation should prove you"? [1]

In our combating of temptation there are six main things to

[1] Tob. 12:13.

be done: (1) forestall temptation by watchfulness and prayer: "Watch ye: and pray that ye enter not into temptation";[1] (2) resist it manfully; (3) avoid the presumption that you can dally with evil and conquer it at will; (4) avoid the occasions of sin—persons, places and things; (5) acquire healthy distrust of self and confidence in God's help, believing firmly that "God is faithful, who will not suffer you to be tempted above that which you are able: but will make also with temptation issue, that you may be able to bear it";[2] (6) resist temptation promptly and perseveringly.

If we are victorious in our struggle with temptation it will be due to God's grace, so it follows that we ought to tender Him our humble thanks. If, on the other hand, we have failed in our struggle, let us not be discouraged but humbly confess our failure, increase our prayers, and return to the practice of penance and mortification. "Rise," says St. Augustine, "from every fall to be more humble, more prudent and more earnest."[3] Father Faber puts it this way: "When we fall we must rise again, and go on our way, wishing ourselves, after a Christian fashion, better luck next time."[4]

Spiritual directors would do well to ascertain whether the diverse internal promptings that urge those under their spiritual care to do good or evil are from good or evil sources. Promptings are said to come from a good principle, if they come from God, the good angels, or the spirit aided by grace. On the other hand, these promptings are said to come from an evil principle if they come from the world, the flesh, or the devil. We shall treat the discernment of spirits more fully in a subsequent chapter when we study the illuminative way, but here it will suffice to say that to beginners who are sinners and whose passions are not curbed, the devil proposes delights and pleasures in order to plunge them deeper in sin. When the conscience of such sinners is stirred with uneasiness or remorse in order to spur them to quit their sad state, such stirrings are from the good spirit.

When some souls have sincerely returned to God, the devil incites them to sadness, and so disrupts their conscience as to make

[1] Matt. 26:41. [2] 1 Cor. 10:13. [3] *De corrept. et gratia*, chap. I.
[4] *Growth in Holiness, op. cit.*, p. 268.

them want to cease in their spiritual progress. Whatever prompts such souls to proceed in their pursuit of perfection is from the good spirit. Whatever is noted in spiritual consolations, given certain beginners, that arouses them to fervor, causes them to weep from true compunction, and brings peace and quiet to the soul, comes from the good spirit. Whenever beginners experience great spiritual desolation, directors might look for one of three causes: (1) punishment for lukewarmness; (2) a trial to see what the soul would do when utterly deprived of spiritual consolations; (3) a lesson, God wishing thereby to show them they are of themselves incapable of securing consolations even as a cure for their pride.

Not infrequently beginners develop a sort of derangement of conscience which causes them to harbor vain fears of having offended God. This condition is by no means confined to beginners, and is found in persons in all three of the ways of perfection, but since it does crop up in those in the purgative way, let us study scrupulosity here and now. The term "scruple" is derived from the Latin *scrupulus*, meaning a small, sharp stone. If we apply this meaning in a metaphorical sense we come to identify a scrupulous person as one who permits minute moral considerations to become as irritating as a small, sharp stone in one's shoe. Persons are so classed who see evil where there is no evil, see mortal sin where there is no mortal sin, and obligations where there are no obligations. Bergier defines it as a pain of spirit, an anxiety of soul which makes a person think that he is offending God in all his actions and that he is unable ever to fulfill his duties perfectly. Tanquerey, in his inimitable way, calls it: "An anxiety about having offended God which certain souls feel for little or no reason."[1] "The scrupulous person," remarks Father Quadrupani, "sees nothing but a series of sins in all his actions, and in God nothing but vengeance and anger."

Care must be taken not to confuse scrupulosity with a doubtful or a tender conscience. A doubtful conscience suspends its judgment, while a certain conscience passes judgment without fear of error. A tender conscience forms an objectively correct judgment with comparative facility, even in finer distinctions, between good and evil; a lax conscience, on insufficient grounds, judges a thing

[1] *The Spiritual Life, op. cit.*, p. 443.

to be lawful which is sinful, or something to be a venial sin which actually is a mortal sin. A scrupulous conscience, prompted by purely imaginary reasons, is in constant dread of sin where there is none, or of mortal sin where there is only venial sin. The basic element of a scrupulous conscience is not so much error as fear. The anxieties are not really rational in character, hence they really do not enter into the judgment of conscience. "There is question here," says H. Jone, O.F.M.Cap., "rather of representations of the fantasy, of sentient judgment, of impulses and movements of the sensitive appetite or emotions." [1]

The following are the symptoms of scrupulosity:

(1) Constant fear that in confession one does not have true sorrow.

(2) Fear of sin in the least thing, such as making a rash judgment, lacking charity, or giving in to evil thoughts.

(3) Inconstancy in doubts, believing one thing light one day and grave the next.

(4) Repeating over and over again minute details or some light circumstances in one's actions.

(5) Not following the advice of the confessor, demonstrating thereby an attachment to one's own opinion over anyone who attempts to guide him.

(6) Constant examination of conscience over petty and even ridiculous matters.

(7) Fear of sin in almost every action.

(8) Trotting to different confessors, fearing that he will not be properly understood by any of them and clinging to his own opinion in the face of their decisions.

The principal objects of the scruples are:

(1) *Prayers*—The scrupulous torture themselves over the manner in which they say their prayers: inattention, distractions, omissions, dissipation and tepidity.

(2) *Confessions*—They worry over past confessions and desire to

[1] *Moral Theology* (Westminister, Md.: Newman Press, 1956), pp. 42–43.

repeat them in general confessions. They think they lacked sorrow, hid some sin, or did not tell all the necessary circumstances.

(3) *Fraternal corrections*—They bother themselves with such points as having heard or repeated gossip or scandal, or for not having stopped such talk through curiosity, or for having been too lax in not correcting evil when they detected it (or thought they did) in others.

(4) *Motives of their actions*—This is a new subject of torture and causes endless distress to the scrupulous, especially in indifferent things and counsels. They think they never have pure intentions. If they give an alms they think they did it from vanity; if they ate something they liked, they think they acted through sensuality, etc.

(5) *On Predestination*—They sometimes get off on this track and seek to know and understand the mystery of predestination.

(6) *Questions they ask themselves*—The scrupulous are torturing themselves with hypothetical questions: "What would I do if I found myself in such and such an occasion of sin or situation?" "What would I do if the Communists captured and tortured me?" etc.

(7) *Temptations*—They are always in hot water concerning the consent given or withheld in temptations. They constantly confuse feeling with consent, and temptation with the will.

The causes of scrupulosity are sometimes *natural* and sometimes *preternatural.* The natural causes are heredity, disorders in health, anaemia, manic-depressive impulses or pressure on the brain, vivid fantasy, excessive introspection, lack of judgment, a secret pride, and lack of confidence in God. The preternatural causes are intervention on the part of God or of the devil. God allows us to be obsessed either as a punishment for our pride, or as a trial to make us expiate our past faults, or to fit us for a higher degree of sanctity. The devil may inject his activity into our morbid state to create havoc and turmoil in our soul.

The remedies for scrupulosity arising from natural causes: (1) the victim must want to be cured; (2) be so disposed that he would thank God for the cross of scrupulosity, inasmuch as it permits of gaining merit; (3) a good program of exercise, fresh air, and nourishing food; (4) abstinence from drugs and stimulants; (5) recreations that provide occasions for laughter; (6) avoidance of idleness; (7) useful, absorbing duties and hobbies; for as St. Teresa says, "Melancholy must be purged, and so outside work will divert the imagination. Charity demands that we bear with faults committed by anyone in this state, having more regard for his needs than our satisfaction." [1] (8) if the person be a scholar, frequent visits, pleasant recreations, walks, vacations, etc. will greatly aid such a one; (9) unconditional and trustful obedience to one's director.

Should the scruples be the fault of the individual, or the result of a preternatural intervention of the devil, most of the foregoing remedies are indicated. Should it be the fault of the individual, he should know himself, and he should keep himself from light faults and dismiss, with vigor, the first scrupulous thoughts, and act promptly and decisively against them. St. Antonine says, "It is a salutary counsel to act promptly against slight scruples and attacks of tepidity."

Cardinal Cajetan advises scrupulants: "When there is a doubt as to whether or not a sin has been confessed, and there is a slight belief that it has, one ought to follow the slight belief, and resolve the matter once and for all." Vasquez says that "scrupulous persons who believe themselves having committed a mortal sin, unless it is clear in their mind and about which there is no doubt, they ought to settle the matter in favor of a light fault." [2] Every time we act against a scruple, we acquire greater resistance to future attacks. This holds true when it is evident that the scruple is the work of the devil. "Resist the devil," says St. James, "and he will fly from you." [3]

Scrupulous persons must learn to *discipline* their mind. It is when one is *first* tempted to scruple over something he has done or neglected to do (in good faith), that he ought to resist it with all the means at his disposal, first by an ejaculatory prayer, and then by promptly turning the mind to some new thought, or engaging

[1] *Foundations*, chap. VII.
[2] *Traité des scrupules*, by M. l'Abbé Grimes (Paris: Tequi, 1926), p. 57.
[3] Jas. 4:7.

the mind in such a practice as taking a letter of the alphabet and trying to see how many words he can think of beginning with that letter. It is much easier to close and bar the door against a wild and vicious animal than it is to eject him from your house.

Prayer is one of the chief means of ridding oneself of scruples, but unfortunately it sometimes serves, as we have already noted, as one of the very areas in which scruples themselves may arise. The spiritual director would do well to explain patiently to one whose scrupulosity concerns prayer that it is a great error to think that prayer is not pleasing to God because it comes from a heart that is disturbed. In fact, the will to do one's best, and the pain experienced trying to banish distraction, as well as the humiliation involved in being a victim of scrupulosity, makes such prayers most pleasing to God. Have we not the example of many saints who were so afflicted and having the same difficulties without being less holy and agreeable to God?

Scrupulous persons ought to be warned against the repetition of prayers to which they are bound by their state in life. They ought to be advised to say such prayers only once as well as they can, and not worry about their indeliberate faults. "Scrupulous persons," says St. Teresa, "ought to despise their distractions, and continue praying without thinking what it is that distracts them, and be persuaded that they are neither voluntary nor sinful."

Directors, on their part, ought to regulate the exercises of piety so that their scrupulous penitents do not overdo it. They ought not to give them long vocal prayers as a penance for they will worry about whether they have said them all, or said them with the right dispositions, or without distractions. A few short ejaculations might serve the purpose.

Directors might have ready answers for the following statements, since they appear to be the most common:

(1) But I do not merit the rejection and the indignation of God.

(2) All my prayers are bad, and God does not hear them.

(3) But my past sins are so numerous and my present weaknesses so awful that God must hate me.

(4) I am different from the saints; they were holy persons and not unworthy like I am.

(5) I have lost all hope.

(6) But then what shall I do? Show me the way out of this difficulty and I shall follow it.

(7) I know the way you have explained is the shortest way to ridding myself of my anxieties but it is against my conscience.

(8) I am prey to a thousand temptations.

(9) I am always distracted; I cannot pray: I am making no progress.

(10) My worst difficulty is in going to confession.

It is a most extraordinary thing for us to disagree with Father Faber, but in the matter of sympathy for scrupulous souls, we most certainly do. Treating of scruples, Father Faber makes these statements: "It is unfortunate that scrupulous persons are always spoken of with great compassion, far more than they deserve"; again, "a scrupulous man teases God, irritates his neighbor, torments himself, and oppresses his director"; and again, "Everyone who is in trouble and disgrace deserves commiseration; but our pity is lessened when the sufferer has no one to blame but himself, and it well-nigh departs altogether when he remains in his sufferings through his own obstinate will. Now this is the case with scrupulous persons during all the earlier stages of their complaints before they become incurable." [1]

As to the first of these three quotations, I would say that scrupulous souls *do* need sympathy and compassion. One might well wonder what might have happened to Louise de Marillac if St. Vincent de Paul had not given a sympathetic hearing when she confided to him her scruples. In spite of her extreme excitement and defiance, he scolded with such sweetness and peace that he was able to correct and cure her.

Concerning the second quotation, we should be slow to say that a scrupulous person "teases God." Scruples that proceed from such inordinate self-love that whatever is done is done from fear of

[1] *Growth in Holiness, op. cit.*, pp. 269–270.

damnation and not from charity, not only tease God, they offend Him. Francesca of Pampeluna saw many souls in purgatory only for scruples; and when this surprised her, our Lord told her there never was a scruple which was wholly without sin, meaning of course those scruples which were the result of self-love and not preternatural scruples permitted by God for the purification of a soul of promise. Certainly the scruples suffered by the Little Flower were the latter type. She writes:

> While I was making my retreat for my second Holy Communion, I was overcome by scruples. What a martyrdom! It lasted about two years, and no one could possibly understand what I had to go through unless they had gone through it themselves. Every single thought and even my most commonplace actions became a source of worry and anxiety. I used to enjoy a momentary peace while I unburdened myself to Marie but this used to cost me a lot because I thought I ought to tell her absolutely everything, even the wildest of my fancies. But this peace only lasted about as long as a flash of lightning, and I was back where I started.[1]

To be sure, the scruples of St. Bonaventure that plagued him so for a while that he could not say Mass, and those of St. Lutgardis who said her office so many times over that God sent an angel to forbid her, make one feel like crying out: "O happy scruples which contributed to the perfection of a St. Thérèse, a St. Bonaventure and a St. Lutgardis!" In fact, St. Francis de Sales says: "The fear that scruples bring to those who have only lately abandoned sin, is an infallible sign of future purity of conscience."

Concerning the third quotation from Father Faber, I feel strongly that there are no incurable scruples, providing the afflicted person *wills* to be cured. It is the duty of the director to make this point clear and to do his utmost to drive home to his penitent the necessity of keeping alive the will to resist and conquer scrupulosity. Prayer must be practiced, the sacraments received, self-will conquered, devotion to the Blessed Virgin and St. Joseph, to the archangels Michael, Raphael and Gabriel encouraged. The axiom: *Obligatio dubia, obligatio nulla*—a doubtful obligation is no obliga-

[1] *The Story of a Soul,* translated by Michael Day, Cong. Orat. (Westminster, Md.: Newman Press, 1955), p. 58.

tion—ought to be given as a guide to direct scrupulous souls in their self-scrutiny. Father P. Dubois lays down these important principles by which scrupulous persons ought to be guided and by which they should guide themselves, namely:

Take no notice whatever of your doubts. Therefore treat as absolutely null and void all laws, obligations and prohibitions which are *doubtful;* and *regard as doubtful* all laws, obligations and prohibitions which are not as certain to you as it is certain that two and two make four. Therefore do, without fear, whatever at first sight and without examination, you do not know to be *certainly* sinful. Therefore do not consider yourself obliged to confess a sin, if you have the least doubt whether it is mortal or not. Therefore do not mention in confession a mortal sin which was *perhaps* confessed before, nor repeat a confession which was *perhaps* bad or invalid.[1]

Tanquerey suggests that in certain cases involving doubts that the penitent commit to writing this governing principle:

I am in conscience bound to take only evidence into account, that is to say, a certitude that excludes all doubt, a certitude as clear as the one that tells me that two and two make four. I cannot, therefore, commit a sin either mortal or venial, unless I am absolutely certain that the action I am to perform is forbidden under pain of mortal or venial sin, and that fully aware of this fact, I will nevertheless do it just the same. I will, therefore, pay no attention whatsoever to probabilities, no matter how strong they may be, I will hold myself bound solely by clear-cut and positive evidence.[2]

In confession, it may be necessary to limit the penitent for a time to a generic confession wherein the victim of scrupulosity simply accuses himself of all the sins since his last confession and all those of his past life.

The qualities of the cleric who is called upon to aid a scrupulous person are: (1) a great charity; (2) firmness in giving orders; (3) avoidance of indecision; (4) positive, clear, direct, and precise advice well-thought-out before delivery; (5) authority; (6) scien-

[1] *L'ange conducteur des âmes scrupuleuses et craintives a l'usage des fideles* (Paris: Desclée), chap. xi.

[2] *The Spiritual Life, op. cit.,* p. 448.

tific approach; (7) experience; (8) patience, remembering that during the first interviews a wise confessor or director permits the person to "talk himself out" no matter how repetitious, and avoids interrupting him; (9) words or gestures that indicate sympathetic understanding will inspire confidence and help get out the whole story. A few sessions will help the adviser ascertain the person's physical health and the seriousness of the motives of his anxiety. It may be found that all one's efforts and the best practices avail nothing in improving or curing the condition; then Father James H. VanderVeldt, O.F.M., Ph.D. and Dr. Robert P. Odenwald suggest that a trained psychiatrist should be consulted. "Certainly," say these famous experts, "not all cases of scrupulosity require a psychiatrist, since age-old experience has shown that prudent, tactful and patient pastoral counseling often leads to a satisfactory solution. On the other hand, numerous cases call for psychiatric treatment." [1]

To the victims of scrupulosity I can only say what St. John of the Cross wrote to a Carmelite nun who suffered from scruples: "Live in faith and hope, though it be in darkness, for in this darkness God protects the soul. Cast your cares upon God, for you are His and He will not forget you. Do not think that He is leaving you alone, for that would be to wrong Him. Read, pray, rejoice in God, your Good and your Health, and may He give you His good things and preserve you wholly, even to the day of eternity."

[1] *Psychiatry and Catholicism* (New York: McGraw-Hill, 1952), p. 339.

7

Characterology and the Purgative Way

IT IS nearer correct to say that a man is influenced by circumstances than to say he is a creature of them. "From the same materials," says Carlyle, "one man builds palaces, another hovels; one warehouses, another villas; bricks and mortar are mortar and bricks, until a man can make them something else. Thus it is that in the same family, in the same circumstances, one man rears a stately edifice, whilst his brother, vacillating and incompetent, lives forever amid ruins: the block of granite which was an obstacle in the pathway of the weak, becomes a stepping-stone in the pathway of the strong."

A good spiritual director should apply himself to a careful study of character if he hopes to be an effective help to many souls. He must realize that a person's character is affected by (1) his constitution, (2) his personality and (3) his environment.

Constitution refers to a man's physical make-up. When we say a person is born with a certain constitution, we mean that such a one is destined to have a definite type of stature, either short or tall, and, likewise, he will have a weak or strong cardiovascular system, one that will break down at thirty, or hold out until he is ninety-nine. The tendency to have various strengths and weaknesses in the body is transmitted through the germ plasm, and such varying physical factors we call constitutional endowments.

Everyone has a unique combination of genes, which are the biological elements which, in turn, are influential in determining the characteristics of the individual. The physical constitution may also be modified congenitally: take for instance a mother who, through carelessness or inability, fails to pay proper attention to her diet during her term of pregnancy, with the result that her blood is nonproductive of the calcium and silicon essential for good bone and dental structure. Such a mother may produce a child who is crippled or deformed, and who, because of these physical handicaps, may develop numerous complexes and frustrations. Noticeable defects can form the basis for introversion, and antisocial acts, due to the fact that other children, noticing these defects, give them stigmatizing nicknames, or otherwise poke fun at them. Or take another example, glands, for instance. Overactivity of certain glands in a pregnant mother may be transmitted to her child, and such a transmission may be a potential source of nervousness and irritability in the offspring. A preponderance of activity or underactivity of even one gland may upset the balance of the whole system. We all have seen sideshow freaks. They became bearded ladies, giants, dwarfs, or fat monstrosities because of defective glands that were in many cases transmitted to them from their parents.

Personality is loosely defined as "the totality of an individual's characteristics." Formally defined, character is an integrative combination of all our cognitive (knowledge), affective (feeling), conative (volition), and even physical qualities. The following things go into the formation of character:

(1) One's attention
(2) One's emotional tendencies and reactions
(3) One's will power
(4) One's moral character, including one's obedience to organized and traditional authority
(5) One's knowledge
(6) One's conscience
(7) One's beliefs and ideals
(8) One's mental attitudes

(9) One's religious attitudes of reverence, etc.
(10) One's intelligence
(11) One's imagination and memory, especially habits of noting and recalling
(12) One's sense of humor
(13) One's wisdom
(14) One's common sense and judgment

Personality is the pattern of an individual life and it includes a person's (1) *abilities* (his acts regarded from the point of view of their efficiency); (2) *dispositions* (his acts regarded from the point of view of his motives); (3) *temperament* (including such traits as emotion, persistence, impulsiveness); (4) *character* (the way in which his motives are integrated and the manner in which he deals with conflicting demands).

Character is a part of personality and not identical with personality. Frequently, the two terms "character" and "temperament" are taken as synonymous. They are not identical, since character is the sum-total of the psychological dispositions, based on temperament as modified by education and will power, and made lasting by habit, while temperament is the sum-total of those fundamental tendencies which flow from the physiological constitution of an individual. Since temperaments provide keys to character-study, let us now turn our attention to them.

Four hundred years before Christ, Hippocrates mentioned that in his day there existed a rough and ready chart for the classification of types of temperaments. Everyone in those days was classified as phlegmatic, sanguine, choleric, bilious, melancholic, lymphatic or nervous, or a combination of several of these temperaments. Not infrequently the phlegmatic is a degree or modification of the sanguine and the choleric of the melancholic. Experience will prove that some persons are placid and tranquil because they are phlegmatic; they cannot be easily excited; there is no danger of over-pungency toward them; they are in their nature like oxen that will bear the goad and whip with patient toughness; while others are extremely sensitive like a fiery Arab steed that cannot even bear to have the whip raised above it, and whom one stroke of the lash would make crazy with rage and excitement.

Let us examine then the seven different types of temperaments and note the peculiarities of each one:

(1) *The phlegmatic type* is described as one in which the vital processes go on slowly. On the bodily side, actions are slow and sluggish. On the mental side, as a rule, the judgment is fairly good, precisely because their passions lack intensity. Look for sensitivity and selfishness in this type. On the spiritual side, they are not attracted to a high degree of virtue. They will resent too much prodding but will be receptive of spiritual advice so long as it does not contain too much for them to do.

(2) *The sanguine type*, as the name seems to indicate, has its origin in a large development of lungs, heart and blood vessels. This all indicates an active temperament. On the bodily side, the vital processes are carried on rapidly, and the movements are light. On the mental side, the feeling of the sanguine is attuned to cheerfulness. The desires are superficial and changeable. Oetinger says "the sanguine would be noblest, if only it had fixity." They are often vain, fickle, frivolous, distracted and love pleasures.

The sanguine type is inclined to undertake more than can properly be done. Persons of this type dislike steady and quiet work. One may often find in this type a tendency to flightiness and childishness. Self-control is frequently lost and they are harsh to those about them.

(3) *The choleric type* embraces all those of irritable temperament, and while they are easily ruffled and subject to disquietude and discomfort, they are, on the other hand, equally easy to please. On the bodily side, the vital processes are carried on vigorously and rapidly. On the mental side, fancy is less prominent than the more decided operations, partly of the senses, partly of the intellect. Transient passions are peculiar to the choleric person. On the spiritual side, they are energetic, long-suffering and tenacious. They are sometimes high-minded, frank, brave, presumptuous, self-willed and irritable. They tend to seek praise and glory. Father Schram says: "The choleric prefers to die rather than to humble himself." [1] If they use their passions and energies for themselves they torture themselves, but if they use them for the glory of God they can become great saints and apostles.

[1] *Theol. Myst.*, II, 66.

(4) *The bilious type* is a seemingly odd classification, but it is simply a strange name for a persevering temperament. It gives the constitution great power of endurance, fits it both for mental and physical exertion and for extensive undertakings. On its spiritual side, it is beneficial in that it indicates strength, durability and exertion toward spiritual progress.

(5) *The melancholic type* designates the suffering temperament. While the sanguine type passes with ease from one feeling to another, from one mental state to another, the melancholic is bound to one and the same state and mood which he cannot quit. On the bodily side it is manifested by sluggishness of the functions with permanency. On the mental side, there is deep and enduring sensibility; the fancy, as arising from receptivity, predominates likewise in this passive temperament. On the spiritual side the melancholy type dwell on their difficulties and exaggerate them. Persons of this type are prone to sadness, to diffidence, and to a kind of misanthropy. They fall prey to discouragement, weariness and scrupulosity. St. Teresa maintains that persons who are highly predisposed to melancholy are not fit subjects for the religious life.[1]

(6) *The lymphatic type*, as the name indicates, is a temperament that is supposed to depend on a predominance of glandular and lymphatic system of vessels. On the bodily side, it is not infrequently evidenced by great weight. On the mental side, we find a slow, languid and sluggish process not easily aroused to activity and if so aroused, will soon sink into a lull again. On the spiritual side, one often finds procrastination as a predominant fault.

(7) *The nervous type* is an over-all classification of those with a lack of emotional control. On the bodily side it is evidenced by diffused motor responses, such as restlessness, moving the fingers, nail-biting, etc. On the mental side the nervous person displays an excessive readiness to react to all outer stimuli but an inability to act in a premeditated way. The behavior is tense and lacks continuity. On the spiritual side nervous people are quick of movement, they are easily drawn to sensual pleasures, and quick to love. A director who can appeal to their heart and turn them to a great

[1] *Foundations*, c. VII.

love of God will be rewarded by seeing persons who will make great spiritual progress.

Temperament is manifested whenever an impression is made upon the mind, whether that impression is caused by external stimuli, by thought, or by the imagination. How a person deports himself, how he reacts when something strongly impresses him, supply the key to his temperament.

Directors may be helped in the determination of temperament by asking such questions as follows:

(1) Are you quickly and vehemently excited by strong external stimuli or forceful thoughts or impressions (choleric) or only superficially moved and excited? (sanguine)

(2) Under such influences, are you inclined to act quickly (choleric) or do you feel inclined to wait and exercise calmness in appraising the whole problem? (sanguine)

(3) Does the excitement of the soul endure (choleric) or does it last for only a moment? (melancholic)

(4) Does the impression continue as if deeply rooted so that, at a later date if the impression is recalled to mind, the excitement is renewed? (melancholic)

(5) Do you conquer such excitement speedily or easily? (persevering or bilious type)

(6) Do you lack emotional control? (nervous type)

(7) Are you of a passionate nature? (choleric and/or melancholic)

(8) How do you act when rebuked? If the hurt fades immediately and the person reacts against feelings of revenge, he is a persevering (bilious) type.

The director will quickly ascertain that *most* people have a mixed temperament and this is a saving thing, since the combination often smooths the rough edges of the leading temperament. Let us look at a few of these combinations:

(1) Sanguine-Choleric: Excitement and reaction are speedy and the impression is longer lasting than with the purely sanguine

temperament. Fortunately, the fickleness and extroversion of the sanguine are modified by the seriousness and stability of the choleric.

(2) Choleric-Sanguine: The excitement is quick as is also the reaction but the impression is not so lasting as with the purely choleric temperament. The pride and arrogance are modified by the sanguine influence.

(3) Melancholic-Sanguine: Impressions are weak, reactions are feeble. The sanguine gives something friendly and cheerful to the otherwise melancholic temperament.

(4) Sanguine-Melancholic: The excitement is quick and reaction superficial and inconstant.

(5) Melancholic-Phlegmatic: The quiet apathy of the phlegmatic temperament helps dispel the morose and gloomy propensity of the melancholic. These personalities do well in community life.

I have cited only a few samples of the combinations, for someone has determined that there are over five hundred possible mixtures, but to the director who knows the principal temperaments, the combinations and the dominant elements will fall into a pattern readily discernible.

Not too long ago, the Swiss psychiatrist Jung used the terms *introvert* and *extrovert* and they are now universally accepted as a convenient mode of separating the individualistic, more or less shut-in type, from the social, talkative, breezy and perhaps superficial person.

The introvert is usually somewhat delicate, quiet, studious, retiring and sensitive. The extrovert, on the other hand, is a robust, energetic, noisy, devil-may-care type. These types represent extremes, since most people are somewhere in between.

In the study of characterology one must be warned that in spite of hereditary tendencies, different constitutions, temperaments and circumstances, one must reckon with the grace of God, and hold boldly to the truth that man has free will and is capable of self-discipline. I once heard a man say that for twenty-eight years the soul within him had to stand, like a watchful sentinel, guarding his appetite for strong drink. To be a man at least under such a handicap, not to mention a saint, is as fine a tribute to grace as could be found. This is certain, that there is enough grace at our disposal to make saints of us but as much grace as would make John a saint would barely keep Peter from knocking a man down —but the point is that the grace is there, but character and temperament may keep one from full and complete cooperation with it.

Environment also enters into this picture and a wise director will endeavor to ascertain facts concerning it. The kind of home, the attitude of parents, place in the family—whether an only child, the middle or the last child, serious sicknesses, poverty or plenty in the home, all these and a thousand more may influence a person's responses. Take for instance the position in the family. Usually the eldest child is constantly struggling to maintain the superior position he has because of his age. The younger child strives to excel the elder. The middle child has the disadvantage of striving to equal the elder and keeping ahead of the younger. These variations modify the goal of dominance or submission. Again the pampered child may grow up into an adult unable to cope with difficulties. The child who does not get enough parental affection may become isolated, stubborn, a day-dreamer.

In the early stages of the direction the spiritual guide might find it helpful to ask questions, such as the following:

Do you have brothers and sisters? (Look for selfishness in an only child.)

Are you the first, middle or last child?

Was your home a happy one?

Did you have your parents in childhood, adolescence, and adulthood?

Did your parents frequently demonstrate their love for you?

Did you have any long childhood illnesses?

Were you the only boy or girl in your family?

Did you look for an over-amount of sympathy from your parents?

Did you think in terms of objects? (extrovert)

Do you think of objects in terms of yourself? (introvert)

Do you show spontaneous and emotional expression? (extrovert)

Are your expressions masked and reserved? (introvert)

Are you inclined to be rough and ready? (extrovert)

Are you inclined to be sensitive? (introvert)

From the foregoing it is patently evident that in reality most characters are the product of constitution, personality and environment, and that it is by courageous and diligent striving to acquire those qualities which one has not received by heritage that one succeeds in overcoming natural defects, in acquiring proper balance, and in producing the best results. Through effort and the grace of God we all can do much to perfect our temperaments and develop a well-ordered character.

And do not say this is impossible. St. Ignatius Loyola, who by nature was choleric, conquered his passions to such an extent that he appeared to be a man without passions, and was considered by his companions as a pure phlegmatic. In like manner, the sanguine St. Francis de Sales, who in his earlier years was noted for his irate excitement and temper, completely subdued his irascible nature, but only at the cost of continual struggle that lasted for years.

It is important for the director of souls to study well the foregoing, since it will stand him in good stead in the full understanding of those seeking his counsel and it will serve to guide him in the proper approach to, and the handling of, those under his spiritual care. For instance, harsh commands or sarcastic remarks will cause the choleric person to resist help. The choleric temperament responds well to well-thought out reasons and motives when presented in a friendly manner. Again the choleric person can be counted on to keep his promises, while the sanguine person is never too reliable in the matter of resolutions. A crude approach or rudeness will make a melancholic person extremely reticent, while kindness will be rewarded by trustfulness and pliability in such persons.

A further reward for a painstaking study of the foregoing will be a better understanding of why some persons never enter into the purgative way or succeed in passing from it into the other stages on the road to perfection. It will certainly help us better understand St. Teresa's teaching concerning those in the various stages of spiritual progress:

There are a great number of souls who dwell but in the courtyard of the mansion or the castle of the soul, and who take no pains to penetrate the interior [that is to say, they never enter into themselves]. These souls, in not exercising any form of mental prayer [i.e., some sort of consideration and reflection on the things of faith], resemble a paralyzed body, who has hands and feet but cannot move them. They are so ill, so accustomed to live in things exterior, they are incurable: it seems that they are unable to any longer enter into themselves. They are so accustomed to live with the reptiles and the animals around the palace that they have become like them. These persons have been offered a share in a noble nature, and the power to entertain themselves with their God, but by their own fault have lost this power.

Such then, are the souls who live but a natural life, the life of the senses, whose Christian spirit is so little developed and who, according to St. Teresa, are grossly exposed to being lost. My, how that description fits so many persons in a parish! They, because of the grace of a good education, a happy temperament or other favorable circumstances have been preserved from great vices and perceptible faults and thus enjoy good reputations in the places where they live and work. In matters of religious practices they do just the essentials: Mass on Sundays and Holy Days, rare prayers, made with little recollection. Pious reading and exercises of devotion inspire but aversion. Their thoughts, their desires, their preoccupations are purely natural. Never, or nearly never, do they reflect on serious thoughts inspired by faith and if they combat their faults they do so from purely natural motives.

The foregoing forms a picture of so many persons in a parish that the very thought of it should be a challenge to every priest in charge of souls to find and use the best means with which to inspire such souls to better dispositions. And what are these means? Well, once and for all we say that the two great means are prayer and penance. Other means include practical instructions on the great truths of heaven, hell, the goodness of God and His providence, the shortness of life, judgment, and the Passion of our Lord.

When a soul sincerely begins to desire to live a true Christian life, it has entered into the purgative way or the first degree of charity. The purgative way or the way of beginners is that wherein a person striving to overcome sin, struggles more or less successfully against faults and vices, and if he relapses from time to time, rises up from his falls and repairs the damage done.

St. Teresa divides the persons in the purgative way into two classes: the *believing souls* and the *good souls*. Regarding the believing souls, the saint says that while they are immersed in worldly things, they have certain good desires. At long intervals they recommend themselves earnestly to our Lord but they pay little or no attention to their spiritual state. Several times a month they give themselves to prayer but with constant distractions caused by the affairs which daily occupy them and the worldly pursuits to which they are so strongly attached—where their treasure is, there is their heart.

Souls in this first class, or believing souls, give themselves to some pious exercises and from time to time entertain salutary reflections, but they do not understand the greatness of God or the importance of their duties to Him. To such, it is enough to live their whole lives determined not to commit mortal sin but that is all they will do.

Such are the traits of Christians who are in the first mansion. It is in this dwelling that St. Teresa says there are many apartments. We can, in fact, distinguish several classes even in this first degree:

(1) *Beginners,* that is to say, children who have only entered upon the Christian way; converts who have recently returned to God and in whom good dispositions are not yet born.

(2) *Habituates,* that is to say, Christians who have retained the same dispositions for years.

(3) *The fallen,* that is to say, those who have reached certain spiritual heights, but who have fallen into a state of lukewarmness.

The director must inspire a desire for higher perfection in this type of believing souls. He must exact regularity and respectful attention in prayer. He must instruct these people on how to act for God in all they do, how to struggle against their passions and venial sins, and he must impress them with the importance of mortification.

St. Teresa gives us an ideal portrait of those in the second degree or mansion or as she calls them—the *good souls*. These souls are those who have begun to give themselves to mental prayer and who understand the importance of not letting themselves remain in the first degree, but who have not the courage to abandon it completely and so they return often to it because they have not avoided the occasions.

Good souls are those who, outside family or common prayers, turn voluntarily to such practices as the rosary or Mass during the week. Their piety is intermittent. While those in the first degree resolve to avoid mortal sin, those in the second degree resolve to avoid deliberate venial sins. When the struggle goes on and on there is a danger of discouragement or lukewarmness or even of scruples. It is here that most souls come to the realization that spiritual direction is advantageous and even necessary. The direction of those in this second degree—good souls—ought to be paternal and kind. When St. Alphonsus was asked what he thought to be a most important factor in spiritual direction, he replied: "I have no doubt on the subject, that the characteristic proper to direction and most conformed to the spirit of God and of the Gospel, is kindness. Did God not show mercy toward the prevaricator Adam; and Jesus Christ who said: 'Learn of Me for I am meek and humble of heart,'[1] did He not support with infinite patience the faults of His Apostles not even excluding Judas?" And he added, "Judge for yourself how well the Jansenists succeeded in France by making our Lord appear as a tyrant."

The director, too, ought to be discreet, prudent, practical, encouraging, and firm, but above all, he ought to be supernatural. In the direction of good souls, as St. Teresa terms those in the second degree of the purgative way, the director ought to spur them to detachment from purely natural things and direct them to spiritual pursuits. This can be done by having them read spiritual books, the Holy Scriptures and the Lives of the Saints and passages from the *Imitation of Christ*.

[1] Matt. 11:29.

In an effort to form a more Christian life the director must impress upon good souls the necessity of frequent reception of the sacraments, prayer, sanctification of ordinary actions, and mortification. About the frequentation of the sacraments nothing need be said here. Both vocal and mental prayer must be stressed, but especially mental prayer. By mental prayer is understood that pious exercise in which one occupies himself in the considering of some mystery of the faith or some article of the faith or other edifying subject: the forming of affections conforming to what is considered in the meditation; the making of general and particular resolutions in the matter of changing one's life or of reforming one's morals.

The director might do well to stress the importance of mental prayer in those seeking to avoid venial sin and for the practice of the virtues so one may more easily reach perfection. The person seeking and making use of direction must never be permitted to lose sight of the goal which is perfection or of the fact that perfection consists in perfect charity which unites us entirely to God. Mental prayer tends to do just that. It is during mental prayer that the intellect occupies itself with God, meditating on His Divinity, on all His Perfections, His Eternity, His Immensity, His Infinity, His Immutability, His Power, His Justice, His Goodness, His Providence, etc. It is in mental prayer that the *will* is united to God by the holy affections of love, joy, and thanksgiving, adoration and praise. It is in mental prayer that the *memory* is so occupied with God that it forgets all earthly things and recalls nothing but the things of heaven.

The director will make clear to those whom he is called upon to guide in spiritual pursuits that certain predispositions are necessary for fruitful mental prayer and these are:

(1) Mortification of the senses and the passions so that the inferior part of man, his body, may be made subject to the soul, and so be more obedient to God and more easily receive His divine communications during the meditation.

(2) Practice as fully as possible the theological and the moral virtues.

(3) Purity of the heart and mind. This to be accomplished by detachment from earthly things so the soul may be attached only to God.

(4) Withdrawal from the world by means of silence, solitude, recollection, and retreat.

(5) A set time for spiritual reading.

(6) Consultation with director upon progress or failure in methods, content, affections and resolutions.

It is a matter of great moment that the director take special pains to instruct those under his guidance in the sanctification of their ordinary actions and the importance of frequent recollection of the presence of God, inculcating such a practice as offering an ejaculatory prayer at the striking of the clock. The adoption of a rule of life will do much to avoid dissipation of time.

Good souls must be always on guard against venial sins, and two practices will aid in this work—namely the daily general examination of conscience and the daily particular examen. The fidelity in these exercises will help a director gauge the earnestness of those whom he is directing, and he should require them to inform him from time to time if they have been faithful to them or missed them.

That the general examination of conscience produce its full effect, namely self-knowledge and self-reform, it should consist of five parts, namely: (1) thank God for His benefits; (2) ask grace to know and root out our sins; (3) demand an account of our souls concerning thoughts, words, actions and omissions, from the time of our last examination to the present; (4) implore God's pardon for our trespasses; (5) make a firm purpose of amendment.

In the general examination the different thoughts and acts since our last general examination are reviewed. How have we acquitted ourselves in:

I. Our duties toward God: (1) prayers; (2) exercises of piety.

II. Our duties toward our neighbor: (1) kindness; (2) charity; (3) obedience; (4) truth.

III. Our duties toward ourselves: (1) patience; (2) humility;

(3) temperance; (4) purity; (5) duties of our state, that is to say the sanctification of our work.

This general examination is ended by our asking pardon of God and promising Him that we shall do better in the future.

The particular examen, as its name implies, is a similar examination but with our attention directed against one fault—the predominant fault, for instance—or toward one virtue we are particularly attempting to acquire. Frequently the particular examination ought to be focused on how we have kept the resolution of our meditation for that day.

According to St. Ignatius, the daily particular examen is of greater importance than the general examination and even more important than meditation, for it enables us to track down our defects one by one and thus overthrow them more easily. The saint suggests, "three times and two siftings."

First, in the morning, immediately on rising, one should resolve to guard carefully against the particular sin or defect with regard to which he seeks to correct or improve himself.
Secondly, after dinner, he should ask God our Lord for the grace he desires, that is, to recall how often he has fallen into the particular sin or defect, and to avoid it for the future.
Then follows the first examination. He should demand an account of himself with regard to the particular point which he has resolved to watch in order to correct himself and improve. Let him go over the single hours or periods from the time he arose to the hour and moment of the present examination, and . . . make a mark for each time he has fallen. . . . Then he is to renew his resolution, and strive to amend during the time till the second examination is to be made.
Thirdly, after supper, he should make a second examination.[1]

Speaking of particular examen, Meschler, the great director of souls, says: "It owes its great efficacy to these three things: first, it divides our enemies, and brings all our forces to bear upon one of them at a time; secondly it attacks our disorders and sinful habits at the root; thirdly, it keeps us at work all day and calls for the exercise of every power of the soul and thus it becomes the

[1] *The Spiritual Exercises of St. Ignatius,* translated by Louis J. Puhl, S.J. (Westminster, Md.: Newman Press, 1954), p. 15.

specific for inveterate and radical defects, which resist all other means of self-reform." [1]

There are three things of high excellence which it is necessary to practice in the spiritual life:

(1) Purify the soul by continual examination and detestation of its vices.

(2) Take no satisfaction save in God alone.

(3) Live in the practice of great fidelity, do not do the least thing which may displease God.

Spiritual directors would be well advised to counsel those seeking their spiritual help that they should strive to subdue their vices before applying themselves to the acquisition of virtue; to correct external faults before working on the purely internal faults; if they are subject to many external faults let them attack those most likely to give scandal; amend deeds before words; and attack with vigor the predominant fault.

Good souls must be brought to the realization that the two great obstacles to any considerable spiritual progress are pride and love of ease. The director will do well to counsel frequently on the nature and practice of humility and draw up a conservative schedule of mortification that will touch not only the appetites and senses but the higher faculties of understanding, will and memory.

Father Lallemant notes that we make little progress in the interior life for the following reasons—reasons, I may add, that should be carefully noted by directors: (1) Exterior objects attract us by the appearance of some good which flatters our pride or our sensuality. This happens especially to those whose feelings are warm and who easily take fire.

(2) The devil, exciting the phantoms of the imagination, awakening the recollection and the image of past things, corrupting and inflaming the humors of the body as occasions offer, produces in us disquietudes, scruples, and a variety of passions. This he effects chiefly in those who, not having their hearts as yet

[1] *The Spiritual Exercises of St. Ignatius Explained.*

thoroughly purged, give him more hold upon them and are more in his power.

(3) The soul does not enter into itself except with pain, seeing there nothing but sin, misery, and confusion. To avoid this distressing and humiliating sight, it instantly hurries out again, and seeks its consolation in creatures, unless it is kept carefully to its duties.

Since a spiritual director is one to whom a person manifests his state of soul and to whom he offers himself to be habitually instructed and urged on in the way of perfection, the prime duty of the director is to know the soul, to teach it and help it to make effective progress. The best way to give direction is by word of mouth rather than by letter. The first few visits should help the director establish character and temperament which should be carefully noted and serve to guide the director in his work. Careful questioning and observation should determine fairly accurately in which of the three ways the soul finds itself—the purgative, the illuminative or the unitive way. If, for instance, it is determined that it is the purgative way, then the director is to think of the person as a beginner—that is, one who habitually lives in the state of grace and has a certain desire for perfection, but who still has attachments to venial sin and is exposed to fall now and then into grievous faults.

If St. Teresa's classical division of beginners into "believing souls" (those who strive to harmonize piety and worldliness) and "good souls" (those who have already been initiated in the practice of mental prayer) be applied, the means to be suggested to each are not too different. To the believing souls, the counsels ought to be directed toward considerations of the consequences of sin, and attempts made to awaken in them a longing for prayer, penance and mortification. The counsels to those in the second class, or the good souls, should be geared to improving their meditation in time and quality and helping them take the offensive against the capital sins. To *all* in the purgative way, mental prayer, through which God's grace is obtained, and mortification, through which they will be led to correspond to grace, must be the main objectives.

Frequently, the director should question those in the purgative way on their progress as follows:

I. *Prayer:* (1) How have you prepared yourself for prayers? (2) Have you prayed this week with fervor to the Blessed Virgin Mary? (3) Have you been faithful to your meditation? How did you make your meditation? Where? When? What resolutions did you make? How have you kept them?

II. *Sanctification of ordinary actions.* Have you often thought of God during the day, offering your work to Him, or recommended yourself to Him by short ejaculations?

III. *Renunciation.* Struggle against defects. How have you made your general examination of conscience? How have you combatted your faults, especially your predominant fault? Have you sinned with full knowledge and full deliberation? Have you made your particular examen daily this week? Have you accepted with resignation and for the love of God all the trials, large and small, encountered this week? How have you mortified yourself this week? What forms did it take? Did you give alms?

IV. *Sacraments.* Have you seriously prepared for your reception of Holy Communion this week? How much time did you spend in thanksgiving? Have you made spiritual communions this week?

Repeat often to those under your care: "Be convinced that no director can render you holy if you are not resolved to meditate and to mortify your own will and passions."

I wish every spiritual director of beginners in the purgative way would commit to memory the seven steps by which man attains to wisdom as set down by St. Augustine in his book *De doctrina Christiana* (Bk. II, Chap. 7). Here they are:

(1) We must turn to God by holy fear, in order to understand His Will and know both what He has forbidden and what He has commanded. This fear ought to bring to mind the thought of death.

(2) Then, piety must render us meek and docile to receive the lessons of Holy Scripture.

(3) This must be followed by knowledge; we must study the Scriptures, in which we learn that God is to be loved for Himself, and our neighbor for God. We must learn from the Scriptures that as long as we are held captive by attachments to temporal things,

we are still far from that great love of God and of our neighbor which they prescribe. Then, thanks to fear, which makes us dread the judgments of God, and to piety which renders us apt to learn the lessons of Holy Scripture, we cannot but weep over ourselves. Thence arise ardent prayers to obtain help from God.

(4) The fourth step is that of fortitude, by which we hunger and thirst after justice, and by which we are detached from the enjoyment of things passing, and become enamoured of things eternal, with God, One and Three, contemplating the Holy Trinity, which shines with so vivid a light and understanding that by reason of our human frailty we cannot bear so great a glory.

(5) This step is called the counsel of mercy, by which we endeavor to purify our souls, still agitated and troubled by the stains which come from their base passions.

(6) Next we must apply ourselves ardently to practice the love of our neighbor, and when we have reached the love of our enemies the eye of the soul is purified and made fit for the contemplation of God, as far as He can be contemplated by those striving with all their might to die to the world. For, only in so far as they die to the world are they able to contemplate God, and in so far as they yet live to the world are they hindered from contemplating Him. In this sixth step, the eye of the soul is so thoroughly purified that truth is preferred before all else, and the heart becomes so upright and so pure that neither to please men, nor to avoid any kind of suffering, would it turn aside from truth.

(7) The last step is reached, which is wisdom, wherein is found the enjoyment of God in peace and tranquility. This wisdom is defined by St. Augustine as "the knowledge and love of the Eternal, the Unchangeable, who is no other than God."

The spiritual director must ever keep in mind that the most desirable state in this life is that of Christian perfection, which consists in the union of the soul with God, and so all his work, his prayers, his conferences and his counsels must tend toward this end. This union which is created by the exercise of divine love, contains within itself an abundance of good things evidenced by such a close familiarity with God that there are no friends on earth who converse oftener or with more facility, more openness, or more unreserved out-pourings of heart. Such a soul enjoys a very deep peace and tranquility; a great liberty of mind which raises her above all things to a state in which she dreads nothing; an extraordinary strength for action; a wonderful guidance in every enterprise; and finally an infinitude of other celestial gifts, such as glorious victories, singular discoveries in the knowledge of supernatural truths, and the solid joys and priceless treasures of spiritual riches.

A most fruitful ministry is assured the spiritual director who follows the lead of the great Jesuit, Father Surin, and stresses the importance of self-knowledge, penance, recollection, interior peace, constancy, and diligence in holy exercises. Let us examine these points in the light of Father Surin's writings.

(1) *Self-Knowledge.* The first step necessary for attaining to divine union is to enter into the deepest recesses of our heart and with the help of the Holy Ghost, own to our weakness and disorders and deplore them in true repentance and effectually correct ourselves of them. Everyone undertaking the pursuit of perfection must incessantly ask God for the light necessary to know himself thoroughly. He must esteem this grace one of the most precious that can be received from God; and from the depth of his misery must utter cries and groans continually, to oblige the divine mercy to grant it to him. Let such a person feel confident that, after long and fervent entreaties, God will grant him this favor.

With a severe and piercing scrutiny let him try to discover the malice of his intentions, corrupted by self-love and self-esteem, and, this done, let him accuse himself of them before God, condemning himself at every turn, and inwardly annihilating himself. "This kind of proceeding," says Father Surin, "may seem to be unreasonable and excessive, but I believe that unless it be undertaken, we shall make but futile efforts toward perfection, and never draw ourselves completely out of the mire of our vices."

The spirit with which Mary Magdalene and the publican clothed themselves at the time of their conversions must animate the soul striving for perfection and in this spirit must it draw near to God and by the grace of the Divine Light examine itself with due severity. The soul so animated must admit of no thought which excuses or lessens its faults, but rather face them in all their grievousness. The more a soul has sorrow for its sins, the more it has peace, because confidence increases when repentance deepens. The more pain it feels for having displeased God, the more the soul will hope that God will grant it mercy and therein rests its joy. The reason the number of saints is so small in the world today is that there are very few persons who have the courage to face up to their transgressions of God's law or are sufficiently constant to continue it long enough for it to prove effective. The foundation of Christian perfection is humility, and humility can be acquired only by a deep knowledge of one's miseries, that is to say, of one's sins at their roots.

(2) *Penance.* It is an all too prevalent error that this humiliation of heart in the exercise of penance is solely an exercise to be performed by those who fall into mortal sin. Indeed, it is essential for even innocent souls, those leading a slothful and imperfect life, that is, if they truly wish to withdraw from their state of lukewarmness and sloth. It is sad to see persons of great spiritual promise remaining in their lukewarm state; and their condition is made more dangerous by their neglecting to conceive great humiliation and shame for the faults they themselves consider slight.

It is on account of this that there are so few saints today; and it is also for this reason that the souls really enlightened by God speak of themselves as if they were the greatest sinners on earth, although they have not committed great crimes or mortal sins. The purgative way is none other than this penitent life, which is the first story of the whole spiritual edifice. The enlightened spiritual director will urge those under his guidance not only to struggle to remove actual sins from the soul, but also to eradicate the roots of these sins, cutting off all the principles of sin, all the inordinate inclinations of nature, to such a degree that they no longer produce any disturbance. This is such a great work and one so far above human strength, it follows that a very great grace from God is necessary. This grace demands generous cooperation and constant fidelity.

This cooperation consists in entering deeply into oneself, in watching over one's actions, examining the motives which induce action, in observing the passions and the disordered impulses of one's weak nature. Having taken notice of them for some days or weeks and discussing them with the spiritual director, under his guidance, the person striving for perfection will come to the knowledge of the cause of the predominant habitual vice or vices. The task of the director involves seeking out the remedies, warning the person concerning occasions of sin and giving sound counsels on perseverance, especially warning against discouragement or weariness.

(3) *Recollection.* To penance must be joined recollection. How can a person know his faults, unless he keeps the ear of his heart always attentive to the voice of God, who warns of them, and the eye of his conscience always open to the light of grace, which points them out along with their remedies? Father Surin says that the *first* duty of recollectedness is to keep the senses closed to all outward things that are not of necessity, nor among the obligations of one's state in life, permitting the senses no freedom. The *second* duty of recollectedness is to employ great vigilance over the use of one's tongue, in other words, great circumspection in speech. In order to have the imagination calm, the mind serene, and disposed to receive the light of God, we must not disturb the ideas that have gathered in us. It is certain that a person who cannot keep silence has little or no solid virtue, and is subject to inconstancy, to levity, and to great distractions. The *third* duty of recollectedness is not to get oneself involved in the affairs of others except when duty demands such involvements. St. Augustine says that by nature we are as curious to know the lives of others as we are idle in correcting our own. The soul that seriously desires to attain union with God must adopt as a rule of conduct the counsel of St. Vincent Ferrer which consists of turning away the eyes of the body and those of the mind from others so that we may be the better able to see ourselves as we are.

The director would be well advised to spend a good deal of time in the early stages of his work with those seeking his special help in spiritual guidance in instructing them in ways and means of closing their senses to all outward things and the shunning of all useless curiosities of the mind. He should warn them that the faculties of the soul, exhausted in their search after vain gratifications, are sometimes found to be incapable of collecting enough strength to apply themselves to their spiritual exercises; thus they lack the vigor to completely unite themselves to God. Too, the director must stress the importance of silence and query his spiritual children frequently on how much progress they are making in this regard. It is the common experience of those who have contracted the habit of chattering that they always say more than they intended, being unable to maintain the just moderation which prudence and charity demand. Again the director must frequently warn against meddling in the concerns of others since out of this failing, all too often, one finds himself full of considerations for others and anxieties to help them. He may neglect his duty out of the fear of displeasing them and this leads to that slavery of human respect which is one of the greatest hindrances to the progress of souls in virtue. The wise director will prescribe this law: *Not to regard what others do, but, taking for granted that they are trying to do right, consider what is one's own duty and the Will of God.*

(4) *Interior Peace.* Peace of soul is so important that one's spiritual advancement absolutely depends upon it. Strange as it may seem, there are those who never possess it and there are those who lose it although they have lived a long time in the practice of spiritual things. Peace of soul is lost in various ways: too much activity of mind, impetuosity, multiplicity of worldly concerns, scruples, uneasiness of conscience, vehement passions, and a thousand other ways.

As to the necessity of peace of soul it suffices to say that a great many souls for the want of establishing themselves in it, accomplish nothing; for to be capable of receiving the operations of God, we must be free and empty. The soul which is not at peace is occupied by the enemies to peace listed above; and thus, it cannot apply itself completely to God. The basic cause of this disorder is the fact that we are generally too occupied with worldly things and give far too little time to the things of God; in other words, we esteem as important things that in reality are of little consequence in the light of eternity.

The soul that prizes God and His service, and that looks upon all else as nothing, is careful not to interest itself easily in any other thing besides God and His Will. That soul which cannot unite itself in this fashion to its God, fills itself with esteem for created things, such as honor, pleasure, knowledge or authority. And because, then, things are disputed at every turn, agitations incessantly arise within such a one, which disquiet and interrupt that interior action, in which consist the love and service of God. The soul becomes a veritable battlefield and this war never ceases until such thoughts are changed and until one comes, by the grace of God, to despise them, until one comes to despise what heretofore was esteemed and to regard with esteem that which was judged worthy of contempt.

The director must strive to inspire his charge with the idea that it is better to correct the least vice than to acquire all the wealth in this world. He must strive too, to make those striving for perfecion surrender their false ideas of the value of human things and to implant the true ones that they may procure that peace without which no one can arrive at union with God. The director should, then, counsel and advise those in any of the three ways, but especially those in the purgative way: (1) to avoid interesting themselves in the affairs of others, unless obliged to do so by justice or charity; (2) to calm all the impulses which arise in the soul with any vehemence, ruling or quenching them promptly by prayer—for instance, St. James says: "Is any one sad among you, let him pray";[1] (3) to take care not to harbor unprofitable thoughts in the mind, but rather to stifle them at the outset; (4) to avoid the occasions that might lead to disturbances and especially those objects which excite the appetites most violently; (5) skillfully to avoid an accumulation of affairs, which induces eagerness and stimulates over-activity.

One of the great fruits of interior peace and recollection is the increase of spiritual light, a light which facilitates the true knowledge of self. The time spent in spiritual reading, especially the lives of the saints, will result in a profound conviction of the multiplicity of one's disorders, and by comparison, of how far one is

[1] Jas. 5:13.

removed from the great models of virtue. The soul will soon come to employ a good deal of the time in recognizing and denouncing its failures and weaknesses, in deploring them, and in procuring remedies.

(5) *Vigilance and perseverance.* At the outset of the pursuit of perfection one must be warned that the path is not an easy one. In order to attain perfection, we must fight against our natural indolence, our tendency to do only that which pleases us, and against the various passions which rise up within us, when we wish to restrain ourselves. But in the end it becomes fairly easy. You see, constant application is absolutely necessary in the work of perfection, because God wills that we should do this work conjointly with Himself. We must, therefore, maintain a constant vigilance and apply ourselves with attention to this work. Continual vigilance must extend to all our actions, whether interior or exterior, even to the smallest and most insignificant.

The simplest action requires an examination of its motives and at the outset of each action, we must see what God requires of us in respect to it. Our ordinary actions are to arise, to eat, to converse, to read, to work, to pray and to retire. If we do such actions as these badly or imperfectly, our life will be bad, it will be imperfect and grovelling. If we content ourselves with exercising virtue on great occasions only, we shall never attain to the possession of virtue. We must always act with an upright intention, in the presence of God, without any evil or impure views. By this means the habit of acting supernaturally and holily will soon be formed within us. Father Surin suggests that if possible, we ought to renew every hour the desire for perfection and the good resolve to strain after it with all our might.

The soul that desires to advance in perfection must not undertake or do anything without having formed the intention of doing all for God. Such a soul must represent to itself continuously how just it is to satisfy God, exciting itself to please Him, until it feels so touched by this noble motive that it acts only from this principle. Constant vigilance must be maintained lest self-glory, pleasure or human respect overcome or divide the heart. It is not entirely adequate to make this exercise of a pure intention but once a day, as is the custom with so many persons; rather, the exercise of a pure intention should be repeated frequently during the day, and by making a halt first in our most important actions, then in those of less consequence, and finally, in the smallest and most insignificant actions. During the brief pause before each action, we should examine the motive or the instinct that impels us. When we discover that it is curiosity or sensuality, or inordinate love of pleasure, or the desire of pleasing some person, or our own satisfaction, we should hold ourselves a little in suspense and then, collecting our thoughts, condemn the intemperance or the imperfection of the motive which moves us. This done, we should think well of what we owe to God, and how just it is to refer all to His glory, thus exciting ourselves to this sublime motive, and only then ought we to proceed to perform our tasks. By the constant practice of the exercise of the purity of intention, little by little, our corrupt nature is repaired and sin is avoided.

The second exercise which must be constantly kept up is the amendment of our life and a change of habits. This change of life is what our Lord and His holy apostles preached to the world: "Be penitent, therefore, and be converted, that your sins may be blotted out."[1] In order to carry out this exercise it is necessary that, besides the general good purpose, which as we said must often be renewed, of not suffering any voluntary imperfection in ourselves we should also undertake in a particular manner the correction of that vice which is most opposed to our spiritual advancement, and which influences the greater part of our actions. It is this vice we must watch most assiduously. We must never permit its attacks to go unresisted, nor pardon ourselves at all in this matter. The vices thus to be fought are an over-activity, a hastiness and vehemence in our movements or actions; a certain levity in our senses, with distraction of mind or an outpouring of ourselves in external objects; an attachment to or a searching after our own pleasures and conveniences, or to the satisfaction of our will in all things; an indolence, carelessness, and self-love, which make us think ever of ourselves, incessantly talking about ourselves; a harshness with regard to others, an aversion for certain

[1] Acts 3:19.

persons, a readiness to judge ill of others; a certain vanity, curiosity, impatience or a gossiping spirit.

When we find any of the foregoing vices in our soul, we must be prepared to spend the rest of our life in combatting and uprooting them: first, all in general, as much as we possibly can, watching unceasingly over ourselves, defending ourselves from them; secondly, in particular, one after another, taking up each one for a month, or for a good space of time sufficient to weaken them.

A fervent soul, and one that desires to advance in solid perfection, will not suffer a single action or an hour of the day to pass, without making a little review of its conduct, to see how all has fared with regard to that which forms the matter of one's particular examen. Such was the practice of St. Ignatius, and it is one of the counsels of St. Teresa: "*Examine yourself,*" she states, "*before each action and at each hour of the day, with a purpose of amendment, and by this means you will attain to perfection.*" And indeed, it is the shortest and straightest road by which to reach perfection, since the soul, thus purifying itself, is best disposed for the divine operations.

The next exercise to which diligence should be applied is that of the realization of the presence of God. It is esteemed one of the most essential of all the spiritual exercises, inasmuch as nature, which of itself inclines to error, riot, and sin, cannot be restrained by any more efficacious curb than the thought of the presence of God. Nicholas Herman in his *Practice of the Presence of God* says: "If I were a preacher, I would preach nothing else than the practice of the presence of God; if I were a director of souls, I would urge it upon everyone, so necessary and even easy do I believe it to be. This exercise does not kill the body. No effort, no strain, no special posture is called for: just glance upwards to God, to speak to God—the holiest, the firmest, the easiest and most efficacious manner of prayer." [1]

The practice of the presence of God consists in this: *that the soul, instructed by faith, represents God to herself not by any*

[1] Lawrence of the Resurrection, *The Practice of the Presence of God,* translated by Sister Mary David, S.S.N.D. (Westminster, Md.: Newman Press, 1957), p. 99.

figure or imagination which she forms, but by a simple knowledge that God is what He is, and that He is within her, full of majesty, of power, and of goodness. So she goes to God and unites herself to Him with a respectful love, as sweetly, as attentively, and as often as she can.

From this exercise, constantly practiced for a considerable time, there grows up in the soul a state of light, which discovers to her her faults and the things she ought to do. It leads too, to a filial fear, which restrains her on a hundred occasions, in which she would otherwise run into evil; a confidence, a tranquility of mind, a purity, a devotion, a holy joy, and an infinitude of good things, but above all, a firmness and stability in virtue and piety, which can be acquired only by this means.

One further exercise that should be practiced with assiduity is the mortification of the appetites of the heart. The soul should make it her study to deprive herself of her pleasure in all those things which give her a base and purely human gratification. The soul should never allow herself to go after that which is gratifying to her curiosity, vanity or sensuality but rather imitate St. Ignatius, who, from the first year of his conversion, when stopping at Manresa, made it his whole study to accede no pleasure to his senses.

To internal mortification must be added corporal penances which are marvelous helps to spiritual progress. It is a common error of our day to make little account of exterior penances, under the pretense that true perfection consists in the interior. Hear Father Surin say: "I do not believe that anyone has ever attained to a degree of eminent virtue without an especial ardour for penances—both interior and exterior."

Nowhere will spiritual directors ever find a more composite plan for guidance than the foregoing five specific points culled from the spiritual letters of Father Surin, and their implementation will assure great spiritual progress. When souls have been taught along these lines, and have spent *three or four years in this work, or more,* according to their particular needs, it frequently happens that our Lord, who conducts them and acts as their guide along the whole of the journey, makes them experience some special grace of His operation. It was this kind of grace that St. Francis prayed for when he asked of God "*His Holy Spirit and His Holy Operation.*"

Once a soul is purified from past faults by penance and grounded in virtue through the practice of mental prayer, penance and mortification and is able to resist disordered inclinations and temptations so that it easily keeps from mortal sin, even if the avoidance of venial sin is not so easy, that soul has entered upon the *illuminative way*. The illuminative way belongs to such, leading them as it does to proficiency in virtue, and to a more complete subjugation of their passions, giving them a facility, not only in avoiding great sins, but also in lessening the number of smaller ones, as well as in practicing the moral virtues.

8

The Illuminative Way and Affective Prayer

I KNOW of few saints whose lives fit so conveniently into the exact pattern of the three degrees of perfection, the purgative, the illuminative and the unitive way, as Saint Norbert. Norbert was born in the year 1080 of one of the most illustrious families of Germany's nobility. His father, whose name was Heribert, was related to the Imperial House itself, and his mother Hadwigis, was a descendant of the ancient house of Lorraine. His parents, belonging to God's nobility as well as of the world, were both virtuous and God-fearing Christians.

Norbert was ordained subdeacon by the Archbishop of Cologne and forthwith appointed to a Canonry in the Imperial Church at Xanten from which the young cleric received a handsome income. The Archbishop, hearing of his natural talents and learning, invited him to come to live at his court in Cologne. Alas, the worldly-minded Norbert, blinded by ambition, obeyed with great eagerness. Soon misled by the flattery of the world, he allowed himself to be entirely carried away by its pleasures and allurements. He forgot the lessons of his pious mother and the obligations of his state in life and became thoroughly worldly. Tiring of the Archbishop's court, Norbert's ambition drove him to ask to be appointed Chaplain to the Emperor Henry V, which came to pass because his father was a distant relative to the emperor—a man who subsequently dared to lay violent hands upon the reigning venerable pontiff Paschal II. When this dastardly deed happened, in all justice to Norbert, he did protest the emperor's action and lost favor with him, and soon he left the royal court and returned to the archbishop's court in Cologne. The change, however, did not improve his manner of living, in fact it seemed that he lived a life more worldly than before.

One summer day in the year 1115, Norbert, bent on pleasure, was on his way to a village called Wredan. He was riding a fiery steed richly caparisoned; his servant rode at his side. Suddenly the heavens opened, and rain, thunder and lightning split the skies. A blinding flash of lightning tore up the earth at the feet of Norbert's horse, and the horse fell and threw its rider, who lay for a long time like one dead. When he awakened, like the apostle Paul, he said: "Lord, what wilt Thou that I do?" At the same moment a voice from heaven said: "Turn away from evil and do good; seek after peace and pursue it."

That was the turning point of his life. Forthwith he returned to Xanten and renounced all his appointments at court. He locked himself in a room and then, prostrate before his crucifix, shed an abundance of tears. It was in this same room that Norbert spent three years of prayer and severest penances. He sought spiritual guidance from the saintly Abbot Conon, and faithfully followed his counsels. Norbert spent three years in the purgative way, and then he who had refused the priesthood so that he might have more freedom to lead a worldly life, now, upon the advice of Abbot Conon, humbly presented himself for ordination, and so Norbert was ordained—no longer the gay courtier and slave of the world, but the humble penitent of Jesus Christ renouncing the world and its pomps. Before the eyes of the vast multitude, he casts aside his princely garments on the floor, and replaces them by a penitential robe of sheepskin, tied around the waist with a rough cord, then, putting the liturgical vestments over his simple tunic, he goes to the altar and presents himself for ordination.

The three years following his ordination were for the most part spent in solitude on a high mountain near Xanten. The sinner was gradually being formed into a saint by prayer, meditation, mortification, and the implementation of the virtues. He spent most of his days and nights in prayer. He never tasted food until sundown each day except on Sundays and walked about bare-footed, even in the midst of winter, wearing only his sheepskin tunic and penitential cape. The two special virtues which were weakest in Norbert were the two virtues which he sought most to acquire and which in the providence of God would most enable him to do the work for which God had destined him: patience and faith. Patience was the virtue he needed to serve as a shield, lest being unarmed, he should yield; faith, for strength, lest being too weak, he should fail. How well he accomplished his work in implementing these two virtues, to say nothing of the other virtues, is borne out by the fact that by faith he wrought many miracles such as raising the dead to life, and by patience, since he had put up with opposition and persecution that would have discouraged a lesser man.

Having completed our study of the purgative way, it is fairly easy for us to trace the various steps St. Norbert had to take to arrive at the illuminative way. His good home, his education, helped to maintain him in the degree called by St. Teresa that of a believing soul, but his worldliness and love of pleasure would have kept him there to his peril if God had not condescended to cause his being thrown from his horse and made known to him that He wanted him "to turn away from evil and do good; seek after peace and pursue it." God uses other less striking means to move us to the same end; these are sermons, retreats, missions, etc. St. Norbert lost no time in deciding that he must do the will of God and seek perfection. He passed quickly, using the three great means of mental prayer, penance and mortification, to the second degree in the purgative way called by St. Teresa the state of a "good soul." It took him three years to subdue the capital sins and to rid himself of his worldliness and ambition. His progress might have been much slower had he not sought and received spiritual direction from the saintly Abbot Conon.

Once St. Norbert had purified his soul from past faults by three years of arduous penance, once he had been grounded in virtue through the practice of mental prayer, of mortifications, and resistance to the disordered inclinations and to temptations, he entered *the illuminative way*.

St. Teresa describes those in the illuminative way (those in the third mansion) as persons who are very desirous not to offend His Majesty, they avoid venial sins, love penance, spend hours in recollection, employ their time rightly, exercise themselves in works of charity to their neighbors, are well-ordered in their conversation and dress, and those who own a household govern it well.[1]

The name *illuminative way* is given to this stage in the soul's perfection because the great aim of the soul is now the imitation of Christ and the positive exercise of the Christian virtues, and since Christ is the light of the world, whoever follows Him walks not in darkness "but shall have the light of life." [2]

What, you ask, are the signs indicative of one's having arrived at the illuminative way? Besides the ones given above as listed in our quotation from St. Teresa, the other signs are: a certain measure of purity of heart; mortification of the passions; avoidance of deliberate venial sins; difficulty in making discursive mental prayer inasmuch as the Holy Ghost inspires such to spend less time in considerations and more time in affections and petitions; and habitual desire to be united to our Lord, to know Him, love Him and imitate Him.

Tanquerey reminds us that there are many classes of souls in the illuminative way; two of these are of immediate importance: devout souls and fervent souls.[3] The *devout* souls he classifies as those possessed of good-will, or ambition to do good, who strive by serious effort to avoid deliberate faults. They are vacillating in their efforts and need to cultivate the virtues of fortitude, constancy, and humility. The *fervent* souls, he says, are more humble, generous, constant and habituated to the practice of Christian self-denial. They need, however, further detachment from things that hinder perfect union with God. These, too, lack constancy and love of crosses.

In noting the signs indicative of arrival at, or transition to, the illuminative way from the purgative way, we mentioned that in the latter state meditation is discursive, while in the illuminative way meditation becomes *affective*. Affective prayer is that form of

[1] *The Interior Castle*, translated by a Benedictine of Stanbrook (Westminster, Md.: Newman Press, 1948), p. 36.
[2] John 8:12. [3] *Ibid.*, pp. 460–461.

prayer in which devout affections predominate, that is, those various acts of the will whereby we tell God how much we love Him and of our desire to glorify Him.[1] When the soul is beginning to devote itself to prayer, a great deal of mental reflection is necessary in order to make it understand the goodness of God and decide to love Him even timidly. But when it advances in knowledge, this reticence disappears and much greater love is reached, although a far shorter time is given to consideration. Thus the passage from meditation to affective prayer comes almost imperceptibly. "Progress," says St. Teresa, "consists not in thinking much, but in loving much." It is noteworthy that the Venerable Father Libermann (1803–1852) writes: "Although meditation leads gradually to affective prayer, this fact does not prevent a great many souls from beginning at this stage without ever having applied themselves to discursive meditation." [2] But under ordinary circumstances affective prayer is a natural *sequitur* to meditation. It does happen that a person who has meditated frequently on a mystery of faith may easily pass to the making of acts of love as soon as the mystery is recalled to mind. When a given mystery has been so often used as a subject for mental prayer, and looked at and considered under every aspect, the results are that the soul's knowledge becomes less speculative and more real and warm, so the result is this, that as soon as the concepts appear before the mind, acts of love pour out from the heart. When this occurs, then almost the whole time of the meditation is taken up with acts of love, and we call this affective prayer. Simply put, instead of engaging in lengthy reasonings on a truth of religion, the mind comprehends it in a general way which is sufficient to touch the heart and inflame it with love. If affective prayer is a great advance in mental prayer it has its pitfalls too. Care must be taken so that one is not deluded into supposing that the vividness of sense emotion is perfection in prayer. Again, because one feels sentiments of love for God, he should not think that he has succeeded in practicing affective prayer. To pray is to make petitions, so naturally, affective prayer must include humble petitions, for this is the only means of obtaining from God the grace one needs in order to

[1] Cf. *ibid.*, p. 461.
[2] *Ecrites sur l'oraison et lettres*, p. 149.

practice virtue. Without petitions, mental prayer or affective prayer is imperfect and incomplete. It will profit little if one meditates on the mysteries of the faith, the commandments, or the vices and virtues, unless in that meditation he humbly petitions God for the grace to be a better Christian. Hear St. Alphonsus say: "What is the advantage of knowing what we ought to do, and yet not doing it—unless to make us more blameworthy in God's eyes? Read and meditate as much as we will, we shall never fulfil our obligations unless we ask God for the grace to do so." The saint continues: "At first during meditation I devoted myself more to producing affections than to praying. . . . But later on, when I realized the necessity and the great utility of prayer, I devoted the best part of the time during my meditation to the prayer of supplication." [1]

When we studied methods of making mental prayer, we stressed but two—namely the Ignatian and the Sulpician methods. We shall do likewise in this study of affective prayer beginning with the method of St. Ignatius. *De facto,* St. Ignatius gives us three methods of affective prayer (1) contemplation, which, by the way, is not to be confused with acquired or infused contemplation; (2) meditated vocal prayer; (3) the application of the senses.

I. *Contemplation.* When we contemplate something, we do not merely look at it; we ponder it, wonder at it and enjoy it. For instance, the first time we see a beautiful painting or a beautiful church or some other historical or rare object of art, we scan it in parts, we notice this or that detail, one after the other. If you can, you go back time and time again to make special note of some new detail or facet. Were we to do this frequently, the time could come when we would no longer stop to examine and admire the details, but we would simply gaze at the picture or the building and say to ourselves: "Oh, what a beautiful piece of work! Oh, what a beautiful building! Oh, what wonderful workmanship!" And we would linger, looking with amazement and love, feasting our eyes on the object of our pleasure.

Meditation might be compared to the gazing at the *details* in some mystery of our faith, the Blessed Trinity, our Lord, the Blessed Virgin, or the saints, and by making use of our intellect and

[1] *The Chief Means of Prayer,* I, 11, p. 4.

memory, we stir our will to make acts of adoration, petition, thanksgiving, and resolution. In the contemplation in affective prayer, we, having so often before meditated on the details, find ourselves able to examine some mystery and no sooner have we brought it to mind, than we linger over it with pleasure and our hearts pour out love and affection. "If I wanted to excite my soul," says St. Ignatius, "I should stop and tarry there, without concerning myself with proceeding further, until my soul has had its fill; for it is not an abundance of knowledge that lays hold on the soul and satisfies it, but the inward relish of the truths it meditates." [1]

Spiritual writers are emphatic in declaring that if this method is to be fruitful we must do *more* than simply ponder on some mystery or some phase of Christ's life, since such meditation or contemplation is not a prayer until and unless we offer adoration, admiration, petition and gratitude toward God. Therefore, we ought to consider the incident as actually placed before our eyes, we must share in it, we must seek to attain some practical result, such as a more intimate knowledge of God, or our Lord, our Lady, a more unselfish love of them and the grace of imitation.

In affective prayer, we give ourselves more to affections of the will than to the considerations of the understanding. For instance, we consider a mystery, a passage of Scripture such as the words, "And the Word was made flesh" (John 1:14). On these words we make acts of faith, hope and charity, admiration, thanksgiving, etc. We take one of God's perfections, such as His Wisdom, His Goodness, His Holiness. We consider how it was communicated to Jesus Christ and the Blessed Virgin, to the angels or some saint; we praise God for it; we ask for a participation in it and dwell as much as we can on the affection with which we are most touched.

Father Rousseau says:

If at the beginning of your meditation or a little later on, you feel great distress in trying to think and you are powerless to be discursive on the subject of your meditation; and if you even feel that the efforts you are making disturb and trouble you and keep you from thinking about God while all the while you feel interiorly occupied, it may be a sign that God wishes you to make your mental prayer by contem-

[1] *Spiritual Exercises;* cf. Tanquerey, *op. cit.*, p. 468.

plation. Follow this attraction without fear; the violence which you do yourself to meditate in this state, is very meritorious.[1]

II. *Vocal Prayer Meditated.* This method, according to St. Ignatius, consists in a leisurely consideration of any vocal prayer, such as the Our Father, the Hail Mary, the Glory Be to the Father, the Angelus, in order to ponder the meaning of each word. In this method, one dwells on the word as long as one finds fresh sentiments that yield some light, strength, or resolution.

III. *The Application of the Senses.* According to St. Ignatius, this method of contemplation consists in the spiritual or imaginative exercise of the senses upon a mystery of our Lord's life, so that the soul might be moved to stir up pious sentiments and resolutions. In it one applies the eyes, the ears, the taste, the touch and the sense of smell so as to attain to a fuller realization of all the circumstances surrounding the mystery.

The Sulpician Method of Affective Prayer. Those who follow the Sulpician method of meditation will find that the transition to affective prayer is more progressive than different. If they would but add prolonged adoration, so that, at times, it takes up nearly half the meditation time, and if the communion becomes chiefly affective so that the soul is stirred to pour out gratitude for lights received and by ardent desires of practicing the virtue upon which the meditation rests and petitions made for the grace of practicing some particular virtue, they may be certain that they are practicing affective prayer.

It is important to point out here that the method proposed by St. John Baptist de la Salle seems the most simple and an outline of it follows:

Part One: To recall the presence of God and dwell on it. To arouse these affections, or make these acts.

With reference to God: faith, adoration, gratitude.

With reference to self: humiliation, shame, sorrow.

With reference to Christ: appropriation of His merits, union with Him, invocation of His Spirit.

Part Two: Some particular subject matter is considered: a mystery, a virtue, or a principle.

[1] *Directions pratiques dans les différents états de l'oraison* (Paris: Lethielleux, 1913), p. 84.

Here also nine acts are elicited.

With reference to Christ: faith, adoration, thanksgiving.

With reference to self: shame, sorrow, application: then these three concluding acts (1) union with the Savior, (2) petition, (3) invocation of the saints.

PART THREE: Retrospect over the results of the hour, thanksgiving and offering.

Three hundred years ago Father Augustine Baker, O.S.B., remarked that at that time "the world is but overburdened with books on discursive prayer or meditation, which with more than sufficient niceness prescribe rules and methods for the practice of it, and with too partial an affection magnify it, the authors of such books neglecting in the meantime, or perhaps scarce knowing what true affective prayer is, which, notwithstanding, is the only efficacious instrument that immediately brings souls to contemplation and perfect union in spirit with God." One wonders what the good and venerable Father would write today after an excursion to Barclay Street and a survey of the bookshelves in our present-day Catholic bookstores. They are bulging with books on discursive meditation, but blessed if you could find more than a couple on affective prayer.

The paucity of books on affective prayer may come from the fact that we do not find in the writings of the fathers and mystical doctors exact instructions touching on the practice of internal affective prayer. The reason why the early fathers did not bother writing on the subject was because there was no need for it. The ancients lived entirely separated from the world, its business and its distractions, having nothing to distract them from union with God, and they lived in continual conversation with God, suffering themselves to be conducted and managed by the Holy Spirit. But in these days, religious persons and others that aspire to spiritual contemplation, who either want the means to enjoy, or have not the courage and strength to support such solitude and austerities, thank God they have the teachings of St. Teresa, St. John of the Cross, St. Ignatius and St. Sulpice to uphold and promulgate the teachings on the importance of affective prayer.

It must be very important, or Cardinal Bellarmine would never have written "that without a diligent pursuit of internal prayer none will ever become truly spiritual, nor attain to any degree of perfection." [1] Little wonder then that Father Baker should say that

> the first excellency of internal affective prayer above all others is that only by such prayer our union in spirit with God is perfectly attained. . . . [Secondly,] by this prayer of the will, the soul entering far more profoundly into God, partakes of the beams of His divine light far more plentifully, by which she discovers God's perfections more clearly, and also sees the way wherein she is to walk more perfectly than by any other prayer. . . . [Thirdly,] not only divine light, but also grace and spiritual strength to put into practice all the things to which supernatural light directs, is obtained by this [affective] prayer of the heart. . . . [Fourthly,] affective prayer is the only action that cannot possibly want purity of intention since it is not impossible for persons to observe fasts, exercise themselves in curious speculations during meditations simply to comply with self-love. . . . [Finally,] affective prayer of the will is that alone which makes all other sorts of prayer to deserve the name of prayer; for were that excluded, meditation is but a useless speculation and curiosity of the understanding, and vocal prayer but an empty sound of words; for God only desires our hearts or affections, without which our tongues or brains are of no esteem at all.[2]

Father Baker might have added that affective prayer is the only form of prayer that can go on uninterruptedly, something that does not hold true for vocal prayer or meditation. It is with affective prayer that we are best able to fulfill the command of our Lord: "that we ought always to pray and not to faint." [3] St. Paul exhorts all Christians indifferently to "pray without ceasing." [4] It is safe to infer that the degrees of grace and sanctity in any man are to be measured according to the power that prayer has upon his actions and that he whose actions do not for the most part flow from the virtue of prayer is not yet rightly disposed toward his last end.

We said in treating of prayer in the purgative way that while aridities and scruples often attack the soul in that degree of perfection, they more frequently appear in the persons who have entered

[1] *Sermones in fer. 2 Rogat.*
[2] *Op. cit.*, pp. 353–355. [3] Luke 18:1. [4] 1. Thess. 5:17.

the illuminative way. Fears are to be repressed in this latter state and it must be remembered that more good comes from prayers of aridity courageously pursued than from prayers of sensible devotion.

Directors must strive to comfort souls caught in the vise of aridity, and encourage generosity of resolution not to seek contentment in nature by internal excuses, nor to quit prayer for any dullness, coldness, or aversion whatsoever. In spite of the aridity, such souls ought to be inspired to make the most efficacious affections possible to them and to force themselves to the love of God by ejaculatory prayers. Blosius gives the following aspirations as suited to the illuminative way:

> "Oh, when shall I perfectly die to myself and be free from all creatures? Oh, would that I were truly meek of heart and humble; truly poor and naked in spirit. Grant, O Lord, that by perfect self-denial, perfect mortification of my vices I may arrive at perfect love of thee. Thou hast commanded that I should love thee: give what thou commandest and command what Thou pleasest. Grant that I may love thee with my whole heart, my whole mind, with all my powers, with my whole soul. . . . Free my soul from all distracting cares; strip from it the images and forms of perishable things. Grant me to dwell with thee in the sanctuary of my soul; grant that by steadfast thought, clear knowledge and fervent love I may always be able to flow into thee.[1]

Tanquerey and Guibert both warn that, even when transition to affective prayer has been made prudently and at the correct time, there are still dangers to be avoided: (1) "violent efforts to elicit acts to make them vehement;" (2) spiritual gluttony—"being intent on tasting sensible affections;" (3) presumption—"the soul thinks that it has made great spiritual progress because it feels lively affections, and so it comes to have too much confidence in itself."[2]

I know of no better way of drawing this chapter to a close than to quote these famous words of a most famous spiritual light, St. Teresa: "It is one thing to desire the grace of devotion, and quite another thing to ask God for it."

[1] *A Book of Spiritual Instruction*, translated by Bernard A. Wilberforce, O.P., edited by a Benedictine of Stanbrook Abbey (Westminster, Md.: Newman Press, 1955), pp. 30–31.

[2] Guibert, *op. cit.*, p. 244.

9

The Illuminative Way and the Practice of the Virtues

ONE day, Charles IX of France asked the celebrated poet, Torquato Tasso, this question, "Who do you think is the happiest being?" "God," answered the poet. "Any child could give that answer," continued the monarch. "What I want to know is, who is the next happiest after God?" "That is very easy," replied Tasso, "the next happiest being after God is he who most closely resembles God, that is to say, whoever is most perfect in virtue."

Undoubtedly, Tasso's answer was correct, for the more virtuous a person is, the more is he like God, and the happier he will be here and hereafter. A Christian without virtue is a husk without a kernel, a spring without water, a vine without grapes, in fact, in vain do we call ourselves Christians, if we are not imitators of Christ.

In our study of the purgative way—the way of beginners—we saw what appertains to the putting off of "the old man." In this present study of the illuminative way—the way of proficients, we must learn what is required to put on "the new man." He is called "the new man" who is clothed with faith, hope, and charity, with prudence, justice and the other virtues. The three principal works in the purgative way are the initiation and development of mental prayer, mortification, and the uprooting of the seven capital sins from our soul. It would be an improvident farmer who would spend all his life eradicating weeds and yet never planting good crops. In like manner, it would be spiritual folly to root out sins from our soul and never develop therein the seeds of virtue. *De facto,* it is the teaching of the fathers and the ascetic theologians that the will for advancement in the spirit of perfection, with a corresponding effort, and an exercising of the powers of mind and body, are necessary for the proficient (one in the illuminative way), and that there is in this the strongest impulse toward every virtue.

Some wise person once remarked, "You cannot tell the depth of a well by the length of the handle on the pump." Nor can you tell the state of perfection by the length of one's prayers. Spiritual progress does not consist in the multiplication of extraneous and sublime works, nor in the multitude of pious exercises, but in doing well, perfectly and after virtue's patterns, those works we daily perform. "They are entirely mistaken," says Cardinal Bona, "who, that their progress may increase, to their usual prayers and bodily penances repeatedly add others, and who formerly fasting twice a week now resolve to fast three or four times, that they may the more advance, it is true, when they ought rather aim at this, to fast twice, indeed, as before, and perform the customary task of prayers, but with greater fervor, piety, spirit and perfection." [1]

In order that our actions be rightly performed and our actions found perfect before God the following rules should be observed:

(1) All things are to be done with the upright and simple intention of their being done for God.

(2) While engaging in exterior affairs not to lose the spirit of interior devotion.

(3) All things to be performed in the presence and sight of God.

(4) Apply ourselves diligently to the work at hand.

(5) Think of the judgment at the end of our life and perform each and every action as if it were to be our last.

(6) Offer all our thoughts, works and actions to God, but uniting them with that oblation by which Christ offered Himself and

[1] *Cursus vitae spiritualis,* part II, chap. 1. This work was formerly ascribed to Abbot Morozzo.

all mankind to God, thus making our oblation one with Christ's.

(7) Have the right intention—that of having God as the end of our work and referring all things to His honor and glory. "To them that love God, all things work together unto good." [1]

The following are the signs of a right intention:

(1) When we are not upset when our undertakings do not turn out well.

(2) When we rejoice over the good done by others as if it were done by ourselves.

(3) When we have no preference for this or that office or employment (if we are religious) but content ourselves with what obedience imposes.

(4) When we neither desire to be praised for the discharge of our duties nor to receive proofs from others of their satisfaction.

(5) When what we do does not divert us from prayer, from attention to conscience, from remembrance of God.

(6) When, with regard to the whole course of life, we are prepared for and indifferent to either alternative, so that, as it may please the divine Will, adversity and prosperity, wealth or poverty, honor or contempt, sickness or health, a long life or short, are embraced with joy. We seek God: What does it matter whether we reach Him by this way or that?

Like most of us, St. Catherine of Siena was confused by the different books and authors, and their prescriptions for perfection. Smart in the wisdom of the saints, she went directly to God and humbly asked Him to tell her how to be perfect. The divine Teacher told her:

Know that the salvation, the perfection of My servants stand on this one thing, that they do My will alone, ever striving to fulfill it in all things; that they attend to Me, and serve Me every moment of their lives. The more diligently they apply themselves to this, the nearer

[1] Rom. 8:28.

they approach perfection, since thus they are in union with Perfection itself. . . . If thou seekest to know My will, that thou mayest perfectly fulfil it, behold in one word that which it is: that thou shouldst love Me with all thy heart, and all thy soul, and all thy strength. On the fulfilment of this precept thy perfection depends; and therefore it is written that the end of the Commandment is charity, and love is the fulfilling of the Law.[1]

You will recall the answer the poet Tasso gave to Charles IX's question "Who is the next happiest to God?"—"The happiest being after God is he who most closely resembles God, that is to say, whoever is most perfect in virtue." Well, Scripture tells us that "God is charity,"[2] and it is only natural to come to the conclusion that the perfection of a Christian life is the effect and consequence of a vivifying charity within the soul. Charity is to be reckoned as the motive-cause of all such virtues, in so far as they are worthy of God and heaven. St. Thomas puts it this way: "Charity, aiming at the ultimate end as its object, moves the other virtues to action. For the virtue which regards the ultimate end always commands the virtues which have regard to the means. And therefore the merit of eternal life belongs first to charity, then to the other virtues, according as their acts are prompted by charity. Hence charity is the principle of all good works referred to the last end."

The word "virtue" comes from the Latin *virtus* meaning strength, and thus gives us a key to its general definition as a choice gift of God, an eminent perfection of man, a most beautiful ornament of the soul, the only refreshment of the mind, full of every pleasure, and abounding in all delights. There are two kinds of virtues: natural and supernatural.

(1) *Natural virtues.* Good habits, acquired through the constant repetition of acts, that render easy the performance of morally good actions. Even pagans can acquire with God's natural concurrence certain virtues; thus the justice of Aristides, the rectitude of Zaleucus, the chastity of Palemon, the patience of Socrates and the meekness of Antigonus.

(2) Some *supernatural or infused virtues* are called Christian

[1] *Dialogue*, translated by A. Thorold (Westminister, Md.: 1950).
[2] John 4:8.

moral virtues and because of their formal object, are essentially distinct from the highest of acquired moral virtues described by the greatest philosophers. There is an infinite difference between Aristotelian temperance with reason as its rule, and Christian temperance with the superadded rule of divine faith and supernatural prudence.

The chief infused virtues are the theological virtues—these are the virtues that unite us directly to God, Faith, Hope and Charity.

The principal or cardinal infused moral virtues—these are the virtues which remove the obstacles to that union and thus prepare for and perpetuate it, are:

I. Prudence

II. Justice { Religion, Obedience }

III. Fortitude

IV. Temperance { Chastity, Humility, Meekness }

"The infused virtues are principles of action which God ingrafts in us, that they may perform in the soul the function of supernatural faculties and may thus enable us to perform meritorious acts." [1] Such is Tanquerey's definition of the virtues, and so, following the plan we initiated in our treatment of the seven capital sins in the purgative way, we shall simply define the individual virtue with the minimum of comment and then state how it is to be exercised, acquired or increased and the general marks of a virtue begotten in the soul and acquired. It is odd to find the experts asserting that all virtues are begotten by human acts, which is true not only of the acquired virtues, but in some manner, even the infused virtues. You see, they explain that although the infused virtues are mercifully given by God, still by repeated acts we merit an increase of them and the reward of eternal life, and so the principle stands.

There are certain conditions necessary in general for the acquisition or increase of any virtue. Let us here list them:

[1] *Op. cit.*, p. 473.

(1) A fundamental knowledge of the virtue itself.

(2) An esteem for the virtue that surpasses our esteem for any other created thing.

(3) As desire for perfection is essential for spiritual progress, so the desire for the virtues is equally essential.

(4) Earnest and continued prayer for the grace to practice the virtue sought after.

(5) Primary concern for the practice of those virtues for which we are best suited by nature and grace.

(6) The resolve to make the practice of virtue a frequent matter for particular examination.

(7) A firm resolve to follow the spiritual director who will be guided in suggesting for practice the virtues which are most frequently demanded, such as humility, patience, temperance, and in the case of religious, the director will most certainly suggest rather the virtue of obedience than that of abstinence, etc.

(8) Concentration on one virtue at a time.

It must be borne in mind that the grace of virtues is a gift beyond the powers of nature, freely given to us by God and for this we ought to exercise the great hope of procuring it, and great courage to use it manfully. While relying on God's grace we must apply ourselves to work as if the whole thing were to be effected by our own labor. Besides God's grace, we ought to have the instruction and guidance of a spiritual father; we ought to meditate frequently on the life of Christ and His Passion and Death, and study the lives of the saints; finally, since habits of virtue are acquired from repeated acts, we ought to practice them separately, one by one, each for the space of some days, eliciting such acts repeatedly in our daily functions, always looking to Christ as our model.

It is difficult to determine exactly whether our actions are the result of true or false virtues, and so, the following rules should be helpful:

(1) That is the action of true virtue which conforms to the words, deeds, example and will of Christ.

(2) That is the action of true virtue which conforms to the principles and morals of saintly men and women.

(3) That is the action of true virtue which is prudent, since without prudence there is no virtue.

(4) That is the action of true virtue which conforms to the teachings and practice of the Church.

It might be worth noting here that there are different degrees of virtues. The first is when a virtue is exercised on account of the dignity and beauty of the virtue itself. The second is when we perform good on account of God, our end supernaturally known, and this is peculiar to the faithful and just, upon whom supernatural light has shone. The third is that in which we practice virtue not only for God's sake, but even with reference to God, to Whom we attain by acts of virtue. The fourth is when we perform acts of virtue not only for God's sake, but do so in some manner divinely.

We must never neglect the practice of virtue whenever the opportunity presents itself, for action is necessary to virtue and such actions ought to be performed with deep fervor, so it may increase the more. Since, as we have seen, it is important that we strive to acquire virtues one at a time, the spiritual director might well determine the order of the virtues to be practiced and he should take care to exact an accounting from his spiritual charge as to the outcome—the successes and failures.

There are certain signs of virtue begotten and increased in the soul. They are as follows:

(1) We honestly feel the vice opposed to the virtue to have become extinct, overcome, or in a great measure repressed.

(2) That our reason has control over our passions and affections.

(3) That there is facility and even delight in performing virtuous actions.

(4) A strong and continued desire to increase the virtues.

(5) When we abound in charity, since the other virtues are influenced by the growth in charity in our soul.

If we keep in mind St. Augustine's definition of supernatural virtue as "a good quality of mind whereby we live rightly, which no one uses amiss, which God worketh in us without ourselves" then we may better understand and appreciate the following treatment of the individual virtues. Let us begin with the theological virtues—faith, hope and charity.

It is certain that there are three theological virtues, for we read in Holy Scripture: "Now there remain faith, hope and charity, but the greatest of these is charity." [1] The apostle in thus enumerating these three virtues teaches us that they form one class of virtues distinct from all other supernatural virtues. St. Gregory the Great says: "As Job had seven sons and three daughters, so the just man has seven gifts of the Holy Ghost, and the three theological virtues."

The theological virtue of *faith* is a "virtue that inclines the mind, under the influence of the will and of grace, to yield a firm assent to revealed truths, because of the authority of God." [2]

Acts of faith are interior or exterior. They are interior when we firmly assent to things revealed by God, and exterior when we make confession of faith. "Notice carefully that the virtue of faith is a permanent habit infused into the soul, which *disposes the soul to acts of faith* when reason develops, and when we are conscious of the obligation of faith. *Acts of faith,* on the other hand, are *transient,* like any other mental or voluntary act, though they tend to produce the acquired habit of faith by constant repetition of acts." [3]

St. Thomas specifies two effects of faith: fear of God and purity of heart. Fear of God in this instance is a filial fear proceeding from the love of God; we avoid evil and live uprightly out of reverence and veneration for God, whom we love. Our love is evidenced in our realizing the gravity of sin; by our doing penance for the past sins; by flying all imperfections, however light; and by keeping God's commandments and walking carefully in His presence. The other effect of faith is purity of heart of which St. Peter says: "Purifying their hearts by faith," [4] for impurity, if any-

[1] 1 Cor. 13:13.
[2] Tanquerey, *op. cit.*, p. 551.
[3] A. P. Madgett, S.J., *Christian Origins* (Cincinnati, O.: Xavier University Press, 1941), II, 176.
[4] Acts 15:9.

thing, consists in this, that it is commingled with things more vile; but a rational creature, since he is more noble than all things temporal or corporal, if he mingles with them, contracts uncleanness, from which he cannot be purified unless he turn to God by a contrary movement; but this conversion has its beginning in faith, and therefore purity of heart is said to be an effect of faith.[1]

The manifestations of purity are, to put off love of visible things; to cast aside too great affection toward self, toward this life and the world; to purge the thoughts of evil and vain apprehensions; to keep oneself unsullied from sins both grievous and light; to cleave mentally to God and heavenly things.

The means of making an act of faith (which holds true too for the other two theological virtues) is to place before the mind the object and the motives of faith. In doing so, it is well not to employ the usual formula, but to express ourselves in our own words. Beginners must especially endeavor to strengthen their faith by thanking God for this great gift and with humility praying the prayer of the apostles: "Increase our faith." [2] The reading of good books calculated to strengthen faith is also indicated. Intellectual pride militates against this virtue and should be countered by complete submission to the articles of the faith and the teachings of the Church. Advanced or proficient souls ought to strive to excel in the practice of the "spirit of faith," for by so doing they accustom themselves to see all things, do all things, judge all things from the point of view of faith. It was these St. John of the Cross had in mind when he wrote: "It is that thou seek God in faith and in love, without desiring to find satisfaction in aught, or to taste or understand more than that which it is well for thee to know; for these two are the guides of the blind, which will lead thee, by a way thou knowest not, to the hidden place of God. Because faith, which is the secret that we have mentioned, is like the feet wherewith the soul journeys to God, and love is the guide that directs it." [3]

The marks of perfect faith are:

(1) Zeal for the salvation of others.

[1] *Cursus vitae spiritualis, op. cit.*, part II, chapter III. [2] Luke 17:5.
[3] *Spiritual Canticle*, 2nd red., I, 11; *Complete Works, op. cit.*, II, 192.

(2) Absolute simplicity and renunciation of all curiosity and inquiry, such as Abraham exhibited when directed to sacrifice his son.

(3) Readiness to sacrifice everything rather than deny any of the teachings of Holy Scripture, tradition or the infallible Church is the minimum for the preservation of faith. Our aim should be to practice not only faith, but the spirit of faith: "the just man liveth by faith."[1]

(4) Frequent and earnest prayer for increased faith, saying with the apostles: "Increase our faith."[2]

Hope is a theological virtue that makes us desire God as our highest good, and expect with firm confidence eternal bliss and the means of attaining it, because of God's goodness and power. In more simple language, hope is a confident expectation that we shall gain heaven, and that God will give us the means to gain heaven.

When we studied the passions, we said hope was a passion and a sentiment, and in so saying, we referred to the natural order. There is also a supernatural hope that sustains us in the midst of the obstacles encountered in the attainment of salvation and perfection, and it is this supernatural virtue that we are here considering.

The chief object of the virtue of hope is a future good, the gain of heaven. It includes the confident expectation that our sins will be forgiven, that we will receive graces and virtues needed for our salvation, that we shall rise again, and that the body and soul will enjoy an eternity with God. Included is the spiritual confidence that God will give us certain temporal helps to this end, like a good moral education, good health, etc. Scripture says: "They that hope in the Lord shall renew their strength, they shall take wings as eagles . . . and not weary."[3]

The virtue of hope is exercised: (1) When we pray with the childlike confidence of St. John, who wrote: "This is the confidence we have toward Him: that whatsoever we shall ask according to His will, He heareth us";[4] (2) When in spite of trials and reverses we can calmly say with David: "Cast thy care upon the Lord, and He shall sustain thee";[5] (3) When the thought of the gravity and number of our sins overwhelms us, we quickly make

[1] Rom. 1:17. [2] Luke 17:5.
[3] Isa. 40:31. [4] 1 John 5:14. [5] Ps. 54:23.

an act of hope in God's pardon and mercy, recalling His words: "If your sins be as scarlet, they shall be made white as snow." [1]

The signs of supernatural hope are: (1) abiding peace of mind and spiritual joy during the labors exacted of us by our state in life and spiritual, physical and mental trials and sufferings; (2) patience with perseverance in our prayers when the answers are long delayed.

Charity is the third theological virtue and the queen of all the virtues. It is defined as a theological virtue that causes us to love God above all things, for His own sake and to love our neighbor for God's sake. Basso says that "since God loves us so intensely, He wills that we should love Him in return with our whole heart, with all our love." "What doth the Lord thy God require of thee but that thou love Him and serve Him with thy whole heart?" says Moses,[2] but our Lord Himself said: "Thou shalt love the Lord thy God with thy whole heart and with thy whole soul and with thy whole mind. This is the greatest and first commandment. The second is like to this: Thou shalt love thy neighbor as thyself." [3] Elsewhere Holy Scripture has our Lord add these words: "You have heard that it hath been said: Thou shalt love thy neighbor and hate thy enemy. But I say to you: Love your enemies; do good to them that hate you; and pray for them that persecute and calumniate you." [4]

Since charity has a two-fold relation, namely, toward God and toward our neighbor, let us treat first of charity toward God and then such as regards our neighbor.

Charity toward God is that by which we love Him above all things, with our whole mind, soul and energies, not through hope of reward or fear of punishment, but for His own sake and His Infinite Goodness.

The virtue of charity is exercised: (1) when we love God because He is worthy of all love; (2) when we avoid sin simply because it offends God; (3) when we elevate our hearts in prayer when we but think of God's goodness, tenderness, and mercy toward us; (4) when we meditate frequently on the Passion and Death of our Lord, doing so simply that our hearts may know

[1] Isa. 1:18. [2] Deut. 10:12. [3] Matt. 22:37–39.
[4] Matt. 5:43–44.

more and more of the extent of His love for us; (5) when we practice fervent and frequent acts of love, especially by ejaculatory prayer such as that used by the Little Flower: "My God, I love Thee."

The signs of the theological virtue of charity are:

(1) Bearing all sorts of trials and sufferings as choice gifts of God.

(2) When our love of God is so intense that it makes our sojourn here on earth a dreary pilgrimage and as a result, we yearn for eternal union with Him.

(3) Habits of prayer that make communion with God our chief delight.

(4) Rejection of creatures inasmuch as they turn us from God. "If creatures," says St. Teresa, "try to enter your heart, drive them back with the words: 'My heart belongs to Jesus. There is no room for you.' "

The theological virtue by which we love God and our neighbor is the same, since God is cause of both loves. Charity toward our neighbor is that whereby we love men of every description, friends as well as enemies. While it is certain that the love of God is more noble than love of neighbor, nevertheless, the love of God is completed and perfected by love of our neighbor, for, as St. John says: "If we love one another, God abideth in us, and His charity is perfected in us." [1]

The motives inducing us to love our neighbor are: (1) the magnificent example of the Son of God Himself; (2) because of its utility—since "Love . . . is the fulfilling of the Law"; [2] (3) our membership in the Mystical Body of Christ; (4) the common Fatherhood of God; (5) the edification of our neighbor, "By this shall all men know that you are my disciples, if you have love one for another"; [3] (6) the fact that our neighbor, actually or potentially, possesses divine goodness by sanctifying grace.

The actions of charity toward our neighbor are: (1) to love all men inasmuch as they are capable of eternal beatitude in God; (2) to share with others our spiritual and temporal gifts insofar as they can contribute to the furtherance of the glory of God and the

[1] John 4:12. [2] Rom. 13:10. [3] John 13:35.

terrestrial happiness of our fellow man; (3) to defend the weak; (4) to excuse the faults of others; (5) to assist others by word, work, counsel; (6) to bear all injuries with patience, because "Charity is patient, is kind, beareth all things, endureth all things." [1]

The noble acts of charity toward our neighbor as drawn up by St. Vincent de Paul are as follows: (1) to act toward others as we would have them act toward us; (2) not to contradict others; (3) to mutually support one another; (4) to share the sufferings and contradiction of others; (5) to treat all others with an honor born of humility; "Who is weak, and I am not weak?" [2] (6) to demonstrate the affection which we feel toward others by kind deeds done and kind words said.[3]

To the body of our neighbor belong the corporal works of mercy, namely, to feed the hungry, to give drink to the thirsty, to clothe the naked, to give hospitality to strangers, to visit the sick and prisoners, to assist at the burial of the dead. To the soul appertain the spiritual works of mercy, that is, to correct sinners opportunely, affectionately and effectually, to teach the ignorant, to counsel the doubtful and console the sorrowful and afflicted and to pray for the neighbor's salvation.

In nothing is charity so nobly exercised as in the matter of fraternal correction. It is here that certain rules will facilitate the task, for instance, we must be kind; we ought to accommodate ourselves to the capacity of all; a deep affection must be maintained even in the face of resistance; we must follow the counsel of our Lord: "If thy brother shall offend against thee, go and rebuke him between thee and him alone." [4] Fraternal correction can be imprudent and should not be used when there is reason to fear it will produce more harm than good.

Zeal is born of love, especially that zeal which embraces the desire to procure the salvation of others. This sort of zeal is most precious to God "Who wishes all men to be saved, and to come to the knowledge of the truth." [5] True zeal is merciful and mild and it can pity and forbear.

[1] 1 Cor. 13:4. [2] 2 Cor. 11:29.
[3] *Vertus et doctrine spirituelle de St. Vincent de Paul,* by Abbé Maynard (Paris: Tequi, 1946), p. 130.
[4] Matt. 18:15. [5] 1 Tim. 2:4.

The practice of zeal consists in the following:

(1) Praying perseveringly for the conversion of others.

(2) Extending our zeal to embrace all mankind.

(3) Being mindful that example is more powerful than counsel. He who blasts the shrines of the false gods does little unless he builds temples to the true God.

The following are the marks of true charity toward our neighbor:

(1) Zeal for the salvation of others.

(2) Perseverance in doing good for our neighbor even when he least appreciates it.

(3) To despise none, even those we are tempted to believe incorrigible.

(4) To forgive all injuries done us.

(5) To seek prompt reconciliation with those we have voluntarily or involuntarily offended.

(6) Patience in the face of opposition and contempt.

(7) When we pray for those who would destroy us.

Superiors of religious communities might well ponder the words of St. Francis de Sales: "Hold yourself well-balanced that you may not distribute your affections or favors only according to the natural qualities of others. How many there are who are not to our taste but who are agreeable to God! Charity considers true virtue and the beauty of the soul, and diffuses itself over all without partiality."

St. Benedict Joseph Labré once remarked that "a Christian ought in a manner to have three hearts in one, one for God, another for his neighbor, and the third for himself." He explains it this way: "It is necessary that the first heart be for God; pure and sincere, that it direct all its actions toward Him, that it breathe only with love for Him and with ardor in His service, that it embrace all the crosses it pleases God to send. The second heart must be for our neighbor: generous, fearing no labor, no suffering in his service; compassionate, praying for the conversion of sinners, for the souls in purgatory, and for those who are afflicted. The third heart, which is for himself, should be firm in its resolutions, abhorring all sin, giving the body to austerity and penance, and constantly cultivating a life of mortification and sacrifice." You will find nowhere a better thumb-nail program for spiritual perfection.

So much for the three theological virtues of faith, hope and charity. Next follows a consideration of the *moral virtues* which have the effect of bringing our actions into conformity with the moral law and thus are called moral virtues because they order our actions in a manner pleasing to God. As the three theological virtues perfect our interior being, so the moral virtues perfect our exterior. There are two sets of moral virtues, the natural and the supernatural. The former are acquired by repeated actions, the latter, like the theological virtues, are infused with sanctifying grace at Baptism. They are differentiated by their motives—natural or supernatural respectively.

The principal moral virtues are seven, namely, humility, obedience, meekness, liberality, temperance, chastity and diligence in what is good; however, all the moral virtues proceed from the four cardinal virtues: prudence, justice, temperance, and fortitude, so named in Holy Scripture, and wherein we read this notation that they "are such things as men can have nothing more profitable in life."[1]

As charity is the queen of the theological virtues, so prudence holds first place among the moral virtues. Prudence is the capacity of the intellect to apprehend the good things of eternity and the means of attaining them. It affects the intellect whose action precedes the operation of the will and then it presides over the other virtues so as to be the rule, according to which all these are directed. This moral virtue is of the intellect; from its guidance in anything that occurs, we know what is lawful, what is unseemly, what is to be desired, what is to be avoided. Simply put, it is the right way of doing things in particular circumstances. "Christian prudence," says St. Vincent de Paul, "consists in judging, speaking and acting, as the Eternal Wisdom of God, clothed in our frail flesh, has judged, spoken and acted."[2]

[1] Wis. 8:7.
[2] Cf. Maynard, *op. cit.*, p. 254.

Cassian recounts that certain hermits came to the great St. Anthony of the Desert to ask him how best to acquire perfection. They spent the whole night in discussion of the various helps, one saying he held out for solitude, another expounded on the merits of works of charity, still another maintained that mortification was the real key to perfection. St. Anthony listened patiently to the discussion and then said: "All these means are necessary to those who thirst after God but none of them is the principal and infallible means, for we have all seen religious who have observed those practices yet came to a deplorable end. They lacked *discretion* [an adjunct of prudence, as we shall see later] and not having acquired this virtue which conducts one in the middle way between extremes, they either fell into an excess of fervor or into the folly of presumption." [1] And Holy Scripture seems to bear out the Saint's words, for we read: "Blessed is the man that findeth wisdom, and is rich in prudence. Length of days is in her right hand: and in her left riches and glory. Her ways are beautiful ways: and all her paths are peaceable." [2]

Prudence is a title coveted by men. That natural prudence which helps man judge rightly and with confidence is a precious quality, but supernatural prudence is most excellent because it is in a way a participation in the Divine Wisdom. God in His infinite wisdom proposes in all His works, and in all the government of His Providence an excellent end, wise, holy, and truly worthy of Him. The supernatural virtue of prudence directs us to choose also a wise and holy end in our actions, so that they are worthy of God, and makes us choose the best means of attaining this end.

The first act of prudence is to take suitable and proper measures by inquiring as to the best means necessary to do something according to the virtue. We should be guided by the following rules: (1) humble prayer for guidance in formulating the proper decision; (2) search for prudent counsel from others; (3) no deliberation at all if the matter is contrary to the laws of God or His Church.

The second act of prudence, after the observance of the fore-

[1] *Manuel de Spiritualité* (Vienna: M. Petschenig, 1886), p. 135.
[2] Prov. 3:13–17.

going rules, is to judge correctly which of the means are most conducive to the attainment of the end. This is called discretion.

The third act of prudence is to determine and command whatever has been decided ought to be performed.

The marks of prudence are (1) slowness in consultation but promptness in execution. St. Vincent de Paul reminds us that the works of God are done little by little. When God wished to save Noe and his family from the flood waters, He told him to build an ark that took a hundred years to complete. When God directed Moses to lead the Chosen People out of captivity to the Promised Land, the journey lasted by Divine Providence forty years. When our Lord came upon this earth, He spent what might be considered by some to be a very long period of preparation—thirty years, in fact; but He was doing the will of His Father. "Go slowly," the saint cautions, "pray diligently to God, and act in harmony with His Will." (2) A careful and consistent self-scrutiny to find if even the least sin is present in the soul that might defy the mind's penetration. (3) A readiness to ask and accept counsel. (4) Custody of the tongue, for "A wise man will hold his peace till he sees opportunity." [1] (5) Examination of all the other virtues, for Christian prudence is never perfect if one of the other virtues is wanting.

The contrary of prudence is worldly wisdom, or the prudence of the flesh. The wisdom of this world consists in discerning what will bring man a temporal advantage or sensual enjoyment and this wisdom is foolishness with God. "Let no man deceive himself. If any man among you seem to be wise in this world, let him become a fool, that he may be wise, for the wisdom of this world is foolishness with God." [2] St. James says: "But the wisdom that is from above, first indeed is chaste, then peaceable, modest, easy to be persuaded, consenting to the good, full of mercy and good fruits, without judging, without dissimulation." [3]

The second of the cardinal virtues is *justice*. It is defined as a supernatural moral virtue, which inclines the will to render unto others at all times what is strictly their due. Carried to perfection, justice is naught else but sanctity: "Blessed are they that hunger

[1] Ecclus. 20:7. [2] 1 Cor. 3:18–19. [3] Jas. 3:17.

and thirst after justice."[1] This virtue in effect leads us to render to God that which is His due, for God has a right to profound respect and to absolute obedience, and if He has been offended, to complete reparation. The least sin is an attack upon the rights of God, and the most heroic act imaginable is nothing more than what is due God or what He has a right to expect. Thus to serve God perfectly is nothing more than justice.

I. RELIGION: Since justice involves rendering to God what is His due, we class *religion* as a moral virtue, and define it as a supernatural virtue that inclines the will to render to God the worship due Him by reason of His infinite excellence and His sovereign dominion over us.

The average parochial school child could tell us that the four principal acts of religion are adoration, praise of God, prayer and finally, devotion. Devotion is simply a certain will to give oneself up to those things which appertain to God's worship and service. As devotion is an act of the will, it is produced from previous considerations of God's gifts and benefits and our own unworthiness and nothingness.

The signs of devotion are: (1) an intense affection toward Christ and His Most Sacred Passion; (2) continual remembrance of the presence of God; (3) frequent use of ejaculatory prayers; (4) custody of the heart from venial sins since they lessen the fervor of charity and impede devotion; (5) care of the mind and mortification of the irregular affections.

To acquire holiness, three things are requisite: (1) to have a high idea of it and a great desire for it; (2) to use great diligence in the pursuit of it, which diligence, again, must have three characteristics; it must not only be fervent, and persevering, but exclusive; (3) to be courageous in resisting the opposition we shall meet with in the fulfillment of our high ideals.

Prayer has been treated elsewhere in this work so it must suffice to say that it is an act of religion by which we worship God and petition from Him graces and spiritual and temporal favors. It is needless to remark that all prayers, mental and vocal, must be performed with attention, devotion, and reverence.

[1] Matt. 5:6.

Penance is a supernatural virtue, akin to justice, which inclines a man to detest his sins because of their offensiveness to God, while inclining him, at the same time, to atone for them. The actions of penance are (1) interior sorrow for having offended God accompanied by a sincere turning from creatures and a turning to God; (2) atonement for sins by prayers, fasts, alms, and bodily penances. St. Jerome says we can no more attain everlasting life without penance, than we can get at the kernel of a nut without breaking the shell; (3) mortification of the senses and appetites, and by interior compunction.

Piety is a virtue by which we show proper regard and duty to country, parents, relatives and others allied to us. By regard we mean honor and respect. By duty we mean service, assistance, and protection.

II. Obedience: Obedience is allied to justice and is defined as a supernatural, moral virtue which inclines us to submit our will to that of our lawful superiors, insofar as they are the representatives of God. It is a virtue which renders a man's private will prompt to perform the orders and precepts of superiors, because they are commanded by persons possessing authority from God.

The motives urging us to acquire this virtue are multiple. The main reasons, however, are: (1) since man can offer no greater thing to God than the surrender of his will and thus, obedience is most meritorious. "Self-will is the source not only of all sins, but of all imperfections as well, moreover it vitiates even our good works which are done wholly to please God and so they lose at least part of their merit, if not all of it." "Self-will," says St. Bernard, "is a great evil when it makes your good works cease to be good." (2) Obedience is a safe and straight road to virtue, for even things indifferent in themselves, such as eating, sleeping or walking, acquire the character of virtue by reason of obedience. (3) It assures victory over demons. "By the other virtues," says St. Gregory, "we fight the demons, but by obedience we conquer them. Yes, those who obey are conquerors because in perfectly submitting their will to the Will of God, they triumph over the rebel angels who fell because of their disobedience." [1] (4) Finally, Christ our Lord left us the example of the practice of the virtue of

[1] *In 1. Reg.* 10.

obedience amongst other virtues. Hear His words: "I came down from heaven, not to do my own will but the will of him who sent me." [1] Again, "My meat is to do the will of him who sent me, that I may perfect his work." [2]

The actions of obedience are (1) to obey promptly and humbly; (2) to undertake gladly those tasks contrary to our will and inclination when asked to do so by superiors; (3) complete submissiveness of will when what is requested appears in opposition to reason. It is related in the life of St. Teresa that our Lord appeared to her and recommended that she start a foundation at Madrid, but Father Gratien preferred the foundation be made in Seville. St. Teresa followed the direction of Father Gratien, saying, "I could be wrong in judging the truth of a revelation but I shall always be right in obeying my superiors." And our Lord appeared to her later and commended her for her obedience to Father Gratien. (4) "In every act of obedience," says Cardinal Bona, "we should unite the interior affection of the will and the agreement of the judgment with the exterior work, and that with love and eagerness of mind and with spiritual joy, so that our obedience may be entire, unimpeded, swift, humble, strong, blind, unfeigned, without excuses, hesitations or murmurs, constant and persevering." [3]

The signs of perfect obedience are:

(1) To obey for the sake of practicing the virtue of obedience and not because the thing commanded is pleasing to us.

(2) To obey out of love for God those whom He has placed over us.

(3) To see God in those in authority.

(4) To obey blindly.

(5) Not to procrastinate or defer difficult and repugnant orders.

Fortitude is the third cardinal virtue and it has for its object the triumph over certain obstacles to right action arising from the dangers and evils of this life. Accordingly, it is a virtue of the soul, affecting the will and irascible appetite, by which we firmly meet and endure labors and dangers, even of death. "In his march toward

[1] John 6:38. [2] John 4:34. [3] *Op. cit.*, part II, chap. VII.

moral good," says Ribet, "man encounters two enemies: pain and pleasure. Pain frightens and pleasure attracts. Fortitude surmounts fear, and temperance moderates pleasure: two cardinal virtues from which others spring." [1]

No one defines fortitude with greater comprehensiveness than does Tanquerey, for he says it is a supernatural, moral virtue that strengthens the soul in the pursuit of arduous moral good, without allowing it to be deterred by fear, even by fear of death.[2]

The function of fortitude is two-fold: one is to bear and suffer toils and dangers that we cannot escape; the other is to approach and undertake the same dangers and toils when it is expedient.

The actions of fortitude are: (1) to undertake with joy any dangers whatever for God's glory, for our neighbor's salvation, and not to grow weary in the doing; (2) to bear manfully every infirmity, grief, exile, destitution, imprisonment, rejection, infamy, and other things of like nature; (3) to bear others' vices with magnanimity; (4) not to be downcast though many obstacles may hinder good works, remembering that true fortitude of soul is proven by constancy. It is well to bear in mind the words of Clement of Alexandria that "the spiritual man increases the perfection of his fortitude by exercising it, for the end of fortitude is to conquer the movements of the soul." [3]

The signs of fortitude are: (1) to be firmly united to God by charity. "Fortitude," says St. Augustine, "is that love which bears all for that which it loves"; (2) to treat passions and appetites as enemies, and to rule and moderate them; (3) to bear cheerfully things contrary to our natural likes; (4) to shun those, who, by promises or threats, suggest anything contrary to virtue.

One of the offshoots of fortitude is patience. Patience is a virtue by which we endure the evils of this world with an even temper, so that on their account we are not immoderately troubled. There are three degrees of patience: (1) to suffer without murmuring; (2) to suffer without letting anyone know about it; and (3) to seek suffering out of love for God or, in other words, to be a willing victim of suffering.

The principal actions of patience are: (1) to endure sufferings

[1] *Les vertus,* chap. 37. [2] *Op. cit.*, p. 506. [3] *Strom.*, c. 7.

calmly, willingly, with thanksgiving and without complaints; (2) to bear even those evils without complaint that they are inflicted upon us by those who have received naught but good from our hands; (3) to bless Divine Providence for all our trials and sufferings; (4) to offer ourselves daily to God and ask Him to do what He wills with us.

The marks of patience are: (1) to bear others' imperfections with a calm spirit; (2) to keep ourselves from flaring up when we are hurt or despised by others; (3) to love and pray for those who try our patience; (4) to beg of God an increase of pain and sufferings in every ailment; (5) to be silent as our Lord was when attacked by His enemies and not speak in our own defense.

"Always bear in mind," says Father Olier, "that patience is a virtue whereby we bear in peace the pains and sufferings of this life and whereby we find joy in the tribulations which it pleases God to send us. Patience, to be Christian, must regard God, by the eyes of faith, as the Author of all the sufferings and all the persecutions that may befall us." [1]

There are four powerful words that, were they meaningfully used, would make every trial, every cross, every pain both bearable and meritorious and those four words are: "For You, my God!"

Temperance is the fourth and last of the cardinal virtues. It is defined as a supernatural, moral virtue, that moderates the attraction toward sense-pleasure, especially the pleasures of the palate, and the flesh, and keeps them within the proper limits of propriety. By this virtue we are made like angels, for by it we check our carnal desires, regulate the entire man, and make of our bodies more suitable temples for our indwelling God.

The sole action of temperance consists in restricting bodily pleasures to proper moderation and so to do nothing for the sake of delight alone. The other external marks of temperance are modesty, gravity of manners, guarded speech, silence, vigilance, and works of penance. The interior marks are control of the thoughts, and control of temptations of the flesh.

Temperance has three great daughters—chastity, humility, and meekness.

[1] *Introduction à la vie et aux vertus Chrétiennes* (Paris: Le Rameau, 1954), p. 104.

Chastity is a virtue by which the body is preserved from defilement of carnal concupiscence, and the mind is kept clean from all impure desires. Chastity is twofold: perfect and imperfect. Perfect chastity proposes to refrain in perpetuity from all carnal pleasures, the imperfect which decides to abstain from unlawful pleasures and to use lawful pleasures with moderation, that is in the case of married persons.

Virginity is perfect chastity and a firm and fixed resolution of perpetual incorruption in corruptible flesh. Purity or modesty is a virtue by which the external senses are restrained lest they aim at anything unbecoming that may hurt chastity.

Tanquerey lists three degrees of chastity: the first consists in restraining from consenting to any thought, fancy, feeling or action contrary to this virtue. The second aims at the immediate expulsion of any thought contrary to the virtue. The third is such mastery over our thoughts and senses so that when we are called upon to perform certain duties relative to this virtue, we will do so with calm. Finally, there are some who by special privilege from God, such as St. Thomas, experience no inordinate feelings whatsoever.

Its two kinds are: (1) continence, proper to the unmarried, and (2) conjugal chastity, proper to persons living in lawful wedlock. These latter should reverence the sanctity of marriage by the purity of their intention and by faithfully and candidly fulfilling their marriage obligations and by establishing moderation in their relations.

"Continence," says Cardinal Bona, "can be taken in two ways: Firstly, that it may mean a certain virtue, by which a man refrains from all lascivious pleasures, and thus it does not differ from chastity; secondly, to signify constancy of soul against onslaughts of the passions, and is a firm resolution of mind, by which a man keeps himself in the quest of reason in opposition to the transports of concupiscence by which he is impelled to pleasures of touch." [1]

The remedies against temptations to impurity are: (1) the desire to be rid of them and the occasions that produce them; (2) the willing embrace of voluntary penances; (3) the help of a good director to help examine the causes and proper cures; (4) fre-

[1] *Op. cit.*, part II, chap. IX.

quenting the sacraments and developing a tender devotion to the Virgin Mother of God; (5) scrutiny of the soul for seeds of pride, for not infrequently, impurity follows in its wake; (6) meditation on the eternal truths and the beauty of virtue; (7) prompt flight from all occasions of sin—persons, places or things.

St. Vincent remarks that there are two kinds of purity: purity of body and purity of soul. Those who have purity of body do not have chastity unless it is joined with purity of spirit, for that is the essence of this virtue. Chastity, in effect, chases from the imagination, the spirit, and the memory all bad thoughts. We ought therefore turn all our efforts against our heart to make ourselves masters of it and drive therefrom every trace of anything that is contrary to the sublime virtue of chastity.

Humility is generally related to temperance inasmuch as it moderates the sense of our own importance. Humility is defined by St. Bernard as "a supernatural moral virtue whereby a man, through a true knowledge of himself, becomes despicable in his own eyes." [1]

There is no other virtue that is so amply treated by spiritual writers as humility, and so it suits our purpose best to state here only the actions and marks of true humility.

The actions are: (1) a deep knowledge of the fact that all our gifts, natural and supernatural, come from God; (2) distrust of ourselves and placing all reliance in God; (3) not wishing to be honored or esteemed by others, referring all praise and honor to God; (4) welcoming occasions when others look down on us; (5) desiring the last place not only in the ranks of the world, but in the esteem of men; (6) living in peace in the midst of false accusations and slanders; (7) welcoming humiliation; (8) looking upon others as our superiors to whom in public we are superior.

St. Benedict lists twelve signs of humility and they are: (1) fear of the Lord proceeding from innermost reverence; (2) to renounce self-will and not to hold out for the accomplishment of our desires; (3) to subject oneself to a superior in all obedience; (4) to endure patiently every injury and vexation for love of obedience and humility; (5) to manifest clearly and openly to one's director evil thoughts and acts; (6) to be content with all meanness and abjec-

[1] *De gradibus humil.*, c. 1., n. 2.

tion and in all our works to judge ourselves as wholly unworthy laborers; (7) to be convinced of our worthlessness not only in words but in our innermost heart; (8) to follow the common rule and avoid singularity; (9) to shun talkativeness and remain silent until questioned; (10) to be modest and circumspect in word and deed; (11) not to be boisterous in language or in laughter; (12) to show humility not only in our heart but also in our actions, our gait, our gestures and our countenance.

It would be well for all of us to engrave these words on the walls of our heart. "No one reaches heaven," says St. Augustine, "except by humility." [1]

Meekness is the third daughter of temperance. It is a virtue which moderates anger. Its sole action is to mitigate the violence of anger, and anger is one of the capital sins. The occasions of cultivating it are numerous, especially when we have been injured by another and yet we hold our peace. The practices of meekness have already been touched on in Chapter Six wherein we treated of anger and its remedies. Our greatest source of help in the increase and practice of the virtue of meekness is found in frequent meditation on the meekness of our Lord. Oh, the fruitfulness of such prayerful considerations as the meekness of our Saviour as He stood before His cruel judges, or again His meekness as He hung on the Cross and yet could pray so effectively for pardon for His executioners and those who had called for His death.

I cannot terminate this section on the virtues without this important quotation of St. Gregory to the effect that "one virtue without the rest is either no virtue at all or it is imperfect." This may be the very reason why so many persons who excel in the practice of one or several virtues never seem to reach the summit of perfection. St. Francis de Sales, commenting on this, poses these questions and supplies more than adequate answers:

What prudence . . . can an intemperate, unjust and cowardly man have, since he makes choice of vice and forsakes virtue? And how can one be just without being prudent, strong, and temperate, since justice is no other thing than a perpetual, strong and constant will to render to every one his own, and since the science by which right is done is called jurisprudence, and since, to give each one his own, we must

[1] *Lib. de salut.* cap. 32.

live wisely and moderately, and hinder the disorders of intemperance in ourselves so as to give ourselves what belongs to us? And the word virtue, does it not signify a force and vigour belonging to the soul as a quality, even as we say that herbs and precious stones have such and such a virtue or property?

But is not prudence itself imprudent in an intemperate man? Fortitude, without prudence, justice and temperance, is not fortitude, but folly; and justice is unjust in the weak man who dares not do it, in the intemperate man who permits himself to be carried away with passion, and in the imprudent man who is not able to discern between the right and the wrong. Justice is not justice unless it be strong, prudent and temperate; nor is prudence prudence unless it be temperate, just and strong; nor fortitude fortitude unless it be just, prudent and temperate; nor temperance temperance unless it be prudent, strong and just. In fine, a virtue is not perfect virtue, unless it be accompanied by all the rest.[1]

"Of all things conducive to the attainment of our present goal, viz., the acquisition of Christian virtues, the earnest desire of continual advancement is of the utmost importance, as the least pause retards us." So says Dom Scupoli, and continuing he writes, "The moment we cease forming acts of virtue, our inclinations, naturally prone to ease and pleasures of the senses, raise in us disordered appetites which overthrow or at least weaken our virtuous habits." [2]

Oh, the depths of wisdom in Dom Scupoli's great spiritual writing *The Spiritual Combat!* One has only to read a paragraph or a line to discover the grasp he had of his subject, for instance, he says, "As often as we beg from God any particular virtue, we simultaneously ask for those means which he appoints for its acquisition. Otherwise our prayer would be fruitless and contradictory; it would be tempting God, who never bestows patience but through tribulation, nor humility but through ignominy." [3]

Those who fear to attempt the important task of exercising the virtues because they calculate it is the work of years and years, will find some impetus in the words of the same authority:

[1] *Treatise on the Love of God*, translated by Henry B. Mackey, O.S.B. (Westminster, Md.: Newman Press, 1953), pp. 483–484.

[2] Lawrence Scupoli, *The Spiritual Combat*, translated and revised by William Lester and Robert Mohan (Westminster, Md.: Newman Press, 1956), p. 112.

[3] *Ibid.*, p. 116.

It is impossible to prescribe generally any determined space of time to be employed in the acquisition of each virtue, as this is dependent on our various states and dispositions, our progress in the devout life, and the direction of our spiritual guide. It is certain, however, that if the diligence and eagerness previously prescribed are not wanting, within a few weeks we shall make considerable progress.[1]

According to Dom Scupoli the marks of progress in virtue are (1) perseverance in exercises of piety, in spite of all disgust, vexations, dryness, and the want of all sensible consolation; (2) when our corrupt inclinations, subdued and kept under by reason, are no longer capable of interrupting us in the practice of virtue, therefore when we feel no repugnance on the part of the inferior appetites, we may be assured of having acquired habitual virtue.

The more we strive to perfect ourselves in the practice of the virtues the more we shall come to the conviction that consistent victory is most difficult of attainment. Our adversaries are as wily as they are strong. If they fail to over-power us, they will try to waylay us; if they are unable to destroy us, they will be content to wound us. We must, therefore, be prepared to meet with reverses. But we must not, on that account, give up the cause as lost, and surrender as discretion. On the contrary, we must redouble our efforts, and display our courage the more by speedily retrieving our losses and converting seeming defeats into evident triumphs.[2]

I think that the following reflections of a great spiritual writer—Archbishop Goodier, S.J.—are worthy of profound study. Hear him as he says:

When I was younger, a novice in religion, and knew myself less, and knew others less, and was full of high ambitions in the spiritual life, and sought in books and in study, in thought-out plans and schemes on paper for guides to the summit of perfection, I set virtues before me, and meditated on their beauty, and proposed to myself to acquire them, sub-dividing them, analysing them, arranging their degrees as the steps of a ladder. This week, as the good spiritual writers bade me, I would acquire the virtue of patience; next week it should be a carefully guarded tongue; the week after that should be given to charity;

[1] *Ibid.*, p. 121.
[2] Louis de la Palma, *Part. exam.*, pp. 23 et seq.

then should come the spirit of prayer; and in a month or two, perhaps, I might have an ecstasy and "see the Lord." But now, when I have grown older, and find myself still struggling for the first of these virtues, and that in a very elementary degree, and have been taught quite other lessons than I dreamt of, in part by the sorry disappointments in my own soul, in part by the progress seen in the souls of others, I am convinced there is one road to perfection better than all else—in fact, that if we neglect this one no other will be of much avail. After all, it is possible to acquire perfection in virtues, and yet to be far from a saint; few men have made better use of the particular examination of conscience, for the acquiring of natural virtues, than a certain well-known atheist, and yet to the end he remained without a spark of religion in him. On the other hand, it is possible to be a great saint, and yet to be imperfect in many respects: ask the saints themselves and they will tell you of their many failures and shortcomings. But one thing is not possible; it is not possible to grow in the knowledge, and love, and imitation of Jesus Christ, without at the same time growing in the perfection of every virtue and becoming more a saint every day. This, then, if I were allowed to begin my spiritual life over again, is the line along which I would try to live it; and is the line along which I would try to lead the lives of many whom God gave into my care. Particular virtues are good things—of course they are; it is much to be always patient, to be diligent in the use of our time, to be considerate with those who try us, to keep our tongue in control; nevertheless, "Do not the heathens this?" And is it not possible to possess all these, and yet, on their very account, to remain as proud as Lucifer? I would go further and say that the devil himself must possess many of these virtues; he can certainly bide his time, he can be very busy, he can speak honeyed words, he can accommodate himself to everybody's needs, he can be the most attractive of companions. But these things are not the main issue; they are often no more than the paint on the surface; and truth, sanctity, only begins when the core of the creature is affected. And this is done, almost alone, by love; when the creature loves, then it is changed, and till then scarcely at all. The knowledge, love and imitation of Jesus Christ include every virtue, make them unconsciously our own, produce them from themselves, and do not merely put them on from without, even as the brown earth gives forth the beauty of spring flowers and does not know it.

Hence, in practice, were I to be asked for an application of all that I have been here pleading for, I would say:

1. Read spiritual books, yes, as much of them and as many of them as may be convenient; but do not measure growth in spiritual life by the number of books you have read . . . Above all, read the Scriptures, especially the Gospels, with an eye less upon ourselves, and more upon Him whom they describe; in that, more than in any other reading, shall we find that knowledge and true spirituality grow together.

2. Hold spiritual conferences, yes, but less about ourselves and our own despicable faults, or even our little virtues and ideals; more, far more, about Him and His superb perfection, forgetting ourselves in the glory of His sunshine. By so doing it is true we may lose the satisfaction of watching ourselves grow in holiness—that is dangerous satisfaction at the best—but instead we shall grow the more naturally and fully, and He will know it, and that is enough.

3. Make meditation yes, pray, yes, give the thirsting soul as much of this as it can take. But do not spend all the time lamenting our own littleness and our own shortcomings, patching up our pretty threadbare resolutions and will-o'-the wisp ideals which, experience has taught us, are only set up that they may topple down again each day. Instead fill the hours of prayer with His absorbing presence, with His invigorating company, the loving admiration of this most Beautiful of the sons of men, the joy of His friendship. the interpretation of His mind, sympathy with the gladness and sorrows of His heart. Fill our prayer with these things, creep through His wounds into His very soul, thence look out through His eyes upon heaven and earth, and our little selves prone at His feet, and though by the process we may forget our own spiritual ambitions, we shall instead unconsciously become what He was.

4. Examine our conscience, yes, but do not turn it into an everlasting pecking of the soul, ceaseless beating of this poor creature, which time has long since shown us comes to little good. Instead, let the eyes of Jesus look at us, let us see ourselves through those eyes the joy we are to Him for our encouragement, the sorrow for our trusting contrition, the smile on His face or the wistful look of disappointment at the sight of us; and it will be strange if the constant sight of Him does not produce its lasting effect.[1]

[1] *A More Excellent Way* (St. Meinrad, Ind.: Grail, 1946), pp. 20–24.

10

The Illuminative Way and the Discernment of Spirits

IN CHAPTER SIX we made mention of the discernment of spirits and said we would treat this subject more fully in our study of the illuminative way. This we shall now do.

By the word *spirit* we understand here an impulse, a movement, an interior inclination of our soul toward something which, to the understanding, is true or false, and to the will, is good or evil. This impulse toward things that are vicious or virtuous, true or false, implies two acts–one of the intellect and one of the will. It is precisely this disposition of the intellect and this movement of the will that we call spirit.[1]

Alvarez de Pas defines "a spirit" as that invisible element by which man is incited interiorly to do some human act, e.g., to live uprightly, to do penance for his sins, to choose a particular form of life or, on the contrary, to perpetrate some disgraceful deed . . . Or, again, a spirit is an internal impulse by which man feels himself urged to do something.

Mention is made of spirits in the Old Testament as we note in the case of Saul, who felt the influence of the evil spirit, and in the New Testament, our Lord Himself is depicted as being led into the desert by the good spirit and there He was tempted by the evil spirit. Again, when St. James and St. John wanted to call down

[1] Scaramelli, *Le Discernement des Esprits,* ch. I, p. 2, n. 7 (Louvain: Voss, 1881).

fire and brimstone upon the city of the Samaritans, our Lord said to them: "You know not what spirit you are."[1] In other words: "You do not know yet what ought to be the inclination of your heart." St. Paul, speaking to the Corinthians, says: "Now, who have not received the spirit of this world, but the Spirit that is of God."[2] St. John says: "Dearly beloved, believe not every spirit: but try the spirits if they be of God."[3]

St. Bernard says that the discernment of spirits is a necessary science, adding: "If this discernment is lacking, all virtue loses its lustre and is changed into abominable vice."[4] This same illustrious saint gives us a list of six different spirits:

(1) The divine spirit which speaks to the heart. "But God put in my heart, and I assembled the princes and magistrates and common people to number them."—2 Esd. 7:5.

(2) The *angelic spirit* which also speaks within us: "And behold the angel that spoke within me went forth."—Zach. 2:3.

(3) The *diabolical spirit* which God permits to suggest many evil thoughts. "Indignation and wrath and trouble, which he sent by evil angels."—Ps. 77:49.

(4) The *spirit of the flesh*, by which many are dominated: "Let no man seduce you . . . walking in the things which he hath not seen, in vain puffed up by the sense of his flesh."—Col. 2:18.

(5) The *spirit of the world*, of which St. Paul says he was exempt: "Now, we have received not the spirit of the world, but the Spirit that is of God."—1 Cor. 2:12.

(6) The *human spirit*, of which St. Paul says: "For what man knoweth the things of a man, but the spirit of a man that is in him."—1 Cor. 2:11.

The above six spirits may be reduced to three general categories: (1) the divine spirit, including that of the angelic spirit since the angels do not operate except in the name of God; (2) the diabolical spirit with the two satellites, the flesh and the world; and (3) the human spirit. Oddly enough, St. Bernard says that the human spirit

[1] Luke 8:55. [2] 1 Cor. 2:12. [3] 1 John 4:1. [4] *Ser.* 49 *in Cant.*

is worse than the diabolical spirit, since by it man can fall all by himself and without any external impulse.[1]

The divine spirit is formed in us by special lights and pious affections which we call actual graces. The state of grace and the infused virtues are not sufficient for us to perform the supernatural acts necessary for our salvation, so God in His goodness sends us special helps either directly or through the mediation of His angels.

The diabolical spirit is the result of the action of the demons who surround us in great numbers. They penetrate our internal senses, and thus incite our disordered affections toward certain objects and appeal to our lower passions and so it is these propensities and tendencies toward evil that we call the diabolical spirit.

The diabolical effect on the senses differs from that produced by the spirit of the flesh and the spirit of the world. Let us have St. Bernard explain these differences.

> When the devil attacks us directly, he always introduces into the soul a definite bitterness, since he excites troubled thoughts, uneasy affections, painful agitations, discouragement, despair, envy, hate, rancour, lonesomeness, and other kinds of torments; when he calls his satellites into play, that is the flesh or the world, he always introduces a spirit of sweetness (but a false sweetness) because in this case, he wishes to arouse in us desires for pleasure, honors, riches, and places before our eyes a false felicity which will finally result in temporal or eternal misfortune. . . . The suggestion itself should be the key to its origin. The spirit of the flesh inspires softness and ease; the spirit of the world speaks of vain things; the diabolical spirit always speaks with bitterness.[2]

The human spirit is the result of original sin which has left our human nature very weak: the intellect is darkened, the will is weakened and the concupiscence of the flesh makes us prone to evil, so it follows that this very nature of ours is a cause of many of our falls.

As to the discernment of spirits, it may be the result of two things: (1) a grace gratuitously given by God to certain persons, such as St. Mary Magdalen dei Pazzi who saw the thoughts of her

[1] *Ser.* 105, *super Cant.*
[2] *Ser. de spiritibus.*

novices; St. Joseph Cupertino who could tell when a person was in sin; and the Curé d'Ars who could do likewise; (2) the other means is by study based on the rules and precepts as found in Holy Scripture, the teachings of the Church, the works of the fathers and in the lives of the saints.

Since the second means is the ordinary means for most of us, the following things are essential for spiritual directors. First, we must pray, for as St. James says: "If any of you want wisdom, let him ask of God who giveth to all men abundantly." [1] Secondly, we must study. Thirdly, we must use our own personal experience as a basis for our judgments or, as Holy Scripture says: "Judge of the disposition of thy neighbor by thyself." [2] Fourthly, we must be humble: "God resisteth the proud, but to the humble He giveth grace." [3] Fifthly, we must maintain a great spirit of detachment, for particular affection for anyone may cloud our judgment. Sixthly, we must develop a spirit of simplicity so as not to confuse and confound the penitent with superfluous subtleties. Seventh, we must take time for serious reflection and not make snap judgments. Finally, we must be able to distinguish between the signs indicative of good or evil spirits. And what are these signs? The answer follows.

The marks of the divine spirit relative to the movements or acts of our *intelligence* are:

(1) The divine spirit always teaches truth and can in no way suggest evil.

(2) The divine spirit never suggests to our spirit anything vain, extravagant, useless, or sterile.

(3) The divine spirit always brings light to the soul.

(4) The divine spirit always inspires docility, humility, and discretion.

The marks of the divine spirit in the movements or acts of the *will* are:

(1) Peace is one of the predominant marks of the divine spirit.

[1] Jas. 1:5. [2] Ecclus. 31:18. [3] 1 Pet. 5:5.

(2) Humility—sincere and in no way affected.

(3) Great confidence in God and distrust of self.

(4) Flexibility of will—great willingness to follow God's inspirations but a facility to follow the advice of others.

(5) Purity of intention in all our works.

(6) Patience in suffering.

(7) Voluntary interior mortification.

(8) Simplicity, sincerity and truthfulness.

The marks of the diabolical spirit in the movements of the *intellect* are:

(1) Proposal of false or erroneous things.

(2) Inconvenient, light, and useless things.

(3) Indiscretions.

(4) Vain things and proud suggestions.

Marks of the diabolical spirit in the movements or acts of the *will* are:

(1) Confusion, uneasiness, and fright.

(2) Manifest pride or false humility.

(3) Despair, defiance, vain security.

(4) Disobedience or obstinacy to those in authority.

(5) Evil motives and intention in one's works.

(6) Impatience and revolt against adversities.

(7) The resurgence of the passions.

(8) Indifference to the imitation of Christ's example.

(9) False charity and false zeal.

What must be done when the director finds some of the above signs of the diabolical spirit in those under his care? First, he must do his best to gain such a person's confidence. Secondly, he ought to advise constant prayer and frequentation of the sacraments. Thirdly, when the devil attacks by thoughts and affections, the person must be warned to act quickly against them and perform contrary acts.

It may happen that you may be called upon to direct someone who, having chosen one state, thinks he or she is called to another. Ordinarily, such a movement of spirit ought to be suspected. St. Paul counsels: "Let every man abide in the same calling in which he was called." [1] We said *ordinarily* one should look with doubt upon desires to change one's state in life, because we do have numerous examples of those who were actually called by God to a higher perfection. In cases where such a belief is well-founded, the director ought to look for the marks of the divine spirit as listed earlier. He ought, too, to judge whether the new vocation is in keeping with the spiritual and physical forces of the person in question.

Whenever anyone feels moved by a certain spirit to do something and he is in doubt whether to consider it as an inspiration of grace from God, the following things ought to be considered.

(1) Is the work to which he feels called good in itself?

(2) Is it prudent and wise?

(3) Is the intention or the end evil or good?

(4) Are the motives prompting the act supernatural?

(5) Does this work betoken abnegation and charity?

(6) Is the inspiration itself accompanied by peace and confidence in God? "One of the best marks of the goodness of all inspirations in general, and particularly of extraordinary ones, is the peace and tranquillity of the heart that receives them." [2]

(7) If the inspiration concerns something important, is the attraction or movement solid and lasting? Inclinations, desires and projects which are the fruit of the imagination participate in the character of this faculty, which is essentially mobile and changeable, and so pass away or are quickly modified. This is even true of diabolical suggestions, inasmuch as Satan frequently overworks the imagination and thus his false inspirations or movements are easily detected by their lack of constancy.

[1] 1 Cor. 7:20.
[2] St. Francis de Sales, *Treatise on the Love of God, op. cit.*, p. 358.

It is not altogether easy to determine if the interior movements are the result of our own nature or whether they proceed from God or from the devil. The *Imitation of Christ* gives these few signs indicative of the human spirit:

(1) It is crafty and always has self as her end.
(2) It works for her own advantage, and considers what gain she may derive from another.
(3) It willingly receives honor and respect.
(4) It dreads shame and contempt.
(5) It loves ease and bodily repose.
(6) It welcomes outward solaces in which her senses may take delight.
(7) It longs to be taken notice of, and to do things which may procure praise and admiration.[1]

It is of importance to note that there are certain illusions whereby the devil fools many unwary souls. We must distinguish between diabolical tricks and diabolical illusions. The former are artifices used to lead a person into an evil which he knows to be really evil. Diabolical illusions, on the other hand, are artifices trumped up to draw a man into evil under the appearance of something good or to keep a man from doing something good by tricking him into thinking it is evil. The illusion is more dangerous than the diabolical ruse or trick because if someone errs, he humbles himself and his error excites him to repentance and amendment; while if he sins under the appearance of good, not only does he not humble himself after his fault but he is actually proud of himself, and he may persevere in a fault which to him appears to be a virtuous act.

Diabolical illusions appear frequently in mental prayer, in the practice of the virtues and in the abandonment of vices: "And no wonder: for Satan himself transformeth himself into an angel of light."[2] Father Bonaventure Péloquin, O.F.M., says that, for instance, "the devil may find a person making mental prayer and touch his heart with sweet affections, inflame him with a false

[1] *Imitation of Christ, op. cit.*, p. 191.
[2] 2 Cor. 11:14.

ardour or make him shed a torrent of tears, all of which are done to make the victim feel he has made great advancement in prayer."[1]

Richard of St. Victor indicates the different ends which the enemy hopes for in exciting such kinds of agreeable or pleasant affections.

The first end is to sow such consolations so as to later introduce error.

The second end is to arouse vain complaisance and self-esteem.

The third end is to weaken and make languid one's nature little by little by consuming impulses of affections so that one cannot possibly persevere in the prayer or in the other exercises of religion.

The fourth end is that by attachment to these kinds of affections (apparently very good), they will keep one from performing the other duties of his state which procure the glory of God, or simply, make such a one feel he is already perfect and needs to advance no farther in the pursuit of perfection.

The best precaution against this sort of illusion is to live constantly in a certain fear and defiance of self. The person who is fearful and distrustful of self is usually a humble person, and humble persons are disposed to expose their soul to their director or confessor and thus will not be long fooled by Satan. "Blessed is the man that is always fearful."[2]

We stated that Satan may delude some persons into believing that certain vices are virtues and certain virtues are vices. The ways are so multiple that one could make a list up of nearly everything we think, say, or do. Here are, however, a few examples. Satan may, for instance, delude a person into thinking that anger is justified if we wrap it in the cloak of zeal. He may delude us into believing our unruly affection for another is actually a spiritual affection.

Vice versa, the devil can hide the beauty of virtue under the cloak of vice. He knows well that corporal penance contributes to our spiritual progress, so what does he do? He makes certain people feel that it is a repugnant thing, so that rather than embrace it, they consider it a nuisance. He, in another way, may induce a person

[1] *Catéchisme du discernement des esprits* (Sorel, Can.: Couvent des Franciscaines, 1951), p. 95.

[2] Prov. 28:14.

to gormandize himself at the table, deluding him into believing that he can do penance by over-eating as well as by abstinence. Still others he may induce to give up the practice of meditation on the eternal truths for some more pleasant subjects, and so his end is achieved.

St. Thomas says the sole remedy against such illusions is to recommend ourselves continually to God, begging of Him the light of discernment so we may ever be enabled to distinguish good from evil and evil from good.[1]

Some of the saints have experienced what St. Teresa calls divine locutions, by which the person hears words distinctly formed but not heard by the auditory sense. Hear the saint describe this experience. The words, she says, "are much more clearly understood than they would be if they were heard by the ear. It is impossible not to understand them, whatever resistance we may offer. . . . In this locution of God addressed to the soul there is no escape, for in spite of ourselves we must listen; and the understanding must apply itself so thoroughly to the comprehension of that which God wills we should hear, that it is nothing to the purpose whether we will it or not, for it is His will, Who can do all things. . . . I know this by much experience; for my resistance lasted nearly two years, because of the great fear I was in." [2]

St. Teresa says there is danger of delusion here and so tries to give us some rules to help us distinguish the locutions which come from the Good Spirit and those which may come from the evil spirit. "When our Lord speaks, it is at once word and work," she says, "and though the words may not be meant to stir up our devotion, but are rather words of reproof, they dispose a soul at once, strengthen it, make it tender, give it light, console and calm it; and if it should be in dryness, or in trouble and uneasiness, all is removed, as if by the action of a hand, and even better; for it seems as if our Lord would have the soul understand that He is all-powerful and that His words are deeds. . . . Locutions that come from Satan not only do not leave any good effects behind, but do leave evil effects. . . . After these locutions of the evil one, the soul is never gentle, but is, as it were, terrified, and greatly disgusted." [3]

[1] *Lec. 4, in II Cor. 11:14.* [2] *Autobiography*, XXV, 2, *op. cit.*, p. 214.
[3] *Ibid.*, 5 and 15, pp. 215–216 and 220.

This great saint strongly advocated fervent and constant prayer to God so that those who experience divine locutions might never be deluded thereby, and she also stressed the importance of complete frankness with and obedience to one's director or confessor. "Whenever our Lord commanded me," she writes, "to do one thing in prayer and if my confessor forbade it, our Lord Himself told me to obey my confessor." [1]

A soul in the earnest pursuit of perfection often experiences consolation or desolation. Spiritual writers say that these movements may indicate that its resolve or action is pleasing or displeasing to God or to the devil, and that it is important to know how to rightly distinguish the one from the other.

St. Ignatius says that he considers as consolation "every increase of faith, hope, and love, and all interior joy that invites and attracts to what is heavenly and to the salvation of one's soul by filling it with peace and quiet in its Creator and Lord." And he considers as "desolation what is entirely the opposite . . . darkness of soul, turmoil of spirit, inclination to what is low and earthly, restlessness rising from many disturbances and temptations which lead to want of faith, want of hope, want of love. The soul is wholly sluggish, tepid, sad, and separated, as it were, from its Creator and Lord." [2]

Tanquerey says that "the distinctive work of the good spirit in a well-disposed soul is true spiritual joy and peace. The evil spirit, on the contrary, labors to destroy this joy, by means of sophistries, subtleties and illusions." [3]

Father Faber points out that there are two classes of spiritual favors. One class consists of the raptures, ecstasies, visions, locutions, touches, wounds, thirsts, stigmata, and transformations, which belong to the saints. The second class includes only two things, *spiritual sweetness* and *spiritual consolations* which, says Father Faber, "are the frequent and often daily gifts of the middle-class Christians, that is, those who rise above mere precept, and walk by counsels, without entering into the higher mystical world of the saints."

The same Spiritual Father distinguishes between spiritual sweetness and spiritual consolation as follows: "Spiritual sweetness," he

[1] *Ibid.*, XXVI, 6, pp. 230–231.
[2] *Spiritual Exercises,* n. 316–317, *op. cit.*, p. 142.
[3] *Op. cit.*, p. 597.

says, "is a grace from God, which produces serenity and tranquility, no matter amid what a tumult of passions and temptations it has entered the soul. We see a difficulty before us at which our infirmity recoils, but sweetness at once smooths it away, leveling the hills and filling up the vales, so that we run, as on a railroad, on an easy level. It lasts longer than consolation. It abides out of prayer, even if it comes in it, and it makes us affable to others, while consolation sometimes leaves us with a temptation to irritability."

Of spiritual consolation, Faber says: "It is, as it were, honey to the palate of the mind. It infuses delight and pleasure rather than peace and tranquility. It attracts the soul to itself, and then floods it with spiritual sensations of the most exquisite delicacy. It is shorter in its duration than sweetness, but is more efficacious. It belongs especially to prayer; but it does not usually come until we are weaned from the world." [1]

St. Bonaventure groups both spiritual sweetness and spiritual consolation together in listing their offices, since while they are distinct, nevertheless, grouped together they come under the title of spiritual favors. As spiritual favors, then, he lists them as (1) filling the memory with holy thoughts; (2) giving a vast intelligence of God; (3) inspiring us efficaciously with conformity to God's Will; (4) causing reverence and composure of body and outward demeanor; (5) leading us to delight in hard work and, if need be, in suffering for God.

With offices so praiseworthy and ends so noble it is easy to see that Faber should write that "all the old spiritual books teach that we are to besiege God for them, like the importunate widow in the Gospel." Continuing, he says, "We must value them and pray for them, yet not be greedy for them. We must desire them, not for their own sakes, but for their divine effects and solid virtuous fruits."

Should God give such a grace to our soul, we ought to be grateful, but should He, for His own purpose, withhold or withdraw it, then we must equally praise and thank Him even in our deepest desolation.

If Satan uses either spiritual sweetness or spiritual consolation

[1] *Growth in Holiness, op. cit.*, pp. 426–427.

as a means of deluding us, we must, with the aid of the spiritual director, determine its falsity and use the general rules for distinguishing what comes from good spirits and what comes from evil spirits, by their effects.

St. Teresa had her own idea of those who *always* sought consolations in their prayers. "When the servants of God," she remarks, "who are men of weight, learning and sense, make so much account as I see them do, whether God gives them sweetness in devotion or not, I am disgusted when I listen to them. . . . It is certain that the love of God does not consist in tears, nor in this sweetness and tenderness which we for the most part desire, and with which we console ourselves; but rather in serving Him in justice, fortitude and humility. That seems to me to be a receiving rather than a giving of anything on our part."[1] It is only fair to say that the saint said that those to whom consolations are given ought to accept them thankfully.

In résumé then, the consolations which proceed from good spirits enlighten the soul to know good and strengthen the soul to do good. When they come from the evil spirits, they cause laxity, softness, love of honors and pleasures, and presumption. Anything that is contrary to God's will or the spiritual welfare of the soul is surely from evil spirits. Thus we must beware of anything inconsistent with our assigned duties or the duties of our state of life. Urges to practice only flashy, showy virtues, or any urge to do anything singular certainly gives signs of being born of the evil spirits.

Father Péloquin, O.F.M.,[2] gives the following rules for the discernment of private revelations. The rules concern:

(1) The person who receives the revelations
(2) The object about which they treat
(3) The effects which they produce
(4) The signs that accompany them

I. *Rules concerning the person who receives them:*

God can reveal things to those whom He pleases, even to sinners.

[1] *Autobiography*, 11, n. 21 and 20; *op. cit.*, p. 86.
[2] *Op. cit.*, p. 139–141.

To prudently interpret such revelations, it is necessary to examine the natural and supernatural qualities of the person who receives them.

(a) Natural qualities:
1. Well-adjusted temperament
2. Good judgment
3. Perfect sincerity

(b) Supernatural qualities:
1. Solid virtue
2. Sincere humility
3. Frankness with the confessor
4. Trials in the spiritual progress

The presence of these will not of necessity prove the existence of a revelation but they render the testimony more creditable.

II. *Rules concerning the object of the revelations:*

We ought to judge the revelation as false if it is:

(1) In contradiction to an article of faith.

(2) Contrary to the moral laws.

(3) Impossible of realization.

III. *Rules concerning the effects produced:*

We may consider the revelation true if:

(1) It produces, at first, great surprise.

(2) There ensues profound peace, joy, and security.

(3) It strengthens such virtues as humility, obedience and conformity to the will of God.

One may exact signs or proofs:

(1) If the thing is very important

(2) If conditionally made

(3) If the choice is left to God.

IV. *Rules for discerning the true from the false:*

A revelation may be basically true while containing some accessory errors. God does not correct prejudices or errors which He finds in those to whom He makes private revelations; He has regard for their spiritual standing and not their intellectual status.

Principal causes of errors:

(1) A mixture of the human activity with the divine.
(2) A bad interpretation.
(3) Personal impairment.

How to act toward a person who claims private revelations. The director ought to:

(1) Imitate the wise reserve of the Church.
(2) Wait for indisputable proof.
(3) Not display admiration.
(4) Treat the person with kindness.
(5) Carefully examine the pros and cons.

As for the person involved:

(1) There must be a simple opening of conscience.
(2) Profound humility.

Helping a person to decide on a religious vocation is a frequent task of confessors and directors and so a limited treatment of this topic will be taken up here, since it is not unusual to hear someone say: "I have a strange feeling from time to time that I ought to be a priest, or a religious."

Any adequate concept of a vocation would embrace these elements: a call from God, the due qualities of soul, mind, and body on the subject, and the express invitation or acceptance by ecclesiastical authorities.

A call from God. My, what a hassle one could get involved in in the consideration of the subjective element in a vocation, by holding with some the extreme "predestination theory" of vocation, or with others the "attraction theory." The most prudent thing we can do is to go along with Pope Pius XI who says: "God Himself liberally sows in the generous hearts of many young men this precious seed of vocation"; [1] and with Pope Pius XII who speaks of the "impulse and invisible action of the Holy Ghost . . . the divine call, etc." [2] One would be safe in saying there is some action on God's part upon the rational faculties of the soul, producing a special effect of moving those powers to know, to desire, to decide to enter the priesthood or religious life. "But," says Father Ignatius Brady, O.F.M., "it is not final, rather inchoative in character, perfectible by formal acceptance, and even previously to be fostered by human agents, parents, teachers, confessors, pastors, seminary superiors, etc." [3] In what precisely this subjective call consists, must be left to others to decide. Father Edward Farrell places it in the virtue of religion, and even more specifically in an intense act of devotion—a gift of God.[4]

Signs of a Religious Vocation. When God chooses one for the priesthood or religious life, He will, in His infinite power and wisdom, prepare that subject by bestowing on him, besides divine grace, such talents of body and mind as are requisite to such a calling.

(1) *The positive signs are:*

(a) Right intention for the service of God and salvation of souls.
(b) Physical qualities making one fit to do priestly work.
(c) Intellectual fitness, that is, positive evidence of sufficient talent, good judgment, common sense, and a spirit of study.
(d) Moral fitness, that is, he must have or at least strive for solid piety and perfect purity of life.
(e) Call of the bishop or formal acceptance by the superior.

The signs or requirements for religious life are given in Canon 538:

[1] Encyclical *On the Priesthood*, NCWC ed., p. 54.
[2] *Menti Nostrae*, 1950, n. 75–76. [3] In *The Cord*, 4, 317.
[4] *The Theology of Religious Vocation* (St. Louis: B. Herder, 1951), p. 98; p. 112.

(a) The Catholic Faith.
(b) Lack of any impediments.
(c) Right intention to pursue perfection through the rule, vows, and way of life of the religious institute.
(d) Fitness to bear the burdens and strain of religious life.

The signs of a lack of vocation to the priesthood are:

(a) A special tendency to sensuality, which after long trial has not been conquered.
(b) Excessive attachment to one's own will that one will hardly be found docile, such as "the intractable, unruly, undisciplined."
(c) Proneness to envy or suspicion, or rudeness in behavior.
(d) Small taste for piety, lack of industry, little zeal for souls.
(e) Melancholy.
(f) Flightiness in judgment and reasoning.
(g) Lack of intellectual ability.

It would behoove all priests but more especially spiritual directors to be ever on the look-out for vocations to the priesthood and the religious life. A great saint and a great educator–St. John Bosco–stoutly maintained that God puts the germ of a vocation into the hearts of at least *one-third* of our young people. If this be true, then in every class of thirty pupils, there should be up to ten vocations. Let us strive therefore to fulfill the injunction of Canon 1353 which imposes upon priests the duty of promoting vocations, stressing as it does that "they should foster in them [boys] the seed of a divine vocation." The Latin text uses the word *germen*–"germ."

Well did St. Vincent de Paul say: "No matter how we seek, we shall always discover ourselves unable to contribute to anything more sublime than the making of good priests" and, we hasten to add, "the making of good religious."

11

The Illuminative Way and Recollection

SILVESTER relates that St. Mary Magdalene, after the Ascension of our Lord, having retired into a desert, in which she lived for thirty-two years, God from the very beginning taught her in what she ought to employ herself to become more pleasing to Him. He, therefore, sent an Angel to plant a cross at the entrance of the cave, into which she had retired, that the saint having this object before her eyes, might always have present in her mind the adorable mysteries which were wrought upon the cross. So that all the time she lived in this solitude, she continually employed herself in meditating on the passion and death of her Saviour and Master.

In the first phase of the spiritual life which we call the purgative way, the soul strives to combat both her internal and her external enemies, to free herself from the tyranny of the senses and to prepare the way of the Lord. Its blueprints are laid down by St. Paul as follows:

(1) "Purge out the old leaven, that you may be a new paste, as you are unleavened"; [1]

(2) "Be renewed in the spirit of your mind, and put on the new man, who according to God is created in justice and holiness of truth"; [2]

(3) "Mortify therefore your members, which are upon the earth"; [3]

[1] 1 Cor. 5:7. [2] Eph. 4:23–24. [3] Col. 3:5.

(4) "That Christ may dwell by faith in your hearts." [1]

By following Christ, who, by adoption, has deigned to make us His brethren, we will therefore possess the true light of the spiritual life and we will enter into the *illuminative* way, which, heretofore, was not ours: "For you were heretofore darkness, but now light in the Lord. Walk then as children of the light, for the fruit of the light is in all goodness and justice and truth." [2] Once the soul is purified from past faults by prayer and penance, and grounded in mortification and meditation and thereby, is enabled to resist the disordered inclinations of nature, it enters the illuminative way, and from there on, applies itself to the practice of the virtues: "That you may declare His virtues, who hath called you out of darkness into His marvellous light." [3] The implanting and exercise of the virtues are facilitated by the practice of affective prayer whereby the soul is especially enlightened or illuminated: "Come ye to Him, and be enlightened, and your faces shall not be confounded." [4]

The Model we must ever keep before our eyes is Christ, the Son of God, and the special aim of those who aspire to and enter the illuminative way must be imitation, the following of Christ by the positive exercise of the Christian virtues. When the way seems rough and the spirit bends under the weight of aridity, discouragement, and crosses, we must be mindful of these words of Holy Scripture: "Afflicted in few things, in many they shall be well rewarded, because God hath tried them and found them worthy of Himself." [5]

Those in the illuminative way must realize that the exercise of the virtues is one of their chief works and, therefore, it is absolutely imperative that they study well the life of Christ and set their hearts on an exact copying of His virtues. St. Bonaventure says that: "He who devoutly applies himself to meditation upon the life and death of Jesus Christ, finds there very abundantly all things he stands in need of and needs to seek for nothing out of Jesus Christ." [6]

The imitation of the virtues of Jesus Christ is what we ought to

[1] Eph. 3:17. [2] Eph. 5:8. [3] 1 Pet. 2:9. [4] Ps. 33:6.
[5] Wis. 3:5. [6] *Collationes in Hexaemeron*, 7.

propose to ourselves in the meditations on His passion and the fruit we ought to endeavor to reap therefrom. St. John Chrysostom says that "The Son of God came into this world principally for two reasons: first, to redeem us by His sufferings and His death; and secondly, to give us a perfect model of all His virtues; and by His own example, to induce us to practice them. It was on this account that at the Last Supper, after He had lowered Himself to such excess of humility as to cast Himself upon His knees before His disciples and to wash their feet, He presently said to them: 'I have given you an example, that you do, as I have done to you.' [1] But what He then said and proposed to us, to do in imitation of Him, ought to extend itself to all other actions."

It is therefore most important that those in the illuminative way meditate frequently on the sufferings and death of our Lord. Hear St. Bernard cry out "that nothing is more efficacious for the curing of the wounds of our conscience, and purifying of our souls, than continually to meditate on the sufferings of Jesus Christ." [2]

The fruits of such meditation—effective prayer—are according to Rodriguez: compassion; sorrow and contrition for our sins; love of God; gratitude and thanksgiving to God; affections of admiration; a lively hope and confidence in God; and finally, imitation of the virtues of our Saviour.

Ludolphus of Saxony relates the story of a holy man who lived in solitude, having once beheld a vision of our Lord covered with wounds and carrying a very heavy cross, and heard Him say: "One of the most pleasing services that My servants can render Me is to help Me to carry this cross; and to do it, they need only accompany Me in spirit, in all my sufferings, and have a lively feeling of them in their hearts."

St. Antonine relates of St. Edmund of Canterbury that the latter was privileged to see our Lord in a vision, and that He commanded him, among other things, to meditate upon some mystery of His life and death and assured him that this would be a great help to him to avoid the snares of the devil, to acquire all the virtues and to die a happy death.

Another great help to all those in pursuit of perfection, but

[1] John 13:15. [2] *Serm. 62, sup. Cant.*

especially those in the illuminative way, is a constant spirit of recollection and its essential adjunct—silence.

Recollection consists in an habitual disposition of soul whereby she transcends all creatures and their images, which thereby come to have little or no dominion over her, so that she remains apt for immediate cooperation with God, receiving His inspirations, and by a return, and as it were, a reflex, tending to Him and operating to His glory. It is called recollection, because the soul in such a state gathers her thoughts, naturally dispersed and fixed with multiplicity on creatures, and unites them upon God.

Recollection consists in these two things:

(1) Closing one's heart, as much as possible, to the preoccupations and to the distractions of earth and opening the heart to the things of heaven.

(2) Avoiding all dissipation and living in the exercise of the presence of God.

Good will is essential in these two tasks. There is little need here to say anything regarding useless visits, vain reading, long conversations and idleness or how they militate against the spirit of recollection. Fortunate are religious, for the rule prescribes certain times for complete silence, but even persons in the world can learn to use their moments of calm and peace after their day's work to practice recollection. Those who aspire to piety ought to abstain from anything that would distract them except what must be done from charity or necessity. They should especially be on their guard against useless thoughts, fancies or day-dreams. The Venerable Marie de Sales Chappuis recommended to those so addicted, that when they come to notice that vain thoughts are in their mind that they ought to dislodge them by thinking of God, and making an act of love for Him.

Recollection is a pre-requisite for a life of union with God and for the fruitful practice of the presence of God, as well as for continual prayer. For a soul to live in union with God, she must destroy all attachments which would impede, in any way, her entire turning to God. It was with this in mind that St. Alphonsus prayed: "Help me, Lord, to detach myself from everything that could distract me from the occupation of loving Thee."

Frequently, the spiritual director is asked for methods and means conducive to remaining recollected and united to God in such a manner that nothing can withdraw one from it. People in all walks of life will mention their manifold tasks such as teaching, nursing, child-care, the management of families, the management of convents and institutions of all sorts, and the director must be diligent in pointing out to all such persons that the great contemplatives did not pass their whole lives on their knees. Take for instance, St. Teresa of Avila, who is spoken of as the model of the contemplative life. She founded a great many monasteries, travelled a good deal, and was extremely busy directing her many foundations. In spite of her many duties, how, you ask, was she able to keep always united to God? The answer, of course, lies in the *will* to love God and in *willing* to live always united to Him. But let St. Teresa herself explain it. "The will being in union with God," she writes, "the soul should be aware of it, and see that the will is a captive and in joy, that the will alone is abiding in great peace, while, on the other hand, the understanding and the memory are so free, that they can be employed in affairs and be occupied in works of charity. . . . Accordingly, the soul is, as it were, living the active and contemplative life at once, and is able to apply itself to works of charity and the affairs of its state, and to spiritual reading." [1]

It must be remembered that, if recollection is compatible with the attention due to the fine performance of one's duties, it is incompatible with vain and useless thoughts and imaginations. These must be governed and dispelled. But involuntary distractions are something else. "They do not," as St. Francis de Sales says, "separate the mind from God; nothing separates the mind from God, but sin." "I have often observed," continues the saint, "that many weak, uninstructed souls, make no difference between God and the sentiment or perception they have of God; between faith and the sentiment they have of faith, which is a very great error. It seems to them, that when they have no actual perception of God, they cease to be in His presence; in this they are grossly deceived. A person who is going to suffer martyrdom for God's sake, has perhaps no sentiment of God, but only of the pain he feels while he is suffering; yet still he ceases not to merit all that

[1] *Autobiography*, chap. 17, n. 5 and 6; *op. cit.*, pp. 134–35.

time, in virtue of his first resolution, and he continues to exercise an act of the greatest charity."

In the light of this explanation, the director should endeavor to assure those who question the possibility of remaining always recollected and united to God while performing all the duties of their state in life, that such things are possible. There are but two things necessary—the fixing of the will on God and the curbing of useless and unprofitable thoughts and reflections.

"This union of spirit with God," says St. Alphonsus, "need not make you neglect your duties or even your recreations; it demands but one thing, that without abandoning your ordinary occupations, you act toward God as you would act toward those whom you love and who love you." [1] St. Francis de Sales gives the same explanation: "The thoughts of men in love, with a merely natural love, are always turned toward their beloved, their hearts full of love for her, her praises always on their lips; when absent they constantly express their love in letters; . . . so those who love God never stop thinking of him, longing for him, seeking him and speaking to him." [2]

The exercise of the presence of God is the shortest and by far the easiest means of gaining perfection, for it contains within itself the efficacy and force of all other methods. Did not God say to Abraham these startling words: "Walk before Me, and be perfect"? [3] Since all men are called to perfection and more especially, religious, the imperative command of God stands out in bold relief: "Be you therefore perfect, as also your heavenly Father is perfect." [4] Here Christ used the imperative, just as it was used in the words addressed to Abraham, "I am the almighty God: walk before me, and be perfect." Thus, as in many other places in Scripture, the future is expressed by the imperative, thereby showing forth the infallibility of success if the command is obeyed. St. Bonaventure affirms that to employ ourselves continually in the exercise of the presence of God is to begin in this life to enjoy the felicity of the blessed in the next.[5]

[1] *Man. de Conv.*, 2. *Oeuv.* t. II.
[2] *Introduction to the Devout Life*, II, 13; *op. cit.*, p. 68.
[3] Gen. 17:1. [4] Matt. 5:48.
[5] Alphonsus Rodriguez, *Practice of Perfection and Christian Virtues*, translated by Joseph Rickaby, S.J. (Chicago: Loyola University Press, 1929), I, 401.

The exercise of the presence of God is a great means of gaining perfection, too, because, for St. Basil it is a sovereign and universal remedy for the overcoming of temptations of the devil and all the repugnances of nature.[1] Just as a child is careful about his words and actions in the presence of the parents; just as a scholar is circumspect in the presence of the teacher, so one who practices the recollection of the presence of God will do much to keep himself from doing, thinking or saying anything that could possibly offend God. "When I consider, O Lord," says St. Augustine, "that Thou beholdest me always and watchest over me night and day with as much care as if in heaven and on earth Thou hadst no other creature to govern but myself alone; when I consider well that all my actions, thoughts, and desires lie open clearly before Thee, I am full of fear and covered with shame." [2] Without doubt they ought to impose upon themselves a strict obligation to live well, who consider that all they do is done in the presence of a Judge who observes all, and from whom nothing can be concealed. If the presence of a great person is sufficient to keep us to our duty, what effect ought not the presence of the infinite majesty of God produce in us.

For thousands of years the inheritors of Adam's nature lived without the fulness of the light and grace and guidance which came to the world with the coming of the Messias. God in His infinite mercy did however send patriarchs and prophets to His people to help lead them back to the narrow path of virtue. The exercise of the presence of God, it would appear, was to be one of the principal means presented for the freeing of the natural life from the distorted instincts which had been ever ready to misguide it since the Fall, and for the correction of habits which those instincts had established.

God made Moses lawgiver to the Hebrews and we note how Moses wrote in the first of his five books for generations after him that God "saw the wickedness of men was great on the earth and that all the thought of their heart was bent upon evil at all times . . . and He said: I will destroy man . . ." [3] The lawgiver would teach his followers that they were always in the presence of God.

[1] Cf. *ibid.*, I, 404. [2] *Ibid.*, I, 402–403.
[3] Gen. 6:5–7.

Did not God Himself say to Abraham: "Walk before Me and be perfect"? [1] And did not David, the Royal Prophet, say that sinners provoke the Lord, and give as the reason for man's transgressions that "God is not before his eyes"? [2] Indeed, David was not content with praising God only seven times a day, but, as he says: "I set the Lord always in my sight: for He is at my right hand, that I be not moved." [3]

That David was to make such a complete recovery from what might have been a terrible life of sin, must, I feel, be attributed to the grace he received to beg God's pardon, to do penance, and thereafter practice the presence of God; for we hear him say: "I have kept Thy commandments and Thy testimonies because all my ways are in Thy sight." [4]

It was no other than the Son of God who told us that the angels who take care, guard, and defend us, acquit themselves in such a manner of their charge that they never lose sight of God: "See that you despise not one of these little ones: for I say to you that their angels in heaven always see the face of my Father who is in heaven." [5]

After the Ascension, we find St. Paul teaching this doctrine of spirituality to the Athenians, by telling them that God "is not far from every one of us. For in Him we live, move and are." [6] But not only the patriarchs and prophets of the Old Testament or the apostles of the New Testament taught and practiced this salutary exercise of the presence of God, but innumerable saints found in it a most efficacious means of sanctification. The great St. Teresa writes that a soul pursuing perfection should "place itself in the presence of Christ, and accustom itself to many acts of love directed to His sacred Humanity, and remain in His presence continually, and speak to Him, pray to Him in its necessities, and complain to Him of its troubles; be merry with Him in its joys, and yet not forget Him because of its joys. All this it may do without set prayers, but rather with words befitting its desires and its needs." [7]

Elsewhere in her Autobiography, St. Teresa writes that the practice of the presence of God is

[1] Gen. 17:1. [2] Ps. 9:5. [3] Ps. 15:8. [4] Ps. 118:168. [5] Matt. 18:10.
[6] Acts 17:27–28. [7] *Autobiography*, Chap. 12, n. 3; *op. cit.*, p. 90.

an excellent way whereby to advance, and that very quickly. He that will strive to have this precious companionship, and will make much of it, and will sincerely love our Lord, to whom we owe so much, is one, in my opinion, who has made some progress. There is therefore no reason why we should trouble ourselves because we have no sensible devotion, as I said before. But let us rather give thanks to our Lord, Who allows us to have a desire to please Him, though our works be poor. This practice of the presence of Christ is profitable in all states of prayer, and is a most safe way of advancing in the first state, and of attaining quickly to the second; and as for the last states, it secures us against those risks which the devil may occasion.[1]

The saintly Catherine of Siena had the consolation and glorious privilege of having this pious exercise confirmed by our Lord Himself when He said to her: "Remember Me always and I shall remember you: perform all your actions as if you saw Me present and I shall see to it that you make progress in perfection."

For those of us who are limping along the rough, narrow road that leads to perfection, there is consolation in the thought that in the exercise of the presence of God we can make up for lost time and find in it a shorter and easier means to gain perfection. Surely this was so in the case of St. Thérèse of the Child Jesus, who so assiduously practiced the presence of God.

It should be stated here, that, as St. John of the Cross says, God "is present in the soul in three different ways." He is present, *first*, by His Essence. This essential presence is imparted not only to virtuous and saintly souls but also to those souls steeped in sin, as well as to all creatures. God communicates life and being to all and without Him they would cease to exist. *Secondly*, God is present by sanctifying grace by which He dwells in the soul. Those who lose sanctifying grace, lose at the same time this special presence. *Thirdly*, God is present in the soul by the effects of spiritual love which makes itself felt in numerous ways in the souls of the saintly and pious by filling them with consolation and joy."

The exercise of the presence of God becomes much more meaningful and intimate when the Pauline doctrine of divine adoption through sanctifying grace received in baptism, the mysterious participation in the Divine Nature, the incorporation with Christ,

[1] Chap. 12, n. 4; *op. cit.*, p. 90.

the mystical priesthood of all Christians, and our identification with Christ, is fully understood and practiced. Much of this has been treated in Chapter Two and there is no point in repeating it here. It suffices to say that in the doctrine that is so eminently Pauline, it is not a matter of offering ourselves to Christ that He might descend to our level and live *our* lives within us, but rather that we offer ourselves to Christ that He might live *His* own life in us. It is only when this is done that we can say with St. Paul: "I live, now, not I: but Christ liveth in me." [1]

Recalling that Christ is not content to glorify His Father only in heaven and in our tabernacles but that He has deigned to form a Mystical Body made up of millions of Christians in which He continues to live, to love, and to glorify His Father, each one of us will live better, pray better and love better, conscious of our role in this great masterpiece of Divine Love. Under the influence of such a doctrine, the Christian comes to the realization that it is not only himself, not only a mere human personality, but that there is in him something of Jesus; he is in a way Jesus Himself; he is divinized through his incorporation with Christ. The challenge resulting from such a conviction is to rid oneself of all that is inordinate, mean, or base, in order to clothe oneself with the breadth of view and the unbounded desires which animated our Lord in His actions, prayers, and sufferings during His mortal life. It demands the complete surrender of self to Christ so as to become purely His instrument, in a word, to surrender oneself wholly to Him, allowing Him to live and grow without hindrance, till our life be one with His.

To bring this about, we must: (1) make this the topic of frequent prayer, meditation and spiritual reading, leaning heavily for the latter, on St. Paul, Dom Marmion, Father Plus and Sister Elizabeth of the Trinity; (2) we must die to self, so that Christ may live and love in us. Our slogan must be: "He must increase, I must decrease"; (3) we must strive to please Christ at all times and in all things, posing this question before each action: "How should I do this in order to please Jesus?"; (4) we must accustom ourselves to do nothing alone but rather to do all things in close union with Jesus, for to do everything with Him is the surest way of doing

[1] Gal. 3:20.

everything for Him: (5) we must mortify ourselves in all things but always from the motive of the love of Jesus, desiring to renounce self entirely in order to let Jesus live in us; (6) we must remind ourselves frequently that Jesus who so loved the cross, desires to satisfy His love of suffering in us. Christ, as He reproduces and continues His own life in us, wishes also to reproduce in us the mystery of His passion. He wills, therefore, through us to continue His work as the Saviour, Redeemer, and Repairer. Thoughts like this will condition us to face sufferings joyfully and to bear them patiently.

May St. Paul's teaching of identification with Christ, rather than just imitation, fill your soul. May you be an apostle spreading the glad tidings to others, for in so doing you will be giving them the key with which the saints unlocked the greatest spiritual treasures.

If this was not known to you heretofore, don't worry. You are in good company. St. Teresa writes:

> In the beginning, it happened to me that I was ignorant of one thing—I did not know that God was in all things: and when He seemed to me to be so near, I thought it impossible. Not to believe that He was present, was not in my power; for it seemed to me, as it were, evident that I felt there His very presence. Some unlearned men used to say to me that He was present only by His grace. I could not believe that, because, as I am saying, He seemed to me to be present Himself, so I was distressed. A most learned man, of the Order of the glorious St. Dominic, delivered me from this doubt; for he told me that He was present, and how He communed with us: this was a great comfort to me.[1]

Now before someone gets the urge to stand up and say, "Hurrah for the Dominicans," let us proceed to examine some of the advantages of this great practice, having thus far considered the excellence of this exercise and how the presence of God in us is accomplished.

The advantages of the practice of the presence of God are many and varied. For instance, it provides, besides added motives for holiness, a great source of encouragement for those in danger of abandoning the pursuit of perfection when the task seems particu-

[1] *Autobiography*, chap. 18, n. 20; *op. cit.*, p. 148.

larly irksome or even impossible of attainment. History is replete with stories of valiant soldiers who were inspired to fight on and even give up their lives in a battle because they fought under the eye of their leader. It is said that sailors under Lord Nelson were electrified into acts of great daring and bravery because their great leader was watching them. It is said, too, that Nelson, in some of his skirmishes, had a sailor stand beside him with an extra wig in his hand, and Nelson would wear one wig while his attendant combed the bullets out of the other. Surely, we should be prepared to undergo the most strenuous labors and make the most noble efforts when we are conscious that not only does our God watch us in our struggles and trials but that His victorious arm ever supports us. St. Ambrose says: "*That as there is not a moment in which man enjoys not the effects of God's goodness, so there ought not to be a moment but he should have God present in his thoughts.*"

Again, the thought of the presence of God should keep us from sin. Who could dare offend the infinite majesty of God while realizing that he is in the presence of an all-holy and an all-just God? The great St. Teresa of Avila writes that "our horror of offending God ought to be great, especially when we consider that our sins are against Infinite Majesty . . . and under His eyes. It is as if one says to God: 'Lord, I know what I am about to do is displeasing to you, I know that You see me, I know that You do not want me to do this thing and I understand this well, but I prefer to follow my own caprice and my tastes rather than do Thy will.' "

The thought of how Sara's laugh—a "secret laugh"—was known to God, should inspire us with a great fear of committing sin and also of the folly of ever saying: "There is none that seeth me." [1]

"Blessed is the man," says the Holy Ghost, "that shall continue in Wisdom and that shall meditate in His justice, and in his mind shall think of the all-seeing eye of God." [2] The one thought that sustained Job in his trials and troubles was that God "considered all his ways and numbered his steps." [3]

St. Jerome says: "That when we find ourselves tempted to commit any sin, if we would think that God beholds us and that

[1] Isa. 47:10. [2] Ecclus. 14:22. [3] Job 31:32.

He is present within us, we should never consent to anything that was displeasing to Him." It is really because we forget God that we fall into sin. A horse without a bridle, according to Rodriguez, casts himself headlong into a precipice, and a ship without a rudder cannot but perish. A man who has not the bridle of God's presence, and is not governed by His fear, runs headlong to his own destruction and abandons himself to all his irregular passions.[1]

Finally, the exercise of the presence of God inspires *trust.* No matter what our trials and sufferings, whether mental or physical, may be, they are more easily borne when we recall that He who is all-powerful dwells within us and invests us with His power and sustains us with His grace. It was this very thought that prompted St. Paul to say: "When I am weak, then am I powerful." [2] The Little Flower in her terrible trials of faith: aridity, obscurities, weariness and temptations, said: "Nothing shall have power to frighten me, neither wind, nor rain, nor thick clouds which would hide the Star of Love. That will be the time to stretch my trust to its uttermost limits . . . knowing that behind those sad clouds, my sweet Sun still shines." One day as she lay dying, her sister, distressed at the sight of her sufferings, got this assurance from the Saint of Lisieux: "Oh, don't worry! If I suffocate, God will give me strength. I love Him. Never will He forsake me."

Having considered the excellence of the exercise of the presence of God, and the manner of this great presence, and finally, the advantages accruing from this exercise, there remains now but to discuss *methods.*

It would seem that a most logical approach to anything that is so important, excellent, and salutary ought to be based on a solid foundation, and so we state that two acts are required for the exercise of the presence of God: an act of the understanding and an act of the will.

The understanding is brought into play by considering that God is everywhere and that He is present in every part of every creature, and that we are filled with God, encompassed and surrounded by Him. Upon this truth make an act of faith because it is a truth that faith teaches us. We ought not imagine God as

[1] Cf. *op. cit.*, I, 403. [2] 2 Cor. 12:10.

far from us, or as if He were not present to us, for He is within us. May I repeat St. Paul's inspired words: "For He is not far from any one of us. In Him we live, move and have our being." [1] We must therefore school ourselves to believe that God is present within us and that He is within us after a more real manner than we are within ourselves.

Some of the saints such as Bernard and Bonaventure practiced the presence of God by representing to themselves God as present by their side or in a certain place or under a certain form. Some imagined Jesus Christ as walking by their side and scrutinizing their every action. Some saints hid themselves in the wounds of Christ, others attached themselves in spirit to the cross on Calvary. This might have served the great saints admirably but to the ordinary person pursuing perfection (and I may say doing a clumsy job of it), there is danger that such an exercise will become not much more than a preamble to a meditation. Most meditation books begin by suggesting for each meditation "a composition of place" and suggest the use of the imagination in conjuring up a mental picture of God, or His adorable Son under human form, as if in effect, They passed before our eyes. The exercise of the presence of God is vastly different from the preamble or composition of place in a meditation. There is nothing fictional or imaginary about the presence of God within us. Rodriguez says: "Jesus Christ, as He is man, is in heaven and in the Blessed Sacrament of the Altar, but He is not so in all places, and therefore when we imagine Jesus Christ present, as He is man, it is in effect a pure work of imagination, but as He is God, He is always present within us, and everywhere about us. Again, we may form an idea of the humanity of Jesus Christ and figure it to ourselves, because He has a Body and a Figure, but we cannot represent to ourselves God, as He is God, or conceive a figure of Him, or of what He is, because He has neither body, figure, but is a pure Spirit." [2]

The good Rodriguez states that imagining a representation of God or of Christ as forming a presence is good if performed well but for the ordinary person he says that all such representations of sensible images "do nothing else but tire the mind and engage the

[1] Acts 17:27–28.
[2] *Loc. cit.*

head." Like the good practical Jesuit he was, Rodriguez answers the question: "How then must we consider God present?" In this way: "by forming a simple act of faith, supposing that He is actually and effectually present; because faith assures us that He is so, without searching any farther how He is present."[1] This marvelous answer seems to fit in with what St. Paul said of Moses: "By faith he left Egypt, not fearing the fierceness of the king. For he endured, as seeing Him *as invisible*."[2]

You will remember that we said the exercise of the presence of God required two acts, one of the *understanding* and the other of the *will*. One is a natural *consequence* of the other, since an act of the understanding is always required and is presupposed for the producing of an act of the will. St. Bonaventure in his *Mystical Theology* says that the act of the will whereby we must elevate our hearts to God, in this exercise of which we speak here, consists in the ardent desires of the soul to unite itself to God, by the bond of perfect charity. He styles these motions and desires "aspirations" because they make the soul raise itself to God and aspire to Him. St. Augustine termed them *ejaculations* because "they are shot forth" like darts one after the other toward God. The Church makes use of such short ejaculations in her liturgical prayers beginning as she does each canonical hour with the words: "Incline unto my aid, O God; O Lord make haste to help me."[3]

St. Basil used this practice to call God to mind. If he ate, he gave thanks to God; if he dressed, he rendered thanks for his poor covering; if he looked up to the sky or beheld the sun or stars, he praised God who created them, and as often as he awoke at night he placed himself in God's presence.

St. Vincent de Paul was a wonderful proponent of this great means of practicing the presence of God. He tried never to let an instant pass without thinking of God's holy and amiable presence. Alone or in public, at rest or in the midst of work, in joy or in affliction, in the silence of his cell or in the bustle of the busy street, at court or assemblies, he was always with God, always united to God by prayer and love. In moments of stress thrust upon him by others, there was evidence of St. Vincent's retreat into the presence

[1] *Ibid.* [2] Heb. 11:27.
[3] Ps. 69:1.

of God. He always made a delay between the question asked him and his answer—a delay that gave him time to say—"In the Name of God," and consult Him for the proper answer. St. Vincent made it a rule to recall the presence of God explicitly four times an hour. When the clock struck the quarter hour, he made the sign of the cross and raised his eyes to heaven. When he rode in a carriage, as he frequently did, he kept his eyes closed and opened them only to contemplate the cross on his rosary which hung from his cincture. So as to see nothing that would distract him from the exercise of the presence of God he would draw curtains on the carriage in which he traveled. Walking on the street he observed the same recollection. On passing a church, he would enter and prostrate himself on the floor. He saw no one, but on-lookers were deeply impressed. Moses talked to God on Mount Sinai through a cloud but his face shone with a radiance that dazzled those who beheld the law-giver long after his descent from that mountain. St. Vincent kept always in the presence of God and little wonder that the children followed him, crying out: "Behold—the Saint is going by."

To render practical the thought of the presence of God, St. Vincent had signs placed in different corners and rooms of Saint-Lazare, reading "Dieu me regarde"—God sees me. The saint used to say often that: "The thought of the presence of God makes easier the fulfillment of the will of God: the remembrance of the divine presence creeps little by little into the soul and by His grace it becomes a habit; and finally, one becomes animated by this divine presence."

In résumé then, the exercise of the presence of God consists in an act of the understanding, and of faith as well, in God's adorable presence in, through, and around your body and soul, and then the employment of the will in making acts of love. These acts of love should take the form of short ejaculatory prayers, such as: "Lord it is for your sake I do this"; "Thy will be done"; "My God I love Thee"; "Praised be Jesus Christ," etc. May I repeat that time ought not be wasted in using the imagination to conjure up a mental picture of God or His adorable Son made Man. After a fervent act of faith is made in His presence within you, nothing more but the affectionate motions of the will are required. The great Cardinal Bona, in his *Cursus Vitae Spiritualis,* confirms this approach when he writes that

> this is the most perfect way, when we behold with purest eyes, God no longer outside us, but present in the recess of our heart and in the depth of our soul, and infusing His blessings into us: that is when forsaking all creatures we become accustomed to betake ourselves within us, and erecting a sort of temple in our heart there to worship God truly present, reverently hear Him, converse with Him in every emergency, as a son to his father and a spouse to her bridegroom. This way is called mental and unitive, to which should be added fervent aspirations, which will be the more ardent and efficacious because the soul having put on God, views Him with itself without forms and images, without any imperfection, with the simplest singleness of spirit and therefore becomes most adapted and proximately disposed for union.

This great spiritual writer points out that there are certain conditions necessary before this exercise will be fruitful. "First," he writes, "we must study purity of heart, because it is written: 'Blessed are the clean of heart, for they shall see God'; secondly, love of God is to be excited by frequent aspirations and self-love destroyed that we might be able to forget ourselves and be mindful of God alone; and thirdly, this gift is to be humbly and constantly implored of God." [1]

If you have made little progress in this salutary exercise, maybe the reasons will be found in the foregoing paragraph. The principal point I would make in closing is to resist discouragement stoutly. "Seek ye the Lord, and be strengthened; seek His face evermore." [2] "Think you," asks St. Teresa, "that it is a small thing to have such a Friend at your side? Believe me, do all you can to live in the company of such an excellent Friend. If you have not succeeded in this practice in a year, take two or more and regret not the time so employed."

So now you have the key with which the saints unlocked spiritual treasures!

It is an oft-told story that St. Arsenius heard these words spoken by a voice from heaven: "Fly; keep silence; rest," and they, to be sure, contain everything that is necessary for us to do on our part

[1] *Cursus vitae spiritualis,* part III, no. 2. [2] Ps. 104:4.

to correspond with the designs of God for us. "We must fly," says Father J. N. Grou, S.J., from all that could draw us away from God; we must keep ourselves in a silence both exterior and interior, that we may hear the voice of God: and we must calm all the agitations and anxieties of our mind and heart, that they may be fixed on God alone." [1]

"If any man offend not in word," says St. James, "the same is a perfect man." [2] How true those inspired words really are and how many there are who make so little spiritual progress and never enter into the spirit of recollection simply because they have never known the value of, nor practiced silence. Silence, you see, preserves peace, fosters recollection and devotion, and disposes the soul to a more intimate union with God.

Silence is a rampart against the attacks of the spirit of the world and its frivolous agitations. In the practice of silence, we find a defensive weapon, a powerful weapon against the enemies of our salvation. The devil fears and hates this religious silence because he has experienced its strength and he tempts less frequently those who honor it. Rarely does Satan gain signal victories over the individual who keeps silence.

Silence observed faithfully and supernaturally becomes a true virtue and becomes for all who observe it a precious source of countless blessings and strength. The great St. John Chrysostom speaks eloquently of silence as follows:

Keep silence, brethren; regard it as a strong wall by means of which you will be enabled to conquer temptations; you will have the advantage over them, for you will combat them from a superior position and can trample them underfoot. Keep silence in the fear of God, and the arrows of thy enemies will not harm you. Silence united to fear of God is a chariot of fire which will carry you up to heaven like the Prophet Elias. Silence is the perfection sought by the recluse, the ladder whereby we ascend to heaven, the road which leads to the kingdom of Christ. It is the parent of compunction and the mirror of the penitent. Silence causes our tears to flow, it engenders sweet consolation, it is the companion of humility, enlightening the mind and imparting spiritual discernment. It is the source of good; by it we learn the science of the saints, we learn how to pray aright. It soothes

[1] *Manual for Interior Souls, op. cit.,* p. 72. [2] Jas. 3:2.

the troubled mind and is a tranquil haven when the tempests rage around. Its yoke is sweet and delightful; it is a rest to the weary, a consolation to the afflicted. Silence checks the wandering eye, and controls the unruly tongue; it restrains the voice of calumny, quells the passions, and awakens love of virtue. United to the fear of God, it is the firm rampart of the warrior who fights to win heaven. Seek therefore to acquire the better part that Mary chose; she is the model of silence, she sat at the Saviour's feet and cleaved to Him alone.

I should say here that there are two kinds of silence. The two sorts I have reference to are *exterior silence* and *interior silence.* Exterior silence is that of the lips, in conformity to the moral law, and the particular rule of one's community, and interior silence is that interior recollection which is the principle and mainstay of the exterior silence. Let us consider these two separately. We shall begin with exterior silence.

In a way, all Christians are bound to observe exterior silence, and, for them, it consists in avoiding those idle words, for which Christ, our Lord, says: "They shall render an account in the day of judgment." [1] An idle word is anything in one's talk that is vapid, useless, and aimless. St. Jerome defines an idle word as "that which profits neither him that speaks nor him that hears." There are three classes of idle words: (1) the idle words of impurity; (2) the idle uncharitable words; (3) the idle words of irreverence. Idle words of impurity are the sin of those who degrade one of the highest gifts of God to do the vilest office of His enemies. Idle uncharitable words comprise gossip, slander, whispering, backbiting, and calumny. Idle words of irreverence are made up of all such pleasantries that bring anything sacred into ridicule.

The rules concerning conversation laid down by St. Paul are binding upon all Christians. The Apostle bids his converts think—and, in consequence, speak—only of things that are true, modest, just, holy, lovely and of good fame.[2] Everyone must bear in mind, too, the words of the wise man—words, alas, which are too often unheeded: "In the multitude of words, there shall not want sin." [3]

If the obligation to watch over one's tongue is binding upon all Christians, it is far more binding upon religious. To such, the

[1] Matt. 12:36. [2] Phil. 4:8. [3] Prov. 10:19.

words of the prophet Jeremias are most applicable: "He shall sit solitary and hold his peace, because he hath taken it upon himself." [1] No one can be ignorant of the vast evils that follow from loquacity, for both the Holy Ghost and experience show that sin is scarcely ever wanting in talkativeness. Hence most saintly men, founders of religious orders, especially St. Benedict, commend nothing more than silence to their brethren. Solon having been asked by Periander, since he happened to say nothing, whether he was silent for want of words or because he was a fool, "No fool," replied Solon, "is able to be silent."

Silence is a particular form of mortification which is within the reach of all. Many who could be validly excused from other forms of corporal mortification by reason of illness, or labor, will find that the mortification of keeping silent will bring rich merits and virtues.

Thus far we have considered *exterior silence*. There is still another kind of silence called *interior silence* and it consists in keeping the faculties of the mind well under control, and in maintaining a calm, regulated disposition. It means a controlled imagination and a state of quietude that implies a cessation or rest from unrestrained and inordinate affections and desires. Interior silence is that which works within the soul, and brings thought, word, and deed under the control of the will. The soul is kept in peace by it so that the presence of extreme disturbances—which is called the tyranny of circumstances—may move but not upset it; it is quiet within, and this commands the respect of others and merits rewards from God.

Interior silence is productive of a calm, clear placidness of mind as opposed to the disturbance of passions, fear, and solicitude. That soul is serene which is lifted above the agitations of earth and time and basks in the clear, unclouded light of God's presence. "Delight in the Lord and He will give you the requests of thy heart," [2] and "Commit thy way to the Lord and trust in Him," [3] so says the Holy Ghost. Thus serenity is won by delighting in God, by resting and trusting in God and committing our lives into His hands. The soul practicing interior silence will find herself in possession of a joy that dwells in the very depths of her spirit and she will find herself neither disturbed nor dissipated by the chances

[1] Lam. 3:28. [2] Ps. 36:4. [3] Ps. 36:5.

and changes of this mortal life. There are no storms at the bottom of the sea: on the surface the waves may mingle with the clouds without ever ruffling its serene depths.

Interior silence is productive of tranquility which is nothing more than that placid and peaceful state of mind attained only by a dedicated and clear conscience. Peace of mind is an incomparable gift and a thing of great value. To enjoy peace of mind, or tranquility, there must be a feeling that we are fulfilling the duties of our state of life to the best of our powers. St. Paul could truly say, "I have learned in whatsoever state I am, to be content therewith. I know both how to be brought low and I know how to abound . . . both to be full and to be hungry: both to abound and to suffer need. I can do all things in him who strengtheneth me." [1]

The person who relies on the inevitable decree and the all-seeing providence of God, who can neither be crossed with disturbing thoughts or discouraging words, nor with events unlooked for, lays a sure and solid foundation for tranquility.

Not the least of the effects of interior silence is that it permits God to speak more closely and intimately to the soul. We read in the Book of Osee: "I will allure her and will lead her into the wilderness, and I will speak to her heart." [2] Indeed, interior silence assures us the fullness of this privilege. It is only when the soul is quiet and recollected that the knock which Christ gently makes on the door of the heart will be heard. He wants the privilege of a close friend–to come in when He wants to. If we reverse this order, and go to Christ only when we want to, we shall find the truth of His words: "You shall seek Me, and shall not find Me." [3]

There is no point in further stressing interior silence since the same motives that make exterior silence take on such importance are equally true, if not more so, of interior silence. In fact, there will be little or none of the former, if the latter be not developed.

Remedies against vices of the tongue and violations of exterior silence are chiefly: fervent prayer; the continual remembrance of God's presence; and the imposition of a personal penance after a fall.

Interior silence is best maintained by constant peacefulness and

[1] Phil. 4:11–12. [2] Osee 2:14. [3] John 7:34.

tranquility of mind and by resisting all disquieting passions of grief, fear, despair and scrupulosity. The heart must be guarded against the pouring out of affection inordinately upon creatures. True peace of mind, which is the main fruit of interior silence, is the supreme state in an internal life, being a stability in one and the self-same tenor—an immutability, indifference, and insensibility as to ourselves and to all creatures and events, by which the soul transcends all, living in God only, and not being concerned in any other things besides God.

Father Marty, in a letter to a superior of the Congregation of the Holy Family wrote these important words: "Silence," he said, "is the road by which to attain the end of our vocation, which is perfect union with God."

12

The Director of Souls in the Illuminative Way

SOULS in the illuminative way are identified for us by St. Teresa. "They are," says the saint, "very desirous not to offend His Majesty, they avoid venial sins, love penance, spend hours in recollection, employ their time rightly, exercise themselves in works of charity to their neighbours, are well-ordered in their conversation and dress, and those who own a household govern it well." [1]

Since the illuminative way consists in the imitation of our Lord through the positive practice of the virtues He exemplified, one must have acquired: (1) purity of heart to the extent, at least, of resisting temptations, avoiding occasions of sin and of combatting the evil inclinations of nature; (2) mortification of the passions to the extent that not only mortal sins are renounced but deliberate venial sins as well; (3) the habit in the practice of meditation of prolonging the time of devout affection and petitions more than formerly when practicing discursive mental prayer, and by so doing, the practice of virtue is made easier until eventually such a one is habitually possessed with a burning desire to be united to our Lord.

There are numerous classifications of souls in the illuminative

[1] *Interior Castle*, *op. cit.*, p. 36.

way but they may be reduced to two main divisions: pious souls and fervent souls.

Pious souls have goodwill, the desire to do good, and they make serious efforts to avoid deliberate faults. *Fervent souls* have confidence in God and distrust of self; they are accustomed to the practice of Christian self-denial and they are more constant than the pious souls. Their love of the cross is not all-embracing and they are markedly attached to their parents and relatives and they have still to learn perfect detachment and to acquire the spirit of recollection.

This list may help the director classify his penitents.

Pious Souls	*Fervent Souls*
Desire to do good	Energetic and constant in practice of self-denial
Strive to avoid deliberate faults	Their abnegation is neither universal nor absolute
They are often vain	Their virtue is not tried by trial
They are sometimes presumptuous	They do not love the cross
They avoid the practice of self-denial	Lack constancy in resolutions
They are vacillating	Attached to parents, friends
Lack steadiness of purpose	Marked attachment toward certain things which hinder their union with God
They lack patience	Sincere desire to apply themselves to the service of God and to the practice of the virtues
Quick to make resolutions	
Imperfectly keep resolutions	
Lack fortitude	
Lack constancy	
Lack humility	

Directors will frequently notice in those beginning to give themselves to God, a certain sweetness in their spiritual exercises. St. John of the Cross explains this in his writings.[1] He says God is like a tender mother fondling her new-born son. As the mother will support and nourish her child, so does God support and nourish the beginner with special graces, filling the soul with spiritual sweetness. Everything is sweetness for the soul. It drinks deeply of the

[1] *Dark Night of the Soul*, I, 1; *Complete Works, op. cit.*, I, 330–331.

milk of spiritual favors. No obstacles appear to impede it and spiritual exercises seem to have a special attraction for it. Such a soul finds happiness in spending considerable time in mental prayer; penances bring happiness and fasts are no burden at all, and the ultimate in consolation comes from frequentation of the sacraments. Saudreau observes that young clerics and novices, as well as regulars, live ordinarily under such influences during the first part of their seminary or novitiate and sometimes much longer, but the time comes when God, like a mother, will set His spiritual child on his own two feet and it may please God to deprive him of consolation and sweetness in order to try him and to test his virtue. It is providential that God does this since there are those who, because they enjoy spiritual consolations, think they have attained to perfection and when these consolations are withheld or withdrawn they are plunged into a deep season of discouragement.

Beginners usually experience what are called *sensible consolations* and these are defined as tender emotions that affect one's sensibilities and cause one to experience a feeling of spiritual joy.

More advanced souls experience what are termed *spiritual consolations* and these being of a higher order, act upon the will by drawing it to the practice of virtue and to prayer, and they act upon the intellect by enlightening it. At times one may have an intermingling of both sensible and spiritual consolations.

Unfortunately, these consolations may come not only from God, but also from the devil and from our nature, and so the director must apply the rules for the discernment of spirits to ascertain their origin. Too, certain dangers may appear in the wake of consolations, such as spiritual greed, vain self-complacency and presumption.

The director will inspire his penitent to pray for such comforts as will increase his spiritual good and the glory of God, while however, he accepts God's will in the giving or the withholding of same. If the comforts come, then gratitude and humility are in order.

Since aridity is the privation of sensible and spiritual consolations, the director will see in them a desire on the part of God to either (1) humble the person; (2) to detach him from all created things; (3) as a means of strengthening the person in virtue. Other causes may be (4) self-complacency or pride; (5) spiritual sloth; (6) human consolations sought when God withdraws His and this is productive of sentimental, personal attachments; (7) lack of frankness with the director.

The director ought to warn his penitent against ever exalting himself in his own eyes during times of spiritual consolation. It is good, too, to instruct such a one to the effect that often smooth sailing is less meritorious than weathering the rough seas, providing it is God who instigates the squall.

Scruples may well appear in the illuminative way and frequently do. The rules heretofore given must be applied.

The particular works in the Illuminative Way are:

(1) Affective prayer

(2) Practice and increase of the theological virtues

(3) Practice and increase of the moral virtues

(4) Discernment of spirits

Affective prayer is, as Tanquerey defines it, "the form of prayer in which devout affections predominate, that is, those various acts of the will whereby we express to God our love and our desire of glorifying Him." [1] When almost all the mental prayer is taken up with acts of love it is called affective prayer.

The transition from discursive prayer to affective prayer in most cases takes time. At first they are intermingled but eventually one all but stops reasoning, so it seems, and the greater part of the prayer is passed in devout colloquies.

The director will be on the lookout for certain signs such as: (1) when convictions are so deeply founded as to take but a moment to recall them; (2) despite earnest effort it is found to be difficult to pursue considerations or draw much profit from them; (3) when the person's heart is detached from sin and is easily attached to God or our Lord; (4) when the heart is drawn to admire the divine perfection; (5) when a sense of wonderment arises and gives birth to acts of gratitude, praise, and delight

[1] *The Spiritual Life, op. cit.*, p. 461.

in God; (6) when there is a strong desire to procure the glory of God; (7) when there is evidence of conformity to God's will; (8) when there is evidence of the presence of the spirit of sacrifice.

The danger signs are: pride and presumption; mental strain evidenced by fatigue or exhaustion; the end sought is solely the quest after spiritual consolation; neglect of duties of state or the practice of the ordinary virtues.

Affective prayer consists of I. Preparation. II. Body of the prayer.

The subject of the prayer ought to be geared to the particular need of the person making it. "It is a great error," says Saudreau, "with many pious souls, especially beginners, to follow step by step their meditation books, and to hold themselves strictly to the thoughts and affections which are therein suggested, and which often correspond neither to the dispositions nor their needs. . . . Pious persons, already familiar with our Lord, ought not to be slaves to the subjects proposed to them but should be moved by love to use what will most greatly facilitate the exercise and be the most profitable to them." [1]

Blessed Peter Julian Eymard recommended to his religious that in affective mental prayer they ought to offer it for the same ends as Christ offers Himself at Holy Mass. The holy man lists these seven acts:

(1) Adoration, but adoration always joined with admiration.

(2) To thank God.

(3) To ask pardon.

(4) Petition for graces for oneself and for all mankind.

(5) Love of complaisance: "O My God, how good You are! I love You and wish to love You more and more!"

(6) Love of zeal: "O my God, so little loved, may Your love extend more and more in the hearts of men; convert sinners; let them not fall into the eternal pit where forever they will curse Thy name. May you have generous friends to rejoice Your Heart and help You make great conquests. To Thee alone be love and glory!"

[1] *Op. cit.*, I, 279.

(7) Love of conformity: "O my God, Thy will be done, not mine."

After having exercised love, the pious soul may recall his personal needs and seek out how he can be more virtuous and better serve his God. This great motto of Blessed Julian Eymard ought to be passed on to those in the illuminative way: "Act like little children: love, and then speak."

III. *Resolutions:* As to resolutions, the affective souls ought not neglect them but rather make positive resolutions that correspond to their needs.

Directors will be watchful for signs of spiritual dryness, which from time to time attacks those given to affective prayer. Those particularly susceptible are: (1) *beginners* who have not made much progress but whom God treats as little children, according them, to encourage their good will, the milk of sensible consolations; (2) *retarded souls*—those who ought to have been more advanced in perfection, but who, not having given their whole heart to the practice of renunciation or detachment, remain in the illuminative way when they should already have advanced to the unitive way. The latter are by far the more numerous.

To all who suffer spiritual dryness, the director will be well advised to encourage mortification. "Mortification and prayer," says St. Jane Frances de Chantal, "are the two wings by which souls fly into retreat, there to find rest in God far from the commerce of men." [1]

Before quitting this topic of affective prayer, I deem it wise to suggest to directors that they, from time to time, ascertain how this type of prayer is actually being performed. Some persons spend too much time thinking of themselves and their needs rather than of God. Blessed Julian Eymard points this up well when he writes: "If you want to be more quickly recollected, more directly united to God, you had better not concentrate so much on yourselves and not always place your miseries between your soul and God. Choose, rather, to see His goodness, His love, to contemplate Him in Himself and in His divine motives. After that, you may attend to yourselves. There are souls who never tell our Lord a word

[1] *Oeuvres,* 3, 259.

about Himself, who hardly greet Him, and who have no homage to offer Him; they are taken up with themselves, with their needs, and come into His Presence only to beg, as soon as they cross His threshold." [1]

The experienced director will register little surprise over the fact that sometimes God is pleased to draw souls to Himself by acting immediately on the affections without passing through the medium of the understanding. According to the Venerable Libermann this occurs frequently, adding, "Although meditation leads gradually to affective prayer, this fact does not prevent a great many souls from beginning at this stage without ever having applied themselves to meditation." [2] Saudreau, in spite of the foregoing, maintains that it is better to follow the usual road, and to begin by mental prayer as outlined by St. Ignatius, or the Sulpicians, or some other accepted ascetical lights. For the vast majority, it is necessary that through meditation they should have formed deep convictions on all the great truths, and once this is done, they are in a better position to give more time to devout affections and petitions and make more solid resolutions, for it is by these means that they are attracted to our Lord's virtues and moved to imitate and practice them.

While the various methods of affective prayer should be explained to those whose souls are purified from past offenses by a long and arduous penance, and who have have been grounded in virtue through the practice of meditation and mortification, it ought not be forced upon them. The passage from discursive meditation to affective prayer comes about almost imperceptibly. "This facility of some people for affective prayer is due," says de Besse, "in a measure to their natural inclinations. The influence of grace is there also without the slightest doubt." [3] The thing most likely to militate against the transition from discursive prayer to affective prayer will be attachment to sin, lack of the spirit of recollection, pride or presumption, or a too great attachment to relatives and friends. Since all are called upon to love God with their whole mind, heart, and strength, everything that impedes that all-embracing love will choke off affective prayer.

[1] *In the Light of the Monstrance, op. cit.*, p. 168. [2] *Ecrits*, p. 149.
[3] *The Science of Prayer* (New York: Benziger Bros., 1925), p. 35.

What the director must urge is the practice of the virtues—the infused theological virtues of faith, hope and charity, as well as the moral virtues, with special emphasis on the cardinal virtues of prudence, justice, fortitude and temperance as well as the principal virtues related to them, such as religion, obedience, chastity, humility and meekness.

The director might well suggest meditation on the following topics for those in the illuminative way:

(1) The indwelling of the Holy Trinity within us.

(2) The paternal attitude of God toward us.

(3) The Life of Christ, and especially His Passion.

(4) His love for us as evidenced in the Holy Eucharist.

(5) To see God in His goodness, His love, contemplate Him in Himself and in His divine motives.

(6) Part played by our Lady, the angels and saints in the Christian life.

(7) The fundamental virtues: humility, temperance, faith, hope, charity, religion toward God, obedience to superiors as exemplified in Christ.

(8) Our Lord as the perfect model of penance, mortification, abnegation, submission, and patient suffering.

(9) The fundamental truths of heaven, hell, death, and judgment.

(10) The Mystical Body and the part we play in it.

Certain difficulties may arise in the practice of affective prayer. The director should beware of certain problems and be prepared to offset them should they arise to disturb the process or the quality of the exercise. For instance:

(1) Some people spend their time making their mental prayer a preparation of the mind for work rather than a stirring-up of the will to pray and to love.

(2) Some people think meditation is preaching to themselves rather than an elevation of the heart and soul to God.

(3) Some people do all the talking, and are so busy in this procedure that they fail to listen to God.

(4) Some people think their meditation is worthless if they do not *feel* their acts. So long as one's acts proceed from the *will* it does not matter if they affect the feelings or not.

The director would do those under him a great spiritual favor if he would endeavor to have those who practice affective prayer extend this prayer into the warp of the whole day's work. Once prayer has become affective—that is, mainly composed of acts as distinct from reflections—it should and can be frequently renewed throughout the day by aspirations—short, original ejaculations in one's own words. It can even be wordless and consist of a look, a sigh, a smile, or a movement of the heart.

Those going through the trial of dryness or distractions may complain that they are praying alone with their *will*, and that devout affections are well-nigh impossible. As long as the *will* to pray is present under these painful conditions, there is no need for worry. "By *willing* to spend all the time of prayer in loving God," says Father Piny, O.P., "and in loving Him more than oneself; in *willing* to pray to God for the grace of charity; in *willing* to remain abandoned to the Divine Will, God is pre-eminently honored. One must clearly understand that if we *will* to love God (leaving aside for the moment the consideration of the part that grace plays in this action), by that very action we actually do love Him. If, by a real act of the will, we *choose* to unite ourselves in loving submission to the Will of Him whom we love, or desire to love—by that very act of the will, we immediately desire to love—by that very act of the will, we immediately effect this union. Love is, in truth, nothing else but an act of the will."

Prayer is a work of partnership between Jesus and the soul. The more affective the prayer is, the closer the union. Thus, those in the illuminative way must give themselves to the practice of affective prayer so as to draw from it the love, the knowledge and the emulation of their Divine Model; and along with this they must develop to a greater degree the theological virtues of faith, hope, and charity which they practiced in the purgative way; and finally, they must practice in a special manner those moral virtues which will remove all the obstacles to union with God.

The director would be well advised to suggest at the start, the practice of the virtue opposed to the fault which one has *truly* determined as predominant.

Father Grou gives this list of means of attaining true and solid virtue:

(1) To *will* it with a sincere, entire, efficacious and constant will.
(2) To pray for this good will.
(3) Follow a rule of life. To be exact in observing what we have prescribed for ourselves.
(4) To try to realize always the presence of God.
(5) Fidelity to mental prayer.
(6) Frequentation of the sacraments.
(7) Spiritual reading—Holy Scripture, Rodriguez, *Imitation of Christ*, Lives of the Saints.
(8) Mortification of the heart—resisting impressions from without and fighting them from within.
(9) Devotion to the Blessed Virgin and our Guardian Angels.
(10) Advice of a good director.[1]

Mental prayer must go hand-in-hand with the acquiring of virtue. Says Blessed Julian Eymard:

If it is a matter of acquiring the Christian virtues, more than destroying sin, we may go about it in two ways, both of which are good. We may use either of them according to the urge of grace.

According to the first, the soul that is energetically bent on acquiring virtue meditates on the moral good, the integral and supernatural beauty of it. She realizes that virtue is the proper thing for a Christian, that without zeal for the Christian virtues one is risking his salvation, that the practice of a perfect Christianity produces fruits without number in this life, but, above all, the fruit of eternal life. This thought lights up in her a great desire for action; she works day by day, hour by hour, advancing step by step. She notices her progress; this en-

[1] *Manual for Interior Souls*, chap. 3; *op. cit.*, p. 9 ff.

courages her and helps her to work on with greater fidelity. That is certainly a good method which ought to lead one to holiness.

But there is a better one: to work out of love, to want to do but one thing, *love*, and in that one thing to want all the rest. It is no longer a matter of acquiring virtues or of gathering the fruits of holiness, but of filling ourselves with this truth, of convincing ourselves of this principle; we must love God, and sanctify ourselves out of love for Him. Love then becomes chastity, poverty, obedience, patience, meekness, and humility; and in all this we aspire to do one thing only: to love, make an act of love, remove an obstacle to love or further our love of God and union with Him.[1]

The illuminative way in the spiritual life is so named because the great aim and ideal of the soul is now the imitation of Christ by the positive exercise of the Christian virtues. Dom Marmion says it so wonderfully: "The Christian is another Christ." That is the true definition of a Christian given by tradition, if not in the same words, at least equivalently. "Another Christ" because the Christian is first of all, by grace, a child of the Heavenly Father and brother of Christ here below in order to be His co-heir above; "another Christ"—plunges its roots in this grace, to be exercised according to the thoughts, desires, sentiments of Jesus, and in conformity with the actions of Jesus: "For let this mind be in you, which was also in Jesus Christ." [2]

"It is this," continues Marmion, "which properly constitutes the Christian:—first of all to share by sanctifying grace in the Divine filiation of Christ; that is the imitation of Jesus in His state of Son of God; and next to reproduce by our virtues the characteristics of this unique archetype of perfection: that is the imitation of Jesus in His works." [3]

It might be well to emphasize that all the virtues, supernatural and natural, are intended to make man what he ought to be. The theological virtues subject man's reason and will to God. The cardinal virtues subject all man's powers to the command of right reason. The supernatural virtues will make man perfect as the child of God and heir to the Kingdom of Heaven. The natural

[1] *In the Light of the Monstrance, op. cit.*, p. 174–176.
[2] Phil. 2:5. [3] *Christ, the Life of the Soul* (St. Louis: B. Herder, 1935), p. 45.

virtues will make man perfect as man. Together they pull all man's powers in perfect order for the attainment of the vision of God.

Tanquerey says the practice of the virtue of faith in beginners should consist in: (1) prayer for increased faith; (2) thanksgiving to God for this unspeakable gift; (3) humble submission and conviction in making acts of faith, saying with the apostles, "Increase our faith." [1] Beginners must be warned against: (1) dangerous books wherein the truths of the faith are attacked or ridiculed; (2) pride of intellect; (3) temptations against faith must be fought as are other temptations; (4) habits of sin—since all sin obscures spiritual vision; (5) worldliness—the greatest enemy of a living faith.

Advanced souls must be encouraged to practice not only faith but the spirit of faith. They must accustom themselves to see all things, to judge all things from the point of view of faith. Their judgments should be based on the maxims of the Gospels; their words should be inspired by Christ's words, and their actions should be Christlike. These should also pray for the spread of the faith, remembering that by word and example the power of faith is made evident to others.

The practice of the virtue of hope consists, as St. Thomas teaches, in the *expectation* of a good difficult to attain, namely, the possession of God, and the means to this end. The principal practice then, must be the strengthening of its foundation or as the Council of Trent says: "that we must all place the most unhesitating confidence in the help of God." [2]

Beginners will be encouraged to meditate frequently on those topics best suited to inspire hope, such as the Nativity, and the Passion and death of our Lord. Jesus is our bridge of hope, or as St. Francis de Sales says: "What will God do with His heaven, if He does not give it to us?" The beginners will beware of presumption, despair, and discouragement.

Advanced souls must not only practice the virtue of hope, but entertain a filial confidence in God, especially in trials, adversities and persecutions. Perfect souls practice hope through entire and holy abandonment.

[1] Luke 17:5.
[2] Denzinger-Rahner, 806.

All must pray daily for final perseverance, for though we cannot merit this great grace, we can, however, obtain it of the Divine Mercy.

The virtue of charity is practiced by loving God without reserve and with fervor, with our whole soul, our whole heart and with all our strength and by loving our neighbor as ourselves. Let us consider *first* how the virtue of charity toward God is strengthened.

Beginners practice love of God: (1) by avoiding sin and its causes; (2) by hating all things which we know to be displeasing to God; (3) by rejoicing at those which please God, whether they be bitter or sweet.

Advanced souls practice the love of benevolence, of complacency, of conformity to the will of God, and thereby arrive at the love of friendship. This is accomplished by mental prayer on the power, goodness, wisdom, and fullness of perfection of God. Such souls are productive of such acts of charity toward God as the following: (1) loving God for His own sake; (2) rejoicing in God's perfections, and because He is adored by the angels and saints; (3) desiring that every creature acknowledge and worship Him, and that infidels be converted to the faith, and sinners to a good life; (4) sorrow for our own sins and those of others because they offend God.

Asks Blessed Julian Eymard:

Do you wish to live of love, and to be happy in that life of love? Keep in mind the thought of the goodness of God, constantly renewed in your favor. Observe in Jesus the work of His love for you. Let also your communings with our Lord begin with an act of love. You will then experience delight in bringing your soul under the influence of the action of Jesus. The reason why you never make much headway is that your first thought is for yourself. Does not the child embrace his mother before obeying her? Love is the only door that opens the heart. You have a difficult duty to perform? Before acting, make an act of love. "My God," you must say, "I love You more than myself, and to prove it to You, I will cheerfully perform this act of charity, of self-denial, of patience." The moment your heart has made that act of love, the difficult duty is, as it were, already done in the eyes of God, and in your own eyes it will take on an altogether different aspect.[1]

[1] *In the Light of the Monstrance, op. cit.*, p. 26.

Directors would do well to explain this carefully to those under their spiritual guidance.

In the practice of fraternal charity, beginners are to be encouraged "to see your neighbor in God and God in him"; says St. John Eudes, "That is, regard him as one who has come forth from the heart and goodness of God, who is created to return to Him one day, and to dwell within His bosom, glorifying God for all eternity; and in whom God will, in reality, be eternally glorified either by His mercy or justice." [1]

They should be encouraged therefore to avoid the faults against charity and practice those acts to which they are bound by precept, especially forgiving injuries and putting up with others, in spite of their faults.

More advanced souls should be encouraged to put into practice the virtue of charity—both interior and exterior charity, as exemplified by Christ Himself. "Our Lord," says Blessed Eymard, "is charitable in His Heart and in His Mind. He loves His neighbor, wishes him well, thinks only of the good He can do him, and lets His mercy, not His justice, direct His judgments concerning him. Charitable in His Heart and His Mind, Jesus is as a matter of course charitable in His exterior. His eyes express neither anger nor indignation . . . He does not shun those who hate Him . . . He knows how to be silent out of charity . . . and what shall we say of the eucharistic charity of Jesus? What patient and merciful meekness towards those who forget Him! The Eucharist is the triumph of the charity of Jesus Christ." [2]

The ultimate in the practice of the virtue of charity toward our neighbors is that love that involves complete immolation of self and a very special love for our enemies.

Before giving a few hints to directors on the practice of the moral virtues, it might be well to set down here Saudreau's suggestions for what he calls the "Probation" of the virtues. He advises those in the illuminative way:

(1) To make a particular virtue the end of one's prayers, meditations, and Communions.

[1] *The Kingdom of Christ Within Us* (New York: Benziger Bros., 1911), p. 29.
[2] *Op. cit.*, p. 87–91.

(2) To apply oneself in particular to acts inspired by the virtue.

(3) To renew each morning resolutions relative to the practice of a certain virtue and to examine oneself each night on the practice of said virtue in question.

(4) To inform one's director on the progress made.

The director cannot over-stress the importance of prayer as the all-important general means of progressing in virtues, whether theological or moral. Nor is he to be discouraged to find that it is difficult to convince people that prayer is an absolute essential in this regard. Tanquerey says: "The infused virtues are susceptible of growth in the soul and do, as a matter of fact, grow there with the increase of habitual grace, whence they flow. This growth is God-given, since He alone can give us an increase of divine life and of the elements that constitute it. Now God causes this increase when we receive the sacraments, perform good works, or recite our prayers." [1]

According to St. Thomas, this increase is effected not by an accession of degree, or of quantity, but by a more perfect and more effective possession of the virtue. It is in this manner that virtues take deeper root in the soul and become more solid and more active.

Besides prayer, then, the director ought to stress the importance of the avoidance of frequent and deliberate venial sins which, while they cannot diminish the virtues, do hinder the exercise of the virtues by lessening the facility acquired by previous acts. Perhaps an instruction on the loss of the virtues would be most effective since, if the penitent was aware that the infused virtues are lost by any act that destroys their formal object, for instance, charity is forfeited by any mortal sin since such sin destroys the formal object of that virtue, they might be moved to a greater hatred and fear of mortal sin. Equally striking is the fact that the infused moral virtues also are lost through any mortal sin, since they are bound to charity and come and go with it.

So, as directors, we must stress the importance of prayer, good works and the frequentation of the sacraments, and the avoidance

[1] *Op. cit.*, p. 474.

of sin, by those seeking progress in the practice of the virtues. Next, we must follow different procedures for those beginning and for those more advanced on the road to perfection. Let us here note some of these procedures in the exercise of the theological virtues.

(I) *The Virtue of Faith*

BEGINNERS:

(1) Should be instructed in the fundamental truths of the faith.

(2) Make frequent acts of faith.

(3) Keep strict check on their reading habits–advising against all dangerous or controversial writings.

(4) Make frequent acts of thanksgiving for the gift of faith.

(5) Pray for an increase of faith, saying with the apostles: "Increase our faith." [1]

ADVANCED SOULS:

(1) Must let their whole lives be influenced by their faith, being guided by the *spirit of faith.*

(2) They must be induced to pattern their lives after that of our Lord so that their thoughts, words and actions bespeak the One who fills their heart. It is in this group that one will find the nucleus for the lay apostolate.

PERFECT SOULS:

Must ever keep in mind that the effect produced by the virtue of faith is to make us believe in the existence of God and in His divine perfections. Perfect souls, then, will ever keep before their minds the object and the motive of this virtue, and in so doing, will be drawn into closer unity with God.

(II) *The Virtue of Hope*

BEGINNERS:

(1) Must be warned against the two great obstacles to the fullest

[1] Luke 17:5.

practice of the virtue of hope—namely, despair and presumption.

(2) The road to perfection is narrow and rugged so care must be taken to withstand discouragement.

(3) Worldliness must be systematically eradicated, or as St. Paul says: "Mind the things that are above, not the things that are upon the earth." [1]

ADVANCED SOULS:

(1) Servile fear must give way to childlike trust and confidence in the goodness and mercy of God.

(2) Should be encouraged to read the Lives of the Saints daily.

(3) In times of worry over spiritual progress, to be urged to meditate upon the words of St. Paul: "For we are saved by hope." [2]

(4) Closer imitation of the virtues of Christ and union with Him, so that with David we can say in all our trials: "I will fear no evils, for thou art with me." [3]

(5) Daily prayers for the grace of final perseverance.

PERFECT SOULS:

Are to be inspired to practice the virtue of hope through abandonment to God. These place themselves at God's disposal, holding back nothing, thinking only of God and His glory.

(III) *The Virtue of Charity*

BEGINNERS:

(1) Practice this virtue by striving with every means at their disposal to avoid sin (especially mortal sin) and the occasions and causes of sin.

(2) Do penance for past sins and infidelities.

ADVANCED SOULS:

(1) By means of prayer and meditation, these must strive to con-

[1] Col. 3:1–2.
[2] Rom. 8:24. [3] Ps. 22:4.

form with the Divine Will so that they may arrive at the love of friendship, and, as St. Francis de Sales says, "attract God Himself." "It is sufficient," the saint continues, "for a heart that loves that he whom it loves more than itself is replenished with eternal happiness, seeing that it lives more in him whom it loves than in him whom it animates." [1]

(2) Advanced souls must be schooled in holy indifference and urged to abandon themselves to God's Will alone: "Not my will, but Thine be done." [2]

(3) Efforts must be put forth to match as far as is humanly possible God's love for us. Such an aim implies generosity, disinterestedness and continuity.

PERFECT SOULS:

(1) Will be urged to love God with their whole heart, soul, mind, and strength, and love their neighbor as themselves.

(2) Will follow the example of Christ Himself and strive in all honesty to say as He did: "I do always the things that please Him." [3]

It is a wise director who will do his utmost to implement and/or augment devotion to the Sacred Heart of Jesus in all three classes —beginners, the advanced souls and the perfect. It was Pope Pius XI who said: "The Sacred Heart is the road which will most surely lead us to know intimately Jesus Christ and will cause our hearts to love more tenderly and to imitate Him more generously than we have hitherto done."

As regards the love of our neighbor:

BEGINNERS:

(1) Must be warned against sins contrary to charity in thought, word and deed, and urged to practice charity toward their neighbors as Christ practiced it.

(2) They must promptly forgive those who have offended them.

(3) Pray for their enemies.

ADVANCED SOULS should be urged to:

[1] *Treatise on the Love of God, op. cit.*, p. 206.
[2] Luke 22:42. [3] John 8:29.

(1) Love even when that love is rejected or misunderstood.

(2) Do their utmost to match Christ's love "that you love one another as I have loved you." [1]

PERFECT SOULS should be urged to:

(1) Entertain special predilection for those who despise or offend them.

(2) Love to the extent that they would be willing to even surrender life itself for the spiritual good of a neighbor. "We ought to lay down our lives for the brethren." [2]

Now let us turn our attention to the moral virtues and see what, as directors, we can do to stimulate the exercise and increase of such virtues.

The Virtue of Prudence:

BEGINNERS:

(1) Must rid themselves of indecisiveness.

(2) Must rid themselves of precipitous action.

(3) Must think things out and pray for guidance.

ADVANCED SOULS:

(1) Study the New Testament for guidance in their thoughts, words and actions, acting as much as possible after the example of Christ.

(2) Study the lives of the saints.

(3) Ask the sage advice of others.

PERFECT SOULS:

Must petition the Holy Ghost daily for the increase of the gift of counsel and take pains to practice the virtue of prudence in its most heroic degrees.

The Virtue of Justice—as regards our neighbor:

[1] John 13:34. [2] John 3:16.

BEGINNERS, the ADVANCED SOULS and the PERFECT SOULS

(1) Must deal justly with others, taking care to avoid deceit or fraud.

(2) Must avoid anything that would harm the honor or good name of another.

As regards God. Virtue of Religion:

BEGINNERS: should be urged:

(1) To pray with more attention and devotion.

(2) To practice the exercise in the presence of God.

(3) To observe with renewed fidelity the laws of God, and of the Church, especially those relating to the observance of Sundays and Holy Days.

ADVANCED SOULS and the PERFECT SOULS ought to be urged:

(1) To glorify God in union with our Lord, the Supreme Worshiper of His Eternal Father.

(2) To special and increased devotion to the Holy Sacrifice of the Mass wherein they can most easily unite themselves to Christ as Victim. At Mass, Father Olier says: "He comes to us then and abides upon earth as a sacrifice of praise in the hands of His priests, that He may impart to us His spirit of victim, have us join in the praise He offers and make us inwardly share in His sentiments of worship." [1]

The Virtue of Obedience:

BEGINNERS should be urged

(1) To observe and obey promptly and in a supernatural spirit the laws of God, of the Church and the commands of those placed over them.

(2) To obey superiors with humility and punctuality.

(3) To make obedience a frequent matter for particular examination.

[1] *Introd. à la vie et aux vertus, op. cit.*, chap. 1.

ADVANCED SOULS should be urged:

(1) To submit their wills to those over them.

(2) To meditate frequently on the examples of obedience as practiced by our Lord.

(3) To perform as accurately as possible whatever has been commanded of them.

PERFECT SOULS should be urged to go much further. They ought to be induced to obey blindly, that is, without stopping to consider the reason for their superior's command.

The Virtue of Fortitude

BEGINNERS should be urged:

(1) To stoutly resist the feelings of fear in fulfilling what they know to be their duty.

(2) To be unmindful of the jests or criticisms of others in the performance of the duties of their state in life.

ADVANCED SOULS should be urged to:

(1) Meditate upon, and strive to imitate, the fortitude of our Lord in the most trying circumstances of His life.

(2) Pray daily for an increase in this virtue.

PERFECT SOULS ought to be urged to:

Desire to immolate themselves for God's glory and the salvation of souls, even to the degree wherein they offer themselves as willing victims of suffering for these sublime ends.

The Virtue of Patience:

BEGINNERS should be urged to:

(1) Accept crosses and suffering without murmurings and without resentment in hope of eternal reward.

(2) Submit themselves to the will of God.

ADVANCED SOULS should be urged to:

(1) Meditate frequently upon the sufferings of the Passion.

(2) Eagerly embrace trials and sufferings, in union with our Lord, for as St. Paul says: "For as the sufferings of Christ abound in us; so also by Christ doth our comfort abound." [1]

PERFECT SOULS should be urged to:

(1) Practice patience inasmuch as they desire, and love sufferings for the sake of our Lord whom they wish to imitate and glorify, and also for the sake of the salvation of souls. St. Paul tells such souls: "If we suffer with Him, that we may also be glorified in Him." [2] "*Love Me and suffer in silence,*" were Christ's own words to Mother Marie Sainte Cécile de Rome, on May 13, 1927.

The Virtue of Temperance:

BEGINNERS should be urged to:

(1) Practice each day some interior and exterior act of mortification and mention these at regular meetings with the director.

(2) Watch carefully to maintain silence and recollection.

(3) Recall frequently the presence of God.

ADVANCED SOULS should be urged to observe besides the foregoing: positive acts of detachment from worldly things and curtail the use of anything that might disorder the affections.

PERFECT SOULS should so practice what has been advocated for beginners and the advanced, that they will come to the time when they can say in all truthfulness what St. Francis de Sales said: "I desire very little, and that little I desire but little."

The Virtue of Chastity:

BEGINNERS must be urged to refrain from consenting to any thought, desire, fancy, feeling, or action contrary to this virtue. Occasions of sin must be diligently avoided.

ADVANCED SOULS must be urged to rid themselves immediately and with great energy of anything that might tarnish the purity of body or soul.

[1] 2 Cor. 6:5. [2] Rom. 8:17.

PERFECT SOULS will by prayer and mortification gain such mastery over the senses and thoughts that when duty requires them to deal with questions relating to chastity, it can be performed with calmness and restraint.

The Virtue of Humility:

BEGINNERS must be urged to wage continuous warfare against all forms of pride.

ADVANCED SOULS set their hearts on the imitation of Christ's humility. Frequent meditation will help in this regard. Father Olier's three degrees of humility are important goals:

(1) To rejoice in the knowledge of self, the knowledge of one's vileness, of one's nothingness, of one's deficits, of one's sins.

(2) Wanting to be known as vile and to be considered as such by all men.

(3) Wanting to be treated as such, and by joyfully accepting all the scorn and all humiliations possible.

PERFECT SOULS, beginners, and the advanced souls might well make this great litany of Cardinal Merry del Val their daily prayer, and the petitions thereof, their goal:

O Jesus, meek and humble of heart, have mercy on me.

From the wish to be esteemed, deliver me, O Jesus.

From the wish to be loved, deliver me, O Jesus.

From the wish to be honored, deliver me, O Jesus.

From the wish to be praised, to be preferred to others, deliver me, O Jesus.

From the desire to be asked for advice, deliver me, O Jesus.

From the desire to be approved, deliver me, O Jesus.

From the fear to be humiliated, deliver me, O Jesus.

From the fear to be despised, deliver me, O Jesus.

From the fear to be rebuked, deliver me, O Jesus.

From the fear to be maligned, deliver me, O Jesus.

From the fear to be forgotten, deliver me, O Jesus.

From the fear to be ridiculed, deliver me, O Jesus.

From the fear to be treated unfairly, deliver me, O Jesus.

From the fear to be suspected, deliver me, O Jesus.

That others be more loved than I, O Jesus, give me the grace of this holy desire.

That others grow in the esteem of the world and I decrease, O Jesus, give me the grace of this holy desire.

That others be entrusted with work and I be put aside, O Jesus, give me the grace of this holy desire.

That others be praised and I be neglected, O Jesus, give me the grace of this holy desire.

That others be preferred to me in all things, O Jesus, give me the grace of this holy desire.

That others become holier than I, provided that I, too, become as holy as I can, O Jesus, give me the grace of this holy desire.

The Virtue of Meekness:

BEGINNERS ought to be urged:

(1) To resist anger and occasions of vexation.

(2) To resist all temptations to seek revenge.

(3) To pray for the increase of this virtue.

ADVANCED SOULS and PERFECT SOULS should be urged to meditate frequently upon the meekness of Christ and should endeavor to imitate Him in the practice of this virtue. All must be warned, however, that great meekness can be acquired only by prayer and the diligent practice of self-control. "Learn of Me," said our Lord, "for I am meek and lowly of Heart, and you shall find rest to your souls." [1]

The director will do well to keep impressing upon those under his guidance that the infused supernatural virtues elevate the perfect natural man and enable him to reach the vision of God. The infused moral virtues enable man to use the world in an

[1] Matt. 11:29.

orderly fashion to bring him to God. The theological virtues order man's intellect and will directly to God. Devoid of virtues, man is like a faulty machine whose operation is shaking and tearing it apart. With the virtues, man is like a well-constructed machine. He is using well all his powers, both natural and infused, in the successful search for happiness.

It would be prudent to follow the instruction of St. Alphonsus Liguori and advocate the following prescription of the great doctor:

> Each month you will especially direct your attention to one of the following twelve virtues: faith, hope, love of God, fraternal charity, chastity, obedience, humility, mortification, recollection, prayer both vocal and mental, abnegation, and love of the cross. You will practice these with great care and extreme energy. In so doing you will focus attention on each of those virtues and in your particular examens you will cover them one after the other. Such examens presuppose wise and opportune resolutions, which under no conditions ought you neglect to make.[1]

St. John Chrysostom advocates much the same thing: "We shall correct our faults in time, one this month, another next month, so that like Jacob's ladder, we shall lift ourselves step by step until we finally reach heaven itself." [2]

The director too, from time to time, ought to delve into the matter of the particular examen, ascertaining fidelity to this important exercise and its results. The obligation of rendering an account to the director will make the person more diligent and more generous.

What Cassian prescribes for the destruction of a fault holds equally true for the conquest of some virtue—one must use every means to win the battle—fasts, better acts of virtue, meditations, the addressing of constant prayers and tears to God. Priests could do a better job of advocating and providing means for monthly and annual retreats for the laity since they are powerful means of leading people to a closer union with God.

The director would do well to advocate a great and tender devotion to the Sacred Heart, our Blessed Mother, St. Joseph, the

[1] Rule, n. 4. [2] *Hom. 82 in Joan.*

angels and saints to those under his guidance. Let us consider these devotions separately, and briefly, for therein are the seeds of great spiritual progress.

St. Bernard, speaking of devotion to the Sacred Heart of Jesus, cries out: "It is good and it is sweet to dwell in this Heart! . . . O precious treasure! O rare pearl! O Jesus, draw me to Thy Heart that I may dwell there, wash from me my iniquities, purifying me of every stain." [1] "If it could have been possible," says St. Bonaventure, "for me to have been the lance with which the Heart of Christ was pierced, do you think that after having entered that Heart I should ever have left it?" [2]

More than once our Lord pointed to His Heart as a font of grace: "Behold My Heart," He said to St. Gertrude, "I wish it to be Thy temple." Another time He said to her: "Behold My Heart, delight of the Holy Trinity; I give it to you to supply what is lacking in you." [3] "If I were to write," says St. Mechtilde, "all the graces that I have received from the amiable Heart of Jesus. I would need a book larger than the breviary to contain the list." [4]

St. John the Evangelist may well have been amongst the first to practice devotion to the Sacred Heart, but the first *apostle* of the devotion is generally conceded to be St. John Eudes who initiated amongst his missionaries a feast in honor of the Sacred Heart. This took place around 1643. In 1674, the Holy Father permitted the saint to establish a confraternity in Its honor. It was, however, to St. Margaret Mary that God confided the mission of propagating this devotion throughout the whole world—a story so familiar to all as to need no comment here.

As to the promises made by our Lord to St. Margaret Mary, for those who practice devotion to the Sacred Heart, the director should point out that the promises ought to be carefully studied as stimulants for their devotion. For instance, our Lord said: "Sinners shall find in My Heart the source and the infinite ocean of Mercy." "Tepid souls shall grow fervent." "Fervent souls shall quickly mount to high perfection."

Father Noldin, S.J., says, "Whosoever desires to practice the

[1] *Tract. de pas. op. cit.*, c. III. [2] *Stim. amoris*, p. I, c. I.

[3] *The Life and Revelations of St. Gertrude* (Westminster, Md.: Newman Press, 1952), III, chap. 15.

[4] *Life*, II, chap. 22.

devotion to the Heart of Jesus fruitfully and profitably must fix upon some prayers to be recited either daily, weekly, or at least monthly. A general resolution to be devout to the Heart of Jesus is of little use, unless at the same time the manner in which the devotion shall be practiced is definitely determined upon. Let only a few practices be chosen which can be performed with recollection, without haste; but what is once begun must not lightly be given up. It is not the number and length of our petitions which render them acceptable to God, but the fervor, the fidelity, the perseverance of the suppliant."[1]

As exercises of devotion Father Noldin suggests:

(1) Membership in the League of the Sacred Heart and the daily recitation of the Morning Offering.

(2) Zeal in seeing that pictures of the Sacred Heart are publicly displayed in homes and rooms.

(3) Keeping the Feast of the Sacred Heart with special fervor and devotion.

(4) Practice of special devotions on the First Friday of each month.

(5) Daily offering of some prayer or pious exercise in honor of the Sacred Heart.

(6) Frequentation of the sacraments and devout visits to the Blessed Sacrament.

(7) Praise of the Sacred Heart by frequent ejaculatory prayers.

(8) Placing of absolute trust in the Heart of Jesus and recourse to It in all necessities.

(9) The making of frequent heartfelt entreaties for pardon, in order to make reparation for the offenses and irreverences committed against the ever-loving Heart of Christ.

(10) Earnest effort to live, to labor, to pray, to suffer in constant union with the Heart of Jesus and by endeavoring to make one's heart more and more like the Heart of Jesus.

It would be most rewarding to follow this suggestion of St.

[1] *The Devotion to the Sacred Heart of Jesus* (New York: Benziger Bros., 1905).

Margaret Mary, for she says: "It would give our Lord singular pleasure if you frequently renewed the entire sacrifice of yourself to Him and practiced it faithfully. If Christ is to live in our heart by His grace and His love, we must die to self, to our concupiscences, our passions, our self-indulgence—to all, in short, that belongs to our unmortified nature."

Directors could do much for souls by explaining, suggesting, and encouraging devotion to the Sacred Heart. Faith in His promises is a goal to be sought and an end to be attained and such will be richly rewarding. "Leave all," says St. Margaret Mary, "and you will find all in the Sacred Heart. How sweet it will be to all after having had a constant devotion to the Sacred Heart of Jesus—of Him who will be our Judge."

His Holiness, Pope Pius XII, in his famous encyclical *Haurietis aqua*, issued May 15, 1956, poses this question:

Is there a devotion more excellent than that to the Most Sacred Heart of Jesus, one which is more in accord with the real nature of the Catholic faith or which better meets the needs of the Church and the human race today? What act of religion is nobler, more suitable, sweeter and more conducive to salvation, since this devotion is wholly directed to the love of God Himself? (Cfr. Ency. 'Miserentissimus Redemptor': *Acta Apostolicae Sedis*, 20, 1928, p. 166).

Finally, what is more powerful than the love of Christ, which devotion to the Most Sacred Heart daily increases and fosters?

This love can truly bring the faithful to live the law of the Gospel.

Elsewhere in the encyclical, His Holiness states:

We have presented for your consideration the real nature and excellence of this devotion—beautiful teachings filled with consolation. But before We close this letter, mindful of Our apostolic office, which was first entrusted to St. Peter after his threefold protestation of love for Christ the Lord, We deem it fitting to exhort you again, venerable brothers, and through you all of Our dearly beloved children in Christ, to strive ever more earnestly to promote this most gratifying devotion.

We are confident that in Our day, as in others, a great many blessings will flow from it.

Indeed, if the evidence on which devotion to the Wounded Heart of Jesus rests is rightly weighed, it is clear to all that we are dealing here, not with an ordinary form of piety which anyone may at his discretion slight in favor of other devotions, or esteem lightly, but with a duty of religion most conducive to Christian perfection.

For if devotion, according to the common theological definition which the Angelic Doctor gives, "is apparently nothing else but the will to give oneself readily to things concerning the service of God," [1] can there be a service to God more required and necessary—and at the same time nobler and more pleasant—than that which pays homage to His love?

What is more pleasing and acceptable to God than that service which submits to divine love and is rendered for the sake of love?

For every service freely rendered is in a sense a gift, and love "has the nature of a first gift in strength whereof all free gifts are given." [2]

That form of religion must be held in highest honor by which man honors and loves God more and more easily, and by which he more readily consecrates himself to divine love, which Our Redeemer Himself deigned to propose and recommend to Christianity and which the Sovereign Pontiffs have defended in their writings and extolled with highest praise.

Therefore, whoever considers of little value this outstanding gift of Jesus Christ to His Church, does a rash and harmful thing and offends God Himself.

There is, then, no doubt that the faithful, in honoring the Most Sacred Heart of the Redeemer, fulfill a most serious obligation by which they are bound to serve God and dedicate themselves and all they have, including their most secret thoughts and actions, to their Creator and Redeemer, and in this way obey the divine commandment: "Thou shalt love the Lord thy God with thy whole heart, and with thy whole soul, and with thy whole mind, and with thy whole strength." [3]

In this same encyclical, His Holiness stresses devotion to the great Mother of God, saying:

By the will of God, the Most Blessed Virgin Mary was inseparably joined with Christ in accomplishing the work of man's redemption, so that our salvation flows from the love of Jesus Christ and His sufferings, intimately united with the love and sorrows of His mother.

It is, then, highly fitting that after due homage has been paid to the

[1] *Sum. Theol.* I–II, q. 82, a. 1.
[2] *Sum. Theol.* I, q. 38, a. 2.
[3] Mark 12:30; Matt. 22:37.

Most Sacred Heart of Jesus, Christian people who have obtained divine life from Christ through Mary, manifest similar piety and the love of their grateful souls for the most loving heart of our heavenly Mother.

As to devotion to our Blessed Mother, it suffices to quote these words of St. Anselm: "O Blessed Virgin, as it is impossible for one who does not honor thee, for one whom thou dost not help, to be saved, so it is impossible for him who commends himself to thee, for him whom thou dost favor, to be lost."

As to Mary's capacity to help her clients, Richard of St. Lawrence writes: "Through the Almighty Son has the Mother become all-powerful," and St. Bridget bears this out by writing that she heard our Lord say to His Mother: "My Mother, ask for whatever it pleases thee, for thy requests will always be granted. Because thou didst deny Me nothing on earth, I can refuse thee nothing in heaven."

As to Mary's desire and willingness to help, our Lord once revealed to St. Catherine of Siena that He had charged Mary to take men, and especially sinners, prisoners, and lead them to Him; and Mary herself told St. Bridget that there was no sinner, no matter how abandoned, who, if he called on her, would not return to God, and, by her mediation, obtain forgiveness. Just as the magnet attracts iron, so does she draw the hardest hearts to herself and to God.

Hear our Holy Father Pope Pius XII, say:

Among the saints in heaven, the Virgin Mary, Mother of God, is venerated in a special way. Because of the mission she received from God, her life is most closely linked with the mysteries of Jesus Christ, and there is no one who has followed in the footsteps of the Incarnate Word more closely and with more merit than she; and no one has more grace and power over the most Sacred Heart of the Son of God and through Him with the Heavenly Father. Holier than the Cherubim and Seraphim, she enjoys unquestionably greater glory than all the other saints, for she is "full of grace"; she is the Mother of God, our Redeemer.

Since she is, therefore, "Mother of mercy, our life, our sweetness and our hope," let us all cry to her, "mourning and weeping in this vale of tears," and confidently place ourselves and all we have under her patronage. She became our Mother also when the Divine Redeemer offered the sacrifice of Himself; and hence by this title, also, we are her children. She teaches us all the virtues; she gives us her Son and with Him all the help we need, for God "wished us to have everything through Mary."

As regards the practice of devotion to our Mother, it is of prime importance that the director suggest that the persons under his spiritual guidance apply themselves to know her as well as possible so as to develop filial devotion toward her and offer her all their actions and have her present them to her Divine Son. It is proof of devotion whenever one sets out to imitate her virtues, so this too must be strongly advocated.

The principal practices of piety toward the Blessed Virgin are: the recitation of the Little Office, the rosary, the scapular of Mount Carmel, and the Sabbatine Privilege, which is joined with the scapular devotion. Speaking of the scapular, Pope Leo XIII said: "Its nobility of origin, its venerable antiquity, its extraordinary spread in the Church, the spiritualizing effects produced by it and the outstanding miracles worked in virtue of it, render the Scapular of Carmel commendable to a wondrous degree."

Father Bowden of the Oratory suggests the following practices and they should be welcomed by directors in their work with souls.

(1) Say three Hail Mary's daily in reparation for the blasphemies uttered against her.

(2) To invoke her sixty-three times a day as "Virgin Mother" in honor of her sixty-three years on earth.

(3) Say the litany for the conversion of a soul for Mary to offer to God.

(4) Say a Hail Mary in honor of St. Gabriel who brought it to this earth.

(5) To practice one mortification daily in her honor.

(6) To say seven Glorys with extended arms, in honor of her seven dolors.

(7) To say a Memorare daily to obtain Mary's help at the hour of death.

(8) To say the Salve Regina for the spread of devotion to her.

(9) To spread devotion to her by giving out scapulars, medals, beads and pictures of her.

(10) To say the three Hail Mary's morning and night with the added ejaculation: "O Mary, my Mother, preserve me from mortal sin this day (or this night)."

Directors ought, too, to inspire devotion to St. Joseph, chaste spouse of our Lady, for if Mary is the intermediary between her Son and mankind, so St. Joseph is the intermediary between Mary and us.

The great Father Lallemant, S.J., was gifted with an extraordinary grace for inspiring everybody with a devotion to St. Joseph. It was his own practice to honor him daily by four short exercises. The first two were in the morning, and the other two after dinner.

The first was to raise himself in spirit to the heart of St. Joseph, and consider how faithful he was to the inspiration of grace: then turning his eyes inward on his own heart, to discover his own want of fidelity, he made an act of humility and excited himself to perseverance.

The second was to reflect how perfectly St. Joseph reconciled the interior life with his external occupations. Then, turning to observe himself and his own occupations, he perceived wherein they fell short of the perfection of his model.

The third was to accompany in spirit St. Joseph, as the spouse of the Blessed Virgin, and to meditate on the wonderful knowledge which he enjoyed of her virginity and maternity, in consequence of the humble submission with which he received the announcement of the angel respecting the mystery of the Incarnation. By this exercise he excited himself to love St. Joseph for his love of his most chaste spouse.

The fourth was to figure to himself the adoration which St. Joseph paid to the Holy Child Jesus, and to beg to participate therein, that he might adore and love the Divine Infant with all the sentiments of the deepest reverence and the tenderest love of which he was capable.

Father Lallemant's devotion to St. Joseph was so intense that he requested that an image of his beloved patron might be put with him in his coffin.

In this same vein, it would be well to speak often of the importance of devotion to the angels, for as St. Francis de Sales writes: "Make friends with the angels, who though invisible are always with you; have a special love and reverence for the angel of your diocese, for the guardian angels of those about you but most of all for your own. Often invoke them, constantly praise them, and make good use of their help and assistance in all your spiritual and temporal affairs." [1]

All the ascetical writers stress the importance of devotion to the saints, especially one's own patron or patroness—those whose names we have received at baptism and confirmation. This can be done by daily pious practices in their honor or the making of novenas to them.

[1] *Introduction to the Devout Life*, II, 16; *op. cit.*, p. 74–75.

13

The Unitive Way

EARLIER I mentioned how easy it was to trace the steps St. Norbert took in his painful journey through the purgative way to the illuminative way. Those who knew him as the gay courtier and former chaplain to the Emperor Henry could hardly recognize the same person three or four years later. His features were completely changed, his body, emaciated from fasting and discipline, was wrapped in a penitential robe of sheepskin. Never once in spite of his spiritual progress did he ever think of giving up his practice of seeking spiritual direction. To spend time in spiritual conversation with the Abbot Conon was always for him a stimulating experience. After these visits, as he himself later testified, long fasts and severe discipline lost even their natural repugnance, and the nights spent in prayer were full of heavenly consolation. And as for the practice of the virtues, hardly a day passed that did not afford more than ample opportunity for their exercise. What biographer could ever attempt even to describe, in general, what Norbert suffered at the hands of his former friends and confreres? The fact that he extended the strict Lenten fast to the whole year and, except on Sundays, never ate a meal until evening, his daily life became a most powerful and continual sermon, and his reformation gave occasion to his brother priests to call him a religious fanatic. But human nature is ever the same, and to see a man strictly perform duties in which we ourselves fail, is for us a constant rebuke. So it was with those who lived in Norbert's day. At first they ridiculed him, then they set out to discredit him in the eyes of his ecclesiastical superiors, finally they even managed to maneuver weak men to make attempts on his life. How the former arrogant Norbert was changed and how he practiced the virtues of humility and patience is borne out by his biographer, saying:

> The saint, remembering his past sins, confessed that he deserved all manner of contempt and ill-treatment and rejoiced at injuries and afflictions. He no longer knew of any revenge but the revenge of the saints, namely to suffer and to forgive. Jesus his Master, had also been falsely accused, ill-treated and even crucified, and he was trying to resemble that divine Master as closely as possible. "Calumny," he later repeatedly told his followers, "is the test of a patient and generous heart, which bears with it rather than to give up working for God." [1]

The virtue which especially characterized Norbert was his deep faith. As we read in the Life of St. Norbert by Blessed Hugh: "Bernard of Clairvaux was especially known for his charity; Milo for his humility; but Norbert for his faith." Seeing God in that clear light of faith, he must needs love Him with his whole heart and seek to make Him loved by others. Thus we see in Norbert a ceaseless, burning thirst for the salvation of souls, and it is difficult for one to keep up with the wonderful development of the saint's great faith. It is written of him:

> The period of his conversion at first indicates only an illustrious penitent; soon the penitent is eclipsed by the apostle. For a moment we lose sight of the apostle and consider the founder of a new religious order. The founder himself seems to disappear when the archbishop commands our attention. How can one follow him at the court of kings, whose oracle he is; among heretics to whom he is a powerful opponent, or in the midst of ravages produced by a schism whose executioner he is? [2]

Volumes might be written concerning Norbert's lively faith in the Holy Eucharist. This great mystery has been called the

[1] Cornelius J. Kirkfleet, *History of St. Norbert* (St. Louis: B. Herder, 1916), p. 32.

[2] Migne, *Orateurs sacres*, t. LIII, col. 344.

"dogma generating true and solid piety." Daily did Norbert offer up the Holy Sacrifice, and on many occasions several times a day (allowed to priests by the custom of the day). God permitted His greatest miracles through the saint when he was celebrating the great Sacrifice, and in Antwerp we find Norbert to be its great advocate and apostle. It was when celebrating Mass that Norbert especially reconciled enemies, drove out evil spirits, and even restored sight to the blind.

Of his austerities, mortifications, and self-denial, enough has been written to convince the most skeptical of Norbert's holy life. His devotion to the Blessed Virgin was so great that he devoted all new foundations to her honor, and dedicated them to her name. In recognition of his filial piety the Queen of Heaven showed Norbert the habit of his order and always protected him and his order in a most special manner.

Until his last breath he not only exercised the great virtues but advocated them. On his death-bed he assembled his brethren and urged upon them the practice of faith and patience, two virtues which all during his life he had most cherished. "As when striking flint with steel," he said, "you thereby obtain sparks of fire, so also, does lively faith striking a heart of stone, produce sparks of divine love. . . . Do you suffer persecution? Be patient. Are you better than your Master?" He then continued to comfort them and to exhort them with a smiling countenance to practice these virtues.

So Saint Norbert's life serves well as an object lesson for the instruction of those who would know how to traverse the rough, narrow path to perfection through the three ways—the purgative, the illuminative and finally the unitive way. Having considered the purgative and illuminative ways, let us examine the last of these ways—the unitive way.

"The unitive way," says Benedict XIV, "includes those who are in the state of perfection, who have their minds so drawn away from temporal things that they enjoy great peace, and are neither agitated by various desires nor moved by any great extent of passion, but have their minds chiefly fixed on God, and their attention turned either always or very frequently to Him." To these belongs the unitive way, which is chiefly union with God by love, by the actual experience and exercise of it. Suarez explains these things at length, in a doctrine clearly derived from St. Thomas:

The first duty which is incumbent on man is to give up sin and resist concupiscence, which are opposed to charity; this belongs to beginners, in whose hearts charity is to be nursed and cherished, lest it be corrupted. The second duty of man is, to apply his energies chiefly to advance in virtue; this belongs to those who are making progress and who are principally concerned that charity may be increased and strengthened in them. The third endeavor and pursuit of man should be to rest in God and enjoy Him; this belongs to the perfect *who desire to be dissolved and to be with Christ.*[1]

Once the soul has been purged and purified and adorned with the practice of the virtues, it is prepared for and should aspire to habitual union with God, and this we call the *unitive way*. The end of the unitive way is, as Father Olier[2] puts it: "To live supremely unto God, in Christ Jesus our Lord, so that our inmost hearts may be penetrated with the interior dispositions of the Son of God, and each may be able to say what St. Paul truly said of himself: 'I live now not I; but Christ liveth in me!' "[3]

Since we of ourselves are incapable of all this, we must unite ourselves in a most intimate manner with our Lord. Apart from being made one with Christ through baptism, we must render this union even closer by the frequent reception of the sacraments and most especially the Holy Eucharist. The learned Suarez says:

When Jesus Christ is worthily received, He unites Himself really to the recipient, for He is truly and properly in him, and in a way becomes identified with him in a corporal manner. From this it results that, inasmuch as Jesus Christ is therein present by sacramental power, He incites or moves him who has received Him to love and cherish that God who is bodily and substantially present within him. This may be proved by the words: "My flesh is meat indeed, and My Blood is drink indeed. He that eateth My Flesh and drinketh My Blood abideth in Me, and I in him."[4]

It may be said that by the Holy Eucharist is effected the most

[1] *Treatise on Heroic Charity*, chap. VI, n. 5. [2] *Pietas Seminarii.*
[3] Gal. 2:20. [4] John 6:56–57.

perfect union of human nature with God after the mystery of the Incarnation. By baptism and sanctifying grace we are united to our Lord, inasmuch as we are made through these means living members of the Mystical Body of which Christ is the Head. He is the vine and we are the branches. He has added these words: "He that abideth in Me, and I in him, the same beareth much fruit."[1] But by the Holy Eucharist He becomes united to our body by His Body, to our soul by His Soul, to our soul and body by His humanity and divinity whole and entire, and that, too, in a real manner.

Father Monsabré, O.P., says:

Christ, the Bread of Life, makes us pass into Him. In the vital act of Communion, at the very moment when we eat His Sacred Flesh, It lays hold of us, penetrates into us, takes entire possession of our life, directing the course of it toward His holy life, moulding our tendencies and our habits to His tendencies and His habits, and working that prodigy which the Apostle proclaims in these terms: "Behold I live, yet it is not I that live, but it is Christ who liveth in me."

St. Bonaventure would have us believe that in drinking the Blood of our Lord we have drunk His Holy Soul, and that that Soul, infinitely more powerful than any of the superior spirits which can haunt our nature, lives united to us by communicating to us His thoughts, His inclinations, His desires, His will, His love, according to the needs of our supernatural life. That is what we will have, according to the saintly doctor, provided we have faith in the promises of Jesus Christ, provided we are persuaded that Holy Communion unites us to Him more intimately than all the other Sacraments.

Here is a special union of Christ with the body of the recipient in the Eucharist. This union consists not only in the fact that the gifts of grace bestowed upon the soul affect the body by restraining the passions and by communicating to it some beginning or foretaste of the state of glory or restitution of the state of original justice, but moreover by the Flesh of Christ although not assimilated like other food to our flesh, our bodies become in a certain mystical sense sanctified, inasmuch as Christ in a special manner consecrates our bodies by contact with His Sacred Flesh, uniting them to Himself by a special relationship or affinity. The Holy Fathers say that by Holy Communion we become relations (*concorporei et consanguinei*) of Christ, that we by

[1] John 15:5.

union with Christ's Body become immortal and incorruptible, and that the Eucharist is the drug or seed of immortality. These and similar expressions of the Holy Fathers show how clearly they maintained the doctrine that our bodies are in a special manner sanctified by the contact of Christ's Sacred Body.

The sanctification can be explained first in a moral way, inasmuch as Christ loves our bodies; for as St. Paul says, "No man ever hated his own flesh, but nourisheth and cherisheth it,"[1] which love is effective and operates in such a manner that our flesh, purified from vices, is made to the likeness of the Flesh of Christ, and tends to the glory of incorruptibility. Therefore our bodies, by reason of Holy Communion, have a special title or right to a glorious resurrection. We can also admit a physical influence of Christ on our bodies, by which concupiscence is restrained and a better harmony is established between our bodies and our souls.[2]

Hear the great Father Monsabré describe the Eucharistic effects upon our bodies:

Doubtless it is to our souls that Jesus Christ more immediately unites Himself, and it is our soul which He espouses in Communion, yet does not separate it from the companion, the instrument, the complement of its life. In nourishing it with His substance, He makes it so living, so instinct with life, that that which it receives from Him overflows and gushes forth upon each one of the elements that it animates, and stamps and marks out each, in some sort, for the resurrection. He joins Himself by means of His Flesh to the bodies of His faithful, so that by the union with Him Who is immortal, man becomes a sharer of incorruption. As one hides a bit of burning coal in the straw to preserve there a spark of fire, Jesus Christ, our Lord, hides His Life in us by His own Flesh, and puts it there as a seed of immortality, chasing from it all corruption. Not, my brethren, that our Savior has taken away the law which condemns us to die, but we have His word of promise that He will cure the sting of death: "He that eateth My Flesh and drinketh My Blood hath everlasting life, and I will raise him up on the last day."[3] Others who have not received the Holy Eucharist will rise and live again. I know it, but in the home above the communicants of the exile here below will be recognized by the super-abundance of their life, by the wondrous splendor of their glorified bodies, and for them

[1] Eph. 5:29. [2] *Eucharistic Conferences: The Communion.* [3] John 6:55.

the eternal Communion will be more exceedingly full of joy, of all manner of delights, and of glory.[1]

The Eucharist is also the principle of union binding the faithful to one another and to Christ, their Head in the unity of the Mystical Body. This doctrine is taught us by the Son of God Himself for did He not say: "Holy Father, keep them in Thy name, whom Thou hast given Me; that they may be one, as We also are . . . that they may also be one in Us . . . I in them and Thou in Me: that they may be made perfect in one."[2] This is the fruit of the Eucharist which Christ asks of His Father. Little wonder then that the Council of Trent should call the Eucharist "the sign of unity, the bond of charity, the symbol of peace and concord."[3] And it represents it to us as the "symbol of that one body of which Christ is the head, to which He wished us as members to be bound by the closest connections of faith, hope and charity."[4]

As Father Monsabré says,

Communion is the vital act of the Christian man. He finds in it the proper food for his divine being; in it he is assimilated to Christ Who causes him to live by His life; in it he receives, with the strength to resist the powers of death that conspire against him, a vigorous and joyous impulse towards the perfecting of his whole being by union with God; he is possessed with a foretaste of the delights and joys of heaven; and finally, he then prepares his incorruptible flesh for the honor of the resurrection morn, and for the eternal communion. The divine life descends into us for the first time at Baptism, and that sacrament, which incorporates us into Christ, is the first cause of our mystical union. Baptized into Christ, we are filled with His divinity; nevertheless, because our participation in the Body and Blood of Christ is the complement—that is, the filling up and perfecting—of the primal vital act by which we were supernaturally born again; because Jesus in becoming our food develops in us the sacred germs of Baptism; because He gives Himself more closely, more personally, more vitally in Communion; because the more abundant communication of the Divine Life rivets more firmly the links which attach the Christian man to the Body of which he is made a member, and renders him more able to ful-

[1] *Loc. cit.* [2] John 17:11, 21, 23. [3] Denzinger-Rahner, 882. [4] *Ibid.*, 875.

fill his duties, because of all these consequences is it that in Communion Christ restores our mystical unity, and that after the Last Supper He addresses to His Father this magnificent prayer: "Holy Father, keep them in Thy name, whom Thou hast given Me, that they may be one in Us, as We also are one. . . ." [1]

The union, strengthened by Holy Communion, must be prolonged by habitual recollection in order that Christ's interior dispositions may become ours and may inspire all our actions so that we may be able to say in truth what the great St. Paul said: "I live now, not I; but Christ liveth in me." [2] To help us attain this great spiritual victory, Christ sends us, through His merits and His intercession, His Holy Spirit. By allowing the Holy Ghost to lead us, by being prompt and generous in obeying His inspirations, we eventually come to the point where we act, speak, and think as Christ would were He in our place. "Then," says Tanquerey, "it is that Christ actually lives in us; with us and through us He glorifies God, sanctifies us, and helps us to sanctify our brethren." [3]

St. Thomas, writing regarding the perfection of charity, distinguishes a threefold perfection in it. The first is that God is loved as much as He is lovable, and this perfection God alone possesses. The second is when the will and affections are always intent upon God, and according to their whole effort and strength always actually exercising this charity and this perfection; and this alone belongs to the Blessed in heaven, and not to wayfarers upon this earth. The third is the perfection possible to man upon this earth, which excludes all that is opposed to charity and to grace. And this can be considered in a twofold sense. In one sense it is that which excludes all that is contrary to charity, and is destructive of it, such as mortal sin. Without perfection in this sense charity cannot exist and hence this perfection is necessary for salvation. The other sense in which perfection on earth is to be understood is inasmuch as it not only excludes that which is contrary to charity but also that impedes charity, or prevents the soul from directing all its affections to God. Without this perfection, charity *can* exist in the soul, as is in the case of beginners and those advancing to-

[1] *The Sixth of the Eucharistic Conferences.*
[2] Gal. 2:20. [3] *Op. cit.*, p. 602.

ward perfection, or in other words, those in the purgative and illuminative ways.

Those in the unitive way are said to be perfect in charity when their souls are so devoted to the practice of virtue as to be prompt and perfect in the exercise of charity by loving God habitually, and by frequent prompt and efficacious acts of that divine charity. It is called the *unitive* way because by love the soul is united to God, and the more perfect the charity the closer and more intimate is this union, and union with God is the principal study and endeavor of this grace. We must always bear in mind, however, that the other virtues also must be exercised as well as charity, and concur toward this union; and that even souls in this state are permitted often by God to suffer trials and temptations in order to purify them the more, and to give them occasion to increase their merit.

The characteristics of the unitive way are:

(1) Delight in contemplating God.

(2) To walk always in the presence of God.

(3) Love of God becomes the principal virtue of the soul.

(4) Simplification of prayer so that reasonings gradually disappear giving place to pious affections and sentiments which in turn become more simple until they form but a lingering, persistent thought of God.

(5) Life takes on an attitude of perpetual prayer and it permeates work, recreation through the conformity of our will to God's will, and we can say with our Lord: "I do always the things that please Him." [1]

Let us examine these in detail, since they make up the study of the unitive way. The first characteristic of the unitive way, we said, was "delight in contemplating God." The dictionary defines contemplation as "an act of considering with attention, or a musing attitude." This is a fine definition of natural contemplation which may be intellectual or imaginative.

Supernatural contemplation is somewhat different in that "while considering something beautiful and lovable in prayer, the contem-

[1] John 8:29.

plation is attended by love and admiration." A formal definition of supernatural contemplation might run something like this: "Contemplation is a free, penetrating and certain view of God and of heavenly things, causing admiration, ending in love and proceeding from love."

Nowhere will you find a more concise summary of what contemplation really is than in the all too meagre writings of Father Lallemant. For instance, he defines contemplation as "a perception of God or of divine things, simple, free, penetrating, certain, proceeding from love and tending to love." He explains his definition as follows:

1. This perception is simple. In contemplation we do not exercise the reason, as in meditation.
2. It is free; because to produce it the soul must be liberated from the least sins, irregular affections, eagerness, and unprofitable and disquieting cares. Without this, the understanding is like a bird, tied by the feet, which cannot fly unless it be set at liberty.
3. It is clear and penetrating, not as in the state of glory, but as compared with the knowledge we have by faith, which is always obscure. In meditation we see things only confusedly, as it were from afar off, and in a dryer manner. Contemplation enables us to see them more distinctly, and as it were close at hand. It enables us to touch them, feel them, taste them, and have an inward experience of them. To meditate on hell, for instance, is to see a painted lion; to contemplate hell is to see a living lion.
4. It is certain; because its objects are the supernatural truths which the divine light discloses to it; and when this disclosure is made immediately to the understanding, it is not liable to error. When it is made either through the senses or through the imagination, some illusion may at times mix with it.
5. It proceeds from love and tends to love. It is the employment of the purest and the most perfect charity. Love is its principle, its exercise, and its term.[1]

[1] *The Spiritual Doctrine of Father Louis Lallemant,* edited by Alan G. McDougall (Westminster, Md.: Newman Press, 1955), p. 265.

Note how contemplation differs from discursive or reasoned prayer since it excludes long reasonings. It differs too, from affective prayer, because it excludes the multiplicity of acts which are characteristic of affective prayer. The difference between discursive prayer and affective prayer on the one hand, and contemplative prayer on the other, becomes more evident through St. Thomas' definition of the latter, when he defines it as a "simple gaze on truth." [1] Perhaps to add St. Francis de Sales' definition would help, since he writes that "contemplation is no other thing than a loving, simple and permanent attention of the spirit to divine things." [2]

The division of contemplation is manifold but it is usually divided into two principal kinds: *infused* and *acquired*. *Infused* contemplation is that which has its rise from grace alone or divine inspiration. *Acquired* contemplation is that which human effort or industry begets, assisted by divine aid. Tanquerey mentions a third kind which he calls *mixed contemplation*, which is alternatively active and passive; in other words in the course of prayer the acts that arise are alternately from our own initiative and the products of the special action of grace.

Undoubtedly the infused contemplation which proceeds from the gifts of the Holy Ghost surpasses acquired contemplation. It is certainly easier because with swiftest movement it searches and penetrates divine things without the long windings of meditations. "Wherefore," says Cardinal Bona, "if anyone is on fire with the desire of contemplation, he ought to devote himself to continual meditations, and be persuaded for certain that all meditation is fruitless that does not pass into contemplation, which it ought to have for its aim; for it will be then as a road without an end, as a voyage without a harbor, as a body without a soul. But as advance is made to facility of meditation by assiduous endeavor of the understanding and will, so by this the faculty of contemplation is gradually acquired, increased and perfected." [3]

Father Louis Lallemant writes as follows regarding what he terms the two kinds of contemplation—the ordinary and the extra-

[1] *Summa Theol.*, II–II, q. 180, a. 1.
[2] *Treatise on the Love of God, op. cit.*, p. 239.
[3] *Cursus vitae spiritualis, op. cit.*, part III, chap. II, no. 2.

ordinary. "Ordinary contemplation," he writes, "is a supernatural habit, by which God raises the powers of the soul to sublime knowledge and illuminations, lofty sentiments and spiritual tastes, when He no longer finds in the soul such sins, passions, affections and cares, as prevent the communications He would make to it."

The other, higher kind of contemplation, he continues, "consists in raptures, ecstasies, visions, and other extraordinary effects." [1] The great spiritual writer makes note that, "when, after a long cultivation of purity of heart, God enters the soul and manifests himself to it openly by the gift of his holy presence, which is the first in order of his supernatural gifts, the soul finds itself so delighted with this new state, that it feels as if it had never known or loved God before." [2] Thus, the first step in contemplation is the gift of the presence of God.

St. Francis de Sales uses these definite words:

> Contemplation is no other thing than a loving, simple and permanent attention to divine things; which you may easily understand by comparing meditation with it. Little bees are called nymphs or *schadons* until they make honey, and then they are called bees: so prayer is named meditation until it has produced the honey of devotion, and then it is converted into Contemplation. . . . The desire we have to obtain divine love makes us meditate, but love obtained makes us contemplate.[3]

The transition from affective prayer to contemplative prayer ordinarily comes after the way is prepared by desire for God and detachment from the world. Says St. John of the Cross:

> When this has been to some extent effected, God begins to bring the soul into the state of contemplation, which is wont to happen very quickly, especially in religious, because these, having renounced things of the world, quickly attune their senses and desires to God; and then having nothing to do save to pass from meditation to contemplation, which happens when the discursive acts and the meditation of the soul itself cease, and the first fervours and sweetness of sense cease likewise, so that the soul cannot meditate as before, or find any help in the senses; for the senses remain in a state of aridity. . . . Wherefore in

[1] *Op. cit.*, p. 258. [2] *Ibid.*, p. 259.
[3] *Treatise on the Love of God, op. cit.*, p. 239 f.

this state the soul must never have meditation imposed upon it, nor must it make any acts, nor strive after sweetness or fervour; for this would be to set an obstacle in the way of the principal agent, who, as I say, is God. For God secretly and quietly infuses into the soul loving knowledge and wisdom without any intervention of specific acts.[1]

The three signs of this transition are given by many authors as the following:

(1) The soul is unable to meditate.

(2) The soul takes no pleasure in using the imagination or fixing it on any particular thing, earthly or heavenly.

(3) The soul delights to be alone, in quiet and repose, waiting lovingly upon God, without reflecting upon anything or even desiring to do so.[2]

Abbot Chapman says that most people who use contemplative prayer are unconscious of anything extraordinary except:

(1) The curious inability to meditate.

(2) The ease of remaining with God.

(3) And sometimes an "experience" that God is there, but there is nothing that surprises or troubles the soul, it all seems quite commonplace and ordinary.[3]

Saudreau lists a number of test points indicative of the contemplative way. He asks, for instance:

(1) Is the soul repelled by considerations and by discursive prayer?

(2) Does it perform duties more from duty than from inclination, seeking consolation in prayer only?

(3) Does it experience a vague, unreasoned but profound distaste for everything that is not God, or does not bear relation to Him?

[1] *The Living Flame of Love,* III, 30–31; *Complete Works, op. cit.,* III, 68–69.

[2] G. Diefenbach, O.F.M., *Common Mystic Prayer* (Paterson, N.J.: St. Anthony Guild, 1947), p. 46–47.

[3] *Spiritual Letters,* edited with a memoir by Roger Hudleston, O.S.B. (New York: Sheed & Ward, 1954), p. 94.

(4) Does it feel a quiet happiness in being alone with God—without having anything special to say to Him? [1]

"Not all those," says St. John of the Cross, "who resolutely devote themselves to the interior life are drawn by God through the channel of the mind to a state of perfect contemplation. The reason why, God alone knows." St. Teresa, too, exhorts souls not to be discouraged if God never grants to them the grace of contemplation. It is enough for them to remain in the way of affective meditation, and to keep well this essential rule: reflect on the truths of religion not to become more learned, but to acquire a greater love and courage in the service of Almighty God. These souls are not free from dryness of spirit. It is for them a passing test; God thus tries their humility and patience, then restores again the spiritual joys of meditation. It is not the same with souls called to the prayer of contemplation. The call is recognized by the three signs which St. John of the Cross has carefully described:

(1) When the soul wishes to pray, the intellectual faculties at once become paralyzed. These powers are of no use whatever to the heart in assisting it to love God. Painful efforts to stir them into action are useless and unsuccessful.

(2) The atrophy is confined only to the time of prayer. If it is endured longer, it would be a sign of disease. On the contrary, outside the time devoted to prayer, liberty of thought and feeling is restored. The mind can apply itself with relish to the study of religious truth. The taste disappears only when the soul desires to pray.

(3) In the midst of this torpor of intelligence and sense, the will remains active. It is profoundly attracted toward Him, perfectly convinced that He is there, and may be adored and loved by gazing upon Him in silence.

St. John gives this prudent counsel: "Just as it is necessary to leave the prayer of meditation at the right moment in order to enter the way of union, so it is equally important not to attempt to

[1] *Op. cit.*, vol. II.

change our state before the time desired by the Spirit of God, lest we should have to retrace our steps." [1]

Father Surin writes: "I can give you an assurance that, amongst all the persons whom I have seen make a full surrender of themselves to God, I have observed none who was not favored with this gift (contemplation), after having had a certain amount of practice in meditation on the mysteries and truths of the faith." [2] From this testimony and the writings of Teresa and John of the Cross, it is safe to conclude that contemplation is the normal goal of the spiritual life; souls who are eager for perfection have a right to try to secure it, and their spiritual guides should endeavor to prepare them for it.

The objects with which contemplation is concerned are God and His infinite perfections, Christ our Saviour and all those things that pertain to the mystery of our redemption; heavenly glory and the entire state of the Church Triumphant, the Blessed Virgin, the Angels and the saints—in a word, all matter of meditation except that meditation inquires, contemplation tastes. Putting it another way, meditation considers objects that move us singly and by parts, while contemplation views the object by simple intuition and moves with greater force and promptitude.

The *effects* of contemplation are manifold, among them the correction of excesses, since through it, the soul is imbued with great light so that the Will of God is recognized even in the slightest matters; next, it plucks up the roots of vices, renounces self-will and private judgment, perfects virtues and ennobles works, collects the senses, rectifies intentions and confers peace. In fine, it elevates the mind to God and produces a black-out of all exterior things and confers on the soul an inexplicable delight.

The *end* of contemplation is union between God and the soul which has been withdrawn from all creatures and inflamed with a most fervent love for God.

As to the *degrees* of contemplation, the various authors disagree as to the actual number. Cardinal Bona lists fifteen and I shall set them down here without comment, since they are ably treated in

[1] *Ascent of Mount Carmel*, II, 13; *Complete Works*, *op. cit.*, I, 108.

[2] *Spiritual Dialogues* (New York: Benziger Bros., 1892), vol. I. bk. IV, chap. 2.

Tanquerey's *The Spiritual Life*, and who could surpass his treatment of this phase of the study? Cardinal Bona's list is as follows:

(1) Intuition of truth
(2) Withdrawal of the soul to things interior
(3) Spiritual silence
(4) Quiet
(5) Union
(6) Hearing of God's speech
(7) Spiritual sleep
(8) Ecstasy
(9) Rapture
(10) Corporeal apparition of Christ and of the saints
(11) Imaginary apparition of the same
(12) Intellectual vision
(13) Vision of God in mist
(14) Admirable manifestation of God
(15) The third mode of intellectual vision, though it belongs not to this but to a future and blessed life, is a clear and intuitive vision of God. According to the probable opinion of theologians it has been granted to but a few holy persons, to the Blessed Virgin Mary, for instance, to Moses, St. Paul, and St. Benedict, even in this life, clearly to see the Divine Essence.

The degrees of contemplation according to others are first, recollection of all the powers of the mind; secondly, semi-rapture; thirdly, complete rapture; fourthly, ecstasy. Any such division as the foregoing expresses not so much the essence of contemplation as its accidents. Richard of St. Victor, for instance, records four divisions:

(1) The wounds of love, *charitas vulnerans;*
(2) The captivity of love, *charitas ligans;*
(3) The languors of love, *charitas languens;*
(4) The faintings of love, *charitas deficiens.*

In the first, love pierces the heart and makes itself master of all the affections; in the second, it takes the mind captive and possesses itself of all the thoughts; in the third, it presents the action of the external senses and the internal powers; in the fourth, it throws the soul into swoons and into a sort of death-like state by the boundless longings of its zeal, which the latter is unable to endure, because it perceives that all it does and all it can do is nothing, and that all it cannot do is infinite.

On page 272 we cited the five characteristics of the unitive way and the first one on that list was "delight in contemplating God." We have treated of the nature, the object, effects, end, and degrees of contemplation, so let us pass to the second characteristic of the unitive way, namely: "to walk always in the presence of God."

Earlier in this work we did treat on the importance of the exercise of the presence of God, and it must suffice here but to *recall* its importance and the different modes of its holy practice.

Continued remembrance of God is of great moment for acquiring all perfection and intimate friendship and union with Him. "I am the Almighty God: walk before Me and be perfect," [1] are the words of God Himself to Abraham.

The divine Presence wards off not only sins but the most trivial imperfections and it renders us prompt in the manful performance of all things pertaining to God and the duties of our state in life. It so imprints on the mind the memory of God that it is difficult not to think of Him. It impels us to respect and reverence His Presence, and it inflames our heart with love and heavenly desires, and unites our soul to its Ultimate End.

We can conceive and contemplate God as ever present in three ways:

The first way is a sensible representation, for instance, if we behold Christ our Saviour in every place and work as if He were present and looking at us, and from such a thought we can give vent to frequent aspirations and affections of the will by which the soul may be excited and disposed to union.

The second way is outside of us, without any sensible image, when we view God with the eyes of faith present to us in His

[1] Gen. 17:1.

Divinity and examining all our works, prayers, and concerns. This is brought about by the keen realization that God encompasses, surrounds, and penetrates us; and from this thought or act of faith, we rise to God Himself by frequent aspirations.

The third way is the most perfect, for by it we behold with purest eyes God no longer outside us, but present in the recesses of our heart and in the depth of our soul and infusing His blessings into us. This is as if we were to betake ourselves within ourselves and there erect a sort of temple in our heart wherein we worship God truly present, reverently listen to Him and converse with Him in a friendly manner as a spouse to her bridegroom. This way is called mental and unitive and is productive of most ardent and efficacious aspirations.

St. Bonaventure describes the presence of God which is wrought by contemplation. "There are three ways," writes the saint, "in which I may know that God is present. For either He is present by an effect proper to Himself. This is contemplation, which is the more eminent in that the effect of divine grace in oneself is more deeply felt, or that God is more clearly seen in His creatures. Or else, God is present to me by a sign which belongs to Himself alone, and this is an apparition. In the third case, God is seen in His own light and as He is in Himself: then God is seen face to face, and this is intuitive vision."

The third characteristic of the unitive way is when "love of God becomes the principal virtue of the soul." It was our Lord Himself who said: "Be ye therefore perfect, as your heavenly Father is perfect." [1] If we ask the meaning of these words, an answer may be found in the explanation which our Lord Himself gives: "But I say to you, love your enemies, do good to them that hate you and pray for them that persecute and calumniate you: that you may be the children of your Father who is in heaven, who maketh His sun to rise upon the good and bad, and raineth upon the just and the unjust." [2] From this teaching of the Master, we conclude that to be perfect means nothing else than to have perfect charity, "which seeketh not its own," but, from a supernatural motive, embraces God and our neighbor with true and efficacious benevolence. St. Paul says: "Above all these things have charity, which is the bond

[1] Matt. 5:48. [2] Matt. 5:44–45.

of perfection."[1] Charity includes under it all other virtues, collecting them into one and directing them to our ultimate end.

Says Father Arthur Devine, C.P.,

Supernatural perfection in this life may be considered as a *habit*, or as an *endeavour* or practice. As a *habit* it consists in the possession of sanctifying grace and the habitual will of not doing anything to banish that grace from the soul. As an *endeavour* it means a state of soul in which a person is no longer occupied with the things of this life more than what necessity requires, and devotes himself entirely to God and Divine things. The perfection of charity consists not only in the habit, and in a high degree of this habit, but in bringing the habit of charity into action, and that with readiness and delight.[2]

This is well explained by Father Buckler, O.P., who says: "Be it ever remembered that the perfection of man is determined by the perfection of his actions, not of his habits as such. Thus, a high degree of habitual charity will not suffice to perfect the soul if the charity pass not from habit to act—that is, if it become not operative. For to what purpose does a man possess virtue if he use it not? He is not virtuous because he can live virtuously, but because he does so. Hence the well-known doctrine that perfection resides in ordinary actions."

Since perfect union with God consists in charity, it necessarily depends on the exercise of love, as is written in Holy Scripture: "My little children, let us not love in word, nor in tongue, but in deed and truth."[3] When we speak of love we should know that it is twofold—love of concupiscence and love of benevolence. We love God by both but the second is the superior kind—the kind by which we, as it were, embrace God with benevolence, not on our own account, or for our benefit, but for His own sake and for His glory. True love, then, of a rational creature toward God is not a sort of simple friendship, but supernatural and incomparable, infused into our hearts by the Holy Ghost, who is given to us, deriving its origin from supernatural knowledge which, residing

[1] Col. 3:14.

[2] *A Manual of Ascetical Theology* (London: R. & T. Washbourne, 1902), p. 462.

[3] 1 John 3:18.

in the will as on an imperial throne, illuminates, perfects and directs the entire soul and its faculties.

The motives that should incite divine love are numerous but the principal ones are:

(1) *God Himself*. Since God is infinitely perfect, the Being who is infinitely amiable, the source of all amiability and perfection, He merits therefore the purest, the most disinterested love, a love that is independent of all other loves.

(2) *Because Christ commands it.* "Thou shalt love the Lord thy God with thy whole heart, with thy whole soul, with thy whole mind, and with thy whole strength."[1] "You command me to love You, O my God!" says Augustine, "as if it would not be for me the greatest misfortune not to love You."

(3) *Because God loves us.* God has manifested His love for us chiefly in this, that "He sent His only-begotten son" to earth for our salvation. Christ Himself says: "God so loved the world as to give His only-begotten Son."[2] He did not send Him to live on earth in regal state, but as a lowly servant; not to live and die as an ordinary man, but to live a life of privation and persecution, and to die on the cross. Thus John admonishes us: "Let us love God, because God first hath loved us."[3]

(4) *Because God continually bestows benefits upon us.* "What hast thou, O man, that thou hast not received,"[4] cries out St. Paul, and does not St. James say: "Every best gift and every perfect gift is from above, coming down from the Father of lights."[5] Life, health, our daily bread, the clothes we wear, the roof that shelters us, all are His gifts and what can we say of God's gift of grace or of Christ's greatest gift—His own Body, Blood, Soul and Divinity in the Holy Eucharist?

From the foregoing it is evident that we must love God, but the question is, "How?" Our dear Lord supplies this answer by saying we must love God with our *whole heart*, our whole soul, with our whole mind and our whole strength. Father Grou interprets this for us by saying that we love God with our whole heart when

[1] Mark 12:30. [2] John 3:16. [3] 1 John 4:19. [4] 1 Cor. 4:7.
[5] Jas. 1:17.

we reserve for God our chief affections and by referring all other affections to Him. God wants to have *all* our heart; He will not share it with anyone. We love God with our whole soul when we are ready to sacrifice everything for Him; our wealth, our honor, our life itself, and when we consent to renounce everything, to suffer everything, to lose everything, rather than transgress the commandment of the love of God. Our love for God must raise us above all the pleasures of sense, above all human respect, above all human fear, above all promises and all threats. We must always believe, and act as if we believed, that if we love all for God's sake we gain all.

We must love God with our *whole mind,* since as Father Grou says, it was given to us so that we might know Him. We must love God always in our thoughts in such a manner that we at once can banish from our mind any thought that might offend Him, or any thought that might distract us. In short, this commands us to lead a serious life, as is fitting for creatures made only for God. "The time," says St. Bernard, "in which we do not think of God is time lost."

Finally, we must love God with our *whole strength,* and according to Father Grou, this means that we must put no limits to our love because the measure of the love of God is to love Him without measure. To pray, to frequent the sacraments, to exercise works of charity, to suffer all pains and sorrows of this life, solely with the view of increasing in us this holy love. This is indeed to love God with all our strength!

This great spiritual author then gives us certain signs or marks whereby to judge whether we love God in the manner above stated:

(1) If there is fear or uneasiness about not loving God enough.

(2) Does our love for God produce effects? If we are courageous in undertaking all for God, and in suffering all for God; if our own consolation counts for nothing in the service of God; if we seek ourselves in nothing; if we persevere in spite of temptations and disgust, and weariness and desolation—these are true proofs of love.

(3) If in proportion as we advance in the spiritual life we reflect

less upon our love for God and our disposition with regard to Him; we abandon ourselves to Him in this matter, as in all others, we love Him without thinking of it, scarcely knowing that we love Him—it is then that we love Him with the greatest purity. St. Francis de Sales says: "We should not be anxious to discover whether we are pleasing to God, but rather whether God is pleased with us."

(4) If there is a direct looking toward God, a constant renunciation of all self-interested views, a continual fidelity in following all the movements of divine grace and a refusal to listen to the promptings of our own spirit.[1] St. Augustine says: "He loves God too little who loves anything besides God; unless indeed he loves it out of love to God."

I cannot terminate this section on the love of God without quoting these important words of St. Francis de Sales wherein he says: "The greater is our love of God, the more meritorious are our actions. God does not regard the greatness of the work, but the love wherewith it is performed." To those who weary of the struggle, these words of the same great saint will bring comfort and courage, for he says: "He who has loved most shall receive the greatest glory."

The fourth characteristic of the unitive way is *simplification of prayer so that the reasonings gradually disappear giving place to pious affections and sentiments which in turn become more simple until they form but a lingering, persistent thought of God.*

Those who have truly set forth upon the unitive way soon find that they can dispense with many considerations. The intellect fixes itself on the soul's light, and the chance reflections which are helpful and beneficial for others, are to them a hindrance rather than a help. Spiritual writers call this way of prayer, "the prayer of simplicity." "It consists," says Father Plus, S.J.,

in a loving attention towards God, varying in intensity, in freedom from distraction and in length, springing forth more or less spontaneously and not needing to nourish itself by separate or especially varied acts. This does not imply that all souls that strive to practice the virtue of simplicity, or that practice it spontaneously, necessarily

[1] *Manual for Interior Souls, op. cit.*, pp. 185–186.

comply with this form of prayer, but that they tend towards it unconsciously, at least in its lower forms. And if the Holy Spirit sometimes seems to direct them towards a more elaborate form of prayer, one which calls for different thoughts, the simple soul is not dismayed and does not ask for explanation. God, Who guides all things, is the Master: He will restore it, when He wills, to the sweetness of a more peaceful intimacy.[1]

The spiritual writers, St. John of the Cross and St. Teresa, describe the effects of simplicity in prayer as the outcome of the Divine Master having taken possession of the soul. The "ego" appears definitely non-existent. It is the fullness of liberty, the self with its tangles and brambles no longer attempting (or at least not succeeding, for it can still make itself felt in the imagination or the emotions) to disturb the resolute unity.

Bossuet describes the prayer of simplicity in this way:

One must accustom oneself to nourish the soul by a simple, loving gaze on God and on Jesus Christ; to attain this result, one must gently free the soul from reasonings, from arguments and from the multitude of affections, in order to keep it simple, respectful and attentive and thus have it draw closer and closer to God, its first principle and its last end. . . . Meditation is excellent in its proper time, and highly profitable at the outset of the spiritual life, but one must not linger there, since the soul by its fidelity in mortifying and in recollecting itself, ordinarily becomes the recipient of a purer and more intimate kind of prayer which one may call the prayer of simplicity and which consists in a single view, regard or loving thought on some object, be it God Himself, or some of His mysteries, or any other Christian truth. The soul puts aside reasoning and employs a gentle contemplation that keeps it at peace, attentive and docile to the divine operations and impressions which the Holy Ghost communicates: it does little and receives much; its labor is sweet, yet very fruitful; and since it approaches nearer to the source of all light, of all graces, and of all virtues, it receives still a greater share in all these gifts.[2]

Certainly no spiritual writer has ever given a better or more

[1] *Simplicity* (Westminster, Md.: Newman Press, 1951), p. 48.

[2] *Méthode courte, facile pour faire l'oraison en foi et de simple présence de Dieu* (Paris: Tequi, 1908).

detailed exposition of just what simplicity in prayer is and what the effects of simple unity are than the description left us by Ludovicus Blosius. After asserting that certain conditions, such as an earnest desire for purity of heart and holy introversion, or recollection of spirit, the absolute renunciation of self-love, self-will and self-seeking are pre-requisites in the soul desiring to approach nearer and nearer to God, Blosius says:

> At last, when the soul's higher powers have been raised up, enlightened and adorned by divine grace, the spirit will attain to a simple unity, and will arrive at pure love without images in the imagination, and at a simple knowledge of the mind without reflections. In this state, since it is now capable of receiving from God a grace of unspeakable excellence, it is brought to the living fountain which floweth forth from eternity and with exceeding abundance refresheth the minds of the saints.
>
> Now the powers of the soul shine like stars, and the soul itself is fit to contemplate the abyss of the Godhead with a calm, simple and joyful intuition, without any imagination and without any reflections in the intellect. When, therefore, the soul in this purified state turns itself entirely to God with love, an incomprehensible light shining in its depths, the eye of reason and intellect is obscured by the dazzling light, but the simple eye of the soul itself remains open and not dazed by the light. This eye is a pure, simple, uniform *thought*, raised above all *reflections* of the intellect.
>
> Moreover, as the natural light of the intellect is darkened by such excess of light, the soul sees nothing in time, but raised above time and place, takes to itself, as it were, a certain characteristic of eternity. . . .
>
> The soul clearly perceives that all these things are infinitely distant from the real truth of the divine essence, and that the essence of God is above all names. The soul does not see the essence of God, of whose presence it is aware.
>
> Hence, with an intuitive knowledge of God, without any exercise of thought, it rests quiet in the love of God, pure, simple, and yet unknown, because above all comprehension . . .
>
> Here the soul receives the hidden word which God speaks in the inward silence and in the secret depths of the soul. This hidden word it receives, and experiences the happy embrace of mystical union.[1]

[1] *A Book of Spiritual Instruction, op. cit.*, pp. 83–84.

The prayer of simplicity comprises two essential acts—(1) *contemplation*, in which one finds first a diminution of reasoning and then a suppression of reasoning which is replaced by an intuitive intellectual gaze, and (2) *love*, which heretofore was expressed by a multiplicity of affections and words is likewise simplified so that the very thought of God or of the sufferings of our Lord suffices to excite in the soul an ardent consuming love.

In making this prayer of simplicity, many of the saints advise certain preparations such as acts of thanksgiving, offering and petition. St. Francis de Sales says one *should* make such a preparation, and as to the choice of a subject, one is free to choose it at will, but this will in no way prevents the Holy Ghost from suggesting another, if He so chooses, otherwise we should proceed with the subject we have prepared. A resolution should be taken at the end of the prayer of simplicity, just as in discursive or affective mental prayer. Not infrequently the resolution will be inspired by the Holy Ghost.

The fifth and final characteristic of the unitive way is that *life takes on an attitude of perpetual prayer and permeates work and recreation through the conformity of our will to God's Will.*

Father Grou, describing a soul in the unitive way, says: "A light that is simple, though indistinct, enlightens him. . . . His soul is almost always the same, even when he is not actually in prayer; if he is reading, or speaking, or occupied with work and ordinary cares, he feels that he is less taken up with what he is doing than with God . . . and that He is really the secret occupation of his spirit . . . he goes simply as God leads him." [1]

St. John of the Cross says of such a soul that: "God gives the soul such ardour and courage and aspiration to the things of eternal life that, by comparison with what it hopes for therein, all things of the world seem to be, as in truth they are, dry and faded and dead and nothing worth. . . . Wherefore, when the heart is thus lifted up above the world, not only can the world neither touch the heart nor lay hold on it, but it cannot even come within sight of it." [2]

Tanquerey puts it this way: "Whilst previously there were set

[1] *Manual for Interior Souls, op. cit.*, p. 255.
[2] *The Dark Night of the Soul*, II, 21; *Complete Works, op. cit.*, I, 443–444.

hours of meditation and prayer, now *life is a perpetual prayer:* whether working, or recreating, whether alone or in the company of others, we continually rise towards God by conforming our will to His: I do always the things that please him.[1] This conformity is but an act of love and of abandonment into His Hands: prayers, ordinary actions, sufferings, humiliations, all are but so many means of manifesting our love for God."[2]

When a soul has truly all the qualities spoken of above, it, by God's grace, achieves what spiritual writers call a union with God. The union takes place in the soul's powers, namely in the understanding and will, for these faculties of the soul reach God, and are united to Him by their own vital actions, and in them contemplation and love essentially consist. In this union the understanding, sprinkled with the clearest light of wisdom, beholds God as a certain whole, in which all is good, so that it cannot be diverted from Him to anything else; and the will is constrained by the most ardent love, which, bursting forth after the manner of fire, seems to consume all things, so that the soul now lives not in itself, nor attends to natural actions, but with its whole affection passes into Him, to whom it is united in the closest embrace.

That sublime rapture by which a soul is carried forward to the most happy union can occur in two ways. For sometimes it is accomplished with our co-operation, sometimes without us: and thus there is a twofold union—one active and the other passive. That is called active union to which the spirit is raised in an active or human manner, by preparing itself for reception of contemplation by its own co-operation and effort. The passive takes place in a wonderful and more excellent manner: the Divine Spirit transports the soul and impels it without effort on its part, and raises it to intimate union with such force and efficacy that it cannot escape the most sweet embraces of God, by which the soul, with the suspension of its faculties, is carried above itself, and is dazzled, pervaded and absorbed by celestial light. But, by whichever way a man may arrive at this blessed union, he is certainly most blessed who is found worthy of so great a boon.[3]

In fine, thus united most purely with God, we shall feel and

[1] John 8:29. [2] *Op. cit.*, p. 603.
[3] *Cursus vitae spiritualis, op. cit.*, part III, chap. IV.

experience those things that can be neither spoken nor written, nor have entered into the heart of man; namely, ineffable delights known to the experienced alone, which God has prepared for those who love Him.

Could there be a more consoling and challenging way to end this chapter on the unitive way than to quote these blessed words of Blosius:

> If the spiritual beginner is careful to exercise his soul daily in the manner laid down, and thus to unite himself to God; if, through interior conversations and loving desires, he strives without ceasing to join himself to God; if he takes care to persevere constantly in self-denial and mortification and never gives up this holy purpose, either on account of his frequent falls or because he becomes discouraged by the innumerable distractions of his mind, he will certainly arrive at perfection and mystical union, if not in this life, at least in death. And even if he should not arrive at it then, most certainly will he arrive at it after the death of the body.[1]

[1] *Op. cit.*, p. 81.

14

The Director of Those in the Unitive Way

WHEN our Lord spoke to Mother Marie Sainte Cécile de Rome, R.J.M., at noon on October 11, 1928, He said: "A great number of souls are being lost because many of My priests do not love Me enough. They do not touch hearts because they are not closely enough united to Me. They count too much on human means–and their own ability, and not enough on My divine action."[1] Surely such words should strike the hearts of all priests and spur them on to greater sanctity. Certainly, the priest called upon to direct souls through the purgative to the illuminative ways and then on to the unitive way must needs be a man closely united to God. What a pity it would be for a priest to be only a sign post pointing the way to others but never moving forward himself.

Presuming then, that any priest who is called upon to direct souls most certainly is himself under the direction of another, it follows that what we now say may well be familiar to him, but in any case it may be well to lay down the following counsels even at the risk of being repetitious.

While some souls particularly favored by God receive from Him special favors that speed up, as it were, the union with Him, the vast majority of those who arrive at the unitive way come to this stage by what St. Teresa teaches "consists in the exact practice of renunciation and of all the Christian virtues." The soul is said to be perfect which is disengaged from all superfluous attachments

[1] *Canticle of Love, op. cit.*

and which habitually wills all that God wills, as He wills, and nothing but what He wills.

It is not always easy to be certain that a soul has truly broken all its attachments and is in a state of perfection or if it is yet in the state we call fervor, where the attachments, while considerably weakened, are nevertheless hidden in the soul itself. Saudreau tells us that one of the marks of the perfect life is present when contemplation becomes habitual and when such persons possess the ordinary disposition of perfect souls. Those in the unitive way have an intense charity, the fruits of which are: love of solitude, a spirit of detachment, a desire for heaven, an anxiety as to the extent of their love for God, a disinterested zeal, a love of the cross and a great thirst for Holy Communion, their energies are calm and tranquil, they have a profound humility which is productive of serenity.

St. Lawrence Justinian says: "Lest anyone should misunderstand his own state, we will give the signs by which may be recognized with certainty, true contemplation and the divine tasks which are found in that interior practice. We are enjoying true contemplation if we are prudent in our conduct, if we know how to recollect our thoughts, to put before ourselves a right intention in our actions, to apply ourselves to spiritual studies, to desire the presence of God, to love Him with a love full of humility, to rejoice above all things in intercourse with Him, if we are inflamed with ardour for celestial goods, and if we enjoy a profound peace." [1] We might add, if we dare, what many of the spiritual masters do in their lists of signs or marks of true contemplation—the desire for heaven, or in other words, a desire to quit this life to be with Christ.

So much for the marks of true contemplation. The question now arises as to how the director should prepare souls for contemplation.

Tanquerey warns against two extremes: that of urging indiscriminately and too hastily all fervent souls to contemplation, and that of not being concerned at all about this matter. As to the first, St. Bernard says that ordinarily only those who after long co-

[1] *The Solitary Life*, chap. I.

operation with grace have made solid progress in virtue, who need no longer revolve again and again in their minds the sorrowful picture of their sins, but, on the contrary, find their delight in meditating day and night and in keeping the law of God, are to be urged to contemplation.

According to St. John of the Cross, the usual law of divine Providence is as follows: begin with meditation: but if one is faithful to the practice of the virtues and of universal detachment, God calls the soul to contemplation, and by contemplation to perfect union with Himself.

The director must, however, mark well these words of St. John, for he writes: "Not all those who walk of set purpose in the way of the spirit are brought by God to contemplation, nor even half of them—why, He best knows. And this is why he never completely weans the senses of such persons from the breasts of meditations and reflections, but only for short periods and at certain seasons." [1]

The spiritual father would do well to stress the practice of the virtue of humility to souls called to contemplation but who falter on the way. "If we are really humble," says St. Teresa, "and deny ourselves not only in our imagination which often deceives us, but if we truly detach ourselves from all things, our Lord will not only grant us this favour but many others that we do not even know how to desire." [2] Again the saint writes: "[God] dearly loves humility: if you think yourselves unworthy to enter the third mansions, He will grant you all the sooner the favour of entering the fifth. Then, if you serve Him well there and often repair to it, He may draw you into the mansion where He dwells Himself." [3] Likewise the director should strongly recommend the virtue of charity, for St. Teresa adds: "If you possess [fraternal charity], I assure you that you will certainly obtain the union I have described." [4]

As to the direction of contemplative souls, Saudreau says it could be summed up in four words: "Renunciation and more

[1] *The Dark Night of the Soul,* I, 9; *Complete Works, op. cit.,* 1, 356.
[2] *The Interior Castle,* IV, 3; *op. cit.,* p. 63.
[3] *Ibid.,* Epilogue; *op. cit.,* p. 246.
[4] *Ibid.,* V, 3; *op. cit.,* p. 102.

renunciation." The great Suso adds: "It is not sufficient to die to self, but we must without ceasing renew this death until the end of our life." This renunciation must extend to the understanding, the memory, the imagination, and the will. The will is truly renounced when it is entirely indifferent and resigned. "To ask nothing, to refuse nothing;" or, as St. Francis de Sales says: "The indifferent heart is like a ball of wax between the hands of God, eager to receive all the impressions of His divine pleasure." Was not this the secret of St. Thérèse of the Child Jesus when she asked that the Child Jesus should treat her as a little toy to take up when He wanted to, or to cast her into the corner at his pleasure?

Here are three things that ought to strike all directors of souls —especially concerning those under them who are well advanced in fervor:

(1) Many people who are in the state of union do not know it themselves or reveal the fact to others, and therefore the director himself has no suspicion as to the nature of the graces being showered upon them.

(2) The number of contemplatives among educated people would certainly increase if they only received the necessary instruction at the proper moment. What is so often wanting is the light which is necessary to enable them to correspond with the grace that is offered.[1]

(3) Many souls are sweetly invited to intimate union with God and are well adapted to it, but they do not react to it: (a) because of a too great sensuality of nature in search of conveniences and comforts, in food, drink, raiment, conversations; (b) because they are excessively presumptuous, in spite of their austerity and prayerfulness; (c) because of their inordinate affection for human favor, praise and complacence; (d) because they are too greatly engaged even in lawful things; (e) because of their excessive curiosity of the understanding in investigating and reasoning. Anyone who desires to be carried on to union ought to seek nothing in his contemplation but what may inflame the affective faculty and appertain to union itself. (f) Finally, there are those who lack perseverance.

[1] De Besse, *The Science of Prayer, op. cit.*, p. 90.

When souls who have attained to union with God experience bitterness, dryness and distractions in the process, the provident director will be ready to encourage and console such sorely tried servants of God. What a consolation to be able to tell them of St. Jane Frances de Chantal, who when asked to describe her prayer said: "It is little more than distraction and suffering. What can a poor weak mind like mine do, filled as it is with every kind of business? I tell you with confidence and simplicity, that for nearly twenty years God has deprived me of the power of praying by means of consideration or meditation. All I can do is suffer and abandon my mind with great simplicity into the Hands of God, by keeping close to His operation with complete cessation of my own activity, doing nothing except when moved by His impulse, waiting calmly for whatever His divine goodness is pleased to bestow upon me." [1]

The director must teach with Blosius that a soul cannot arrive at intimate union with God unless it has become entirely pure and simple and thus has a likeness to God. In order then that it may deserve to be united to God it must preserve itself from all sin, from all pleasure indulged in for its own sake, and become free in heart and mind from everything created. By true and deep humility the soul must always acknowledge itself to be the most vile and unworthy, must always subject itself absolutely to the Will of God and keep itself raised up to Him.

The director, too, must prepare himself for disillusionments resulting from sin in those who would appear to have made great spiritual progress. Negligence, surprise, exposure in a rash moment and under specious pretexts to some dangerous occasion of sin, is often sufficient to cause the most lamentable falls. According to St. Francis de Sales, a fall even into mortal sin does not impede the progress of a soul in the way of perfection, provided only that it does not remain in that state for any length of time. Sin is the most powerful humiliation of all for destroying self-love; in everything else there is room for pride. In such cases, the confessor-director may console the penitent by pointing out the truth of St. Paul's

[1] *Instruct. Spirit.* I, dial. 12 (Paris: Plon, 1893).

words: "All things work together unto good, to such as . . . are called to be saints." [1] "All things," St. Augustine adds, "even sin."

The mechanics of prayer must be known to the director who would do a superb job of guiding others to perfection. Many, many books have been written on prayer and the priest-director ought to make a serious study of all the facets of prayer by acquiring several of the most prominent books on the subject and poring over them until he is expert in the art of prayer. For instance, he should know that there are certain types of prayer for each of the three ways. "The soul," says the great Jesuit Père Jean Crasset (1618–1692),

> arrives at divine union, and at the nuptials of the Lamb by three operations, by meditation, by affection and by contemplation. Meditation purges it of its vices and errors, affection inflames it, and causes it to practice good works, contemplation elevates it, and introduces it into the Chamber of the Spouse. Meditation is for beginners, affection is for those who are advancing, contemplation is for the perfect. In meditation the mind seeks, in affection, the heart desires, in contemplation the soul finds what it sought, enjoys what it desired. The mind works in meditation, the heart aspires in affection, both of them repose in contemplation. Thus divine union is an enjoyment of God, whom the soul has sought by meditation, whom she has attracted by affection, and whom she has found by contemplation.[2]

The study of the science of prayer will reveal that the prayer proper to the state of contemplation is aspirations. "Internal prayer proper to the state of active contemplation," writes Father Baker, O.S.B., "consists of certain most purely spiritual operations of the will, longing and thirsting after God, such as 'My God, when shall I love Thee alone?' 'O Infinite, Universal God!' etc. . . . Now the reason why aspirations are less hindered by external businesses than are meditation or immediate acts is because in aspirations the understanding is scarcely employed at all, and, therefore, may well enough attend to other businesses; and moreover, the will, abounding and even over-flowing with divine love, will not find herself

[1] Rom. 8:28.
[2] *Considerations on the Principal Actions of a Christian,* no. XIV.

interested in affection, and consequently, not distracted by such employments." [1]

Blosius suggests certain aspirations for those in the unitive way. "Often," says this spiritual master, "one or other of these aspirations will serve for a whole exercise; nevertheless, it will be useful on another occasion at leisure, to complete them, at least sometimes, and that in mind only, unless, perchance, he should find it suit him better to pronounce them with his lips. Even the words: 'O Lord God,' alone, if from time to time they are pondered and repeated with a devout heart, may keep a man in the presence of God, or in God, and shut out from his mind wandering imaginations and vain thoughts." [2] "O good Jesus. O my hope and my refuge. . . . O most dear of all loved ones. O my only love. O spouse ever fresh in beauty; spouse sweet as honey. O sweetness of my heart, and life of my soul. . . . What do I desire but thee? Thou art my true and eternal good. . . . Tear me away and separate me from everything that is not thee. . . . Inebriate my spirit with the wine of perfect charity." [3]

Aspirations of union suggested by Blosius are as follows: "O dearest of all friends, O my one love! . . . O Lord my God! O most Holy Trinity, one God, brighter than light, giving all delight, feed me, feed me; feed my soul with thy inflowing grace. . . . O my God and my all! O abyss most sweet, most worthy of love!" [4]

While it is evident that these aspirations must arise spontaneously in the soul, it would be quite in order for the director to suggest certain aspirations to those under him, and endeavor from time to time to learn just what aspirations are prompted within the soul itself.

The director of those in the unitive way ought to stress that God wishes them to live lives of grace and not purely of nature, lives inward and recollected, not outward and bustling; lives of fervor and of vigilance, not of lukewarmness and of carelessness, considering as nothing all that is purely human while being affected only by what relates to God, as creatures that are wholly sacrificed to Him, to be His victims by the cross, and by love of Him with

[1] *Holy Wisdom, op. cit.*, p. 514.
[2] *Op. cit.*, p. 32. [3] *Ibid.*, pp. 31–32. [4] *Ibid.*, p. 130.

His Son, Jesus Christ, if it be His good pleasure. They must be as souls lost in God, with no desires but to love leisure and freedom to attend to God, and to serve Him. They must look at nothing in the world but the service of God. In a word, they must be encouraged to rise above nature and every created thing, to a region of purity where they are stripped of all and see only God, being attached to His Holy Will alone.

No better counsel could any director give those under his spiritual guidance than that uttered by Blosius: "However far the servant of God may have advanced, he must never lay aside the desire for further progress. For, during our time of exile in this world, there is no union with God so deep or exalted that it may not every moment become more sublime and more profound. However far, therefore, a man may have advanced, he must be as careful as on the first day of his spiritual combat to humble himself, considering all he does as of little worth and to persevere in diligent labor and self-conquest."

To my sacerdotal confreres I offer the hope that all of us will have learned something of value from this work and that we may be inspired to follow the narrow path that leads to union with God in this world, and more especially in the next. Our task is doubly hard for we must lead others to sanctity as well as walk this same road ourselves. The responsibility is awesome, especially when we read the words spoken by our Lord to Mother Marie Sainte Cécile: "My priests rule the entire religious society. If they were really holy, their mere presence anywhere, at church, on the street, or elsewhere would evoke a thought of Me: they would draw souls to Me. In meeting him, one would feel as if another Christ were passing by. The devil fears a single soul in whom I act freely more than an army of lukewarm and indifferent souls in whom My action is paralyzed, because in the former I operate with My power, while I am forced to leave the latter to their own weakness."

Holiness, then, must be our goal! May God help us achieve it. *Oremus pro invicem.*

Index of Names